Sustainable Development Goals Series

The **Sustainable Development Goals Series** is Springer Nature's inaugural cross-imprint book series that addresses and supports the United Nations' seventeen Sustainable Development Goals. The series fosters comprehensive research focused on these global targets and endeavours to address some of society's greatest grand challenges. The SDGs are inherently multidisciplinary, and they bring people working across different fields together and working towards a common goal. In this spirit, the Sustainable Development Goals series is the first at Springer Nature to publish books under both the Springer and Palgrave Macmillan imprints, bringing the strengths of our imprints together.

The Sustainable Development Goals Series is organized into eighteen subseries: one subseries based around each of the seventeen respective Sustainable Development Goals, and an eighteenth subseries, "Connecting the Goals," which serves as a home for volumes addressing multiple goals or studying the SDGs as a whole. Each subseries is guided by an expert Subseries Advisor with years or decades of experience studying and addressing core components of their respective Goal.

The SDG Series has a remit as broad as the SDGs themselves, and contributions are welcome from scientists, academics, policymakers, and researchers working in fields related to any of the seventeen goals. If you are interested in contributing a monograph or curated volume to the series, please contact the Publishers: Zachary Romano [Springer; zachary.romano@springer.com] and Rachael Ballard [Palgrave Macmillan; rachael.ballard@palgrave.com].

Drew Dalton • Angela Smith
Editors

Gender, Sexuality and the UN's SDGs

A Multidisciplinary Approach

palgrave
macmillan

Editors
Drew Dalton
Faculty of Education and Society
University of Sunderland
Sunderland, UK

Angela Smith
Faculty of Arts and Creative Industries
University of Sunderland
Sunderland, UK

ISSN 2523-3084 ISSN 2523-3092 (electronic)
Sustainable Development Goals Series
ISBN 978-3-031-31045-4 ISBN 978-3-031-31046-1 (eBook)
https://doi.org/10.1007/978-3-031-31046-1

Cover illustration: Barbara Boensch/Alamy Stock Photo

This Palgrave Macmillan imprint is published by the registered company Springer Nature Switzerland AG.
The registered company address is: Gewerbestrasse 11, 6330 Cham, Switzerland

Contents

Notes on Contributors

Donna Chambers is Professor, Cultural and Creative Industries at Northumbria University, Newcastle. She is a critical scholar who is interested in how people and places are represented primarily through cultural and heritage tourism, and postcolonial and decolonial epistemologies in research and teaching. Importantly, she is also interested in how women are represented in tourism through the lens of critical race theory and Black feminism. Donna has been Associate Editor of *Annals of Tourism Research* since 2013, a member of the Editorial Board and Managing Editor of *Leisure Studies* since 2016 and 2019 respectively.

Pierre Chartier is a PhD student in Language Sciences (Discourse Analysis) at the University of Western Brittany, Brest. His research focuses on the naming and (de)legitimisation processes of protest violence—and the identities of those who use it—in social discourse, specialising in Internet-mediated discourse, particularly on Twitter and YouTube. Recent publications include work on media and political discourse around the figure of the 'casseurs'. He is also a member and co-founder of the 'Confrontation' study group, which brings together researchers in language sciences to examine the issue of polemical discourse on digital social networks.

Drew Dalton is Senior Lecturer in Sociology at the University of Sunderland. Drew has worked in the Third Sector for 20 years in a range of roles, from international development, working with vulnerable young people, human rights and campaigns. He is the Founder and CEO/Chair of ReportOUT, a global human rights organisation which investigates human rights abuses of sexual and gender minorities in different nation states. Drew has published previously on topics such as HIV and austerity, LGBTQI+ populations and the weaponisation of COVID-19 by nation states, the impact of the Climate Emergency on LGBTQI+ people globally and the barriers faced by queer Muslims. In 2021 Drew was very proud to be ranked at number 64 on the Pride Power List of the top 100 influential LGBTQI+ people in the UK.

Alex Fairlamb is Senior Leader in charge of Teaching and Learning and CPD, based in North East England. She is Specialist Leader in Education and Evidence Lead in Education. Alex is a proud member of the Historical Association Secondary Committee and the Schools North East Steering Board. Alex is a History teacher and former Lead Practitioner of History and Teaching and Learning, with a strong commitment to ensuring that curriculums are diverse. Her research interests centre on diversity within the curriculum, evidence informed teaching and learning practice within schools, and social justice in education. Alex tweets as @lamb_heart_tea.

Kim Gilligan has worked at the University of Sunderland since 2004. She is currently the Learning and Teaching Enhancement and Sustainability Manager in the Centre for Excellence in Learning and Teaching (CELT). Her research interests lie in the intersections between gender and critical literacies and how these two areas can underpin the development of sustainable values and skills of graduates leaving university into employment.

Tina Kristensen is a PhD candidate at the University of Sunderland. She works in the field of linguistics where she primarily works with critical discourse studies. Her thesis focuses on the intersection of race and gender in the #MeToo movement on Twitter. Her research interests are feminist movements on different social media platforms.

Caitlin Martin is a BSc Sociology and MSc Inequality and Society graduate from the University of Sunderland. For her MSc thesis, Caitlin examined heteronormativity within Agenda 2030 and the Sustainable Development Goals and explored how heteronormative discourse can be resisted and challenged to ensure inclusive development agendas for all. Caitlin is also Human Rights Researcher and Lead Sustainable Development Goals Officer at ReportOUT.

Alex Powell is Lecturer in Law at Oxford Brookes University. His research draws predominantly on the work of Michel Foucault, as well as queer theorists such as Judith Butler, to analyse the relationship between legal apparatus and cultural discourses. However, Alex is also a trained qualitative interviewer. He has particular expertise in narrative analysis approaches. As such, he seeks to bring together critical scholarship and empirical socio-legal research. Currently, he is focused on how the UK addresses asylum claims based on a fear of persecution arising from sexual or gender minority status.

Barbara Sadler is Senior Lecturer in Media and Cultural Studies at the University of Sunderland. She is programme leader for the BA(Hons) Film and Media degree. Barbara has research interests in television adaptations and audience studies.

Angela Smith is Professor of Language and Culture at the University of Sunderland, UK. She has published widely in the areas of gender, politeness theory, and media discourse. She co-edits the Bloomsbury Library of Gender in Popular Culture, and co-convenor of the Ross Priory Broadcast Talk International Research Seminar series.

Joanna Thornborrow is Emeritus Professor of English Language and Linguistics at the University of Western Brittany, Brest. Her research interests are broadly within the field of discourse and conversation analysis, particularly in the areas of mediated interaction, narrative and political discourse. Recent publications include *The Discourse of Public Participation Broadcasting: From Talk Show to Twitter* (2015), *Discours des réseaux sociaux: enjeux publics, politiques et médiatiques*, co-edited with Marcel Burger and Richard Fitzgerald, (Deboeck 2017), co-authored chapters in *The Mediated Politics of Europe: A Comparative Study of Discourse* (eds. M. Ekström and J. Firmstone, Palgrave 2017).

Megan Todd is Senior Lecturer in Social Science at the University of Central Lancashire. Her research focuses on gender, sexualities, and abuse.

Katie Ward is an independent researcher currently working in accessibility in learning resources for a UK exam board. Katie completed her PhD at the University of Sunderland in 2019 focusing on language use in trans and gender variant communities. Her research interests include language and gender, membership categorisation analysis, and critical discourse analysis.

Jodie Weatherston is Lecturer in Social Studies at the University of Sunderland. Her research interests lie within human rights and international development exploring gender-based violence across the globe. Specific areas of interest include sexual violence, female genital mutilation, child marriage, conflict and natural minerals, femicide and women's rights globally.

Helen Williams is Senior Lecturer in Criminology at the University of Sunderland, UK. Her current research centres on sexual violence and the criminal justice system, and particularly the treatment of victim/survivors from marginalised communities. She is interested in the gendered and classed inequalities of sex and relationships and the state and social regulation of sexuality. She has previously written about slut-shaming and digital activism.

List of Photos

List of Tables

CHAPTER 1

Introduction

Caitlin Martin and Angela Smith

At the dawn of the new millennium, world leaders joined together with the unparalleled aim of eradicating disease, poverty and hunger. These Millennium Development Goals (MDGs) of 2000 were set to run for 15 years, with eight goals announced to converge around the need to eradicate extreme poverty. On 25 September 2015, the 2030 Agenda for Sustainable Development was adopted by all 193 United Nations Member States, an ambitious blueprint which calls for peace and prosperity for people and the planet, now and into the future (UNSDG, 2022). The 2030 Agenda for Sustainable Development pledges work towards sustainable economic growth, social inclusion and environmental protection (World Health Organisation, 2018). Embedded within Agenda 2030 are 17 Sustainable Development Goals, which in a global partnership between all United Nations Member States are an urgent call for action to resolve

C. Martin (✉)
Sunderland, UK
e-mail: bh18kl@student.sunderland.ac.uk

A. Smith
Faculty of Arts and Creative Industries, University of Sunderland, Sunderland, UK
e-mail: angela.smith@sunderland.ac.uk

D. Dalton, A. Smith (eds.), *Gender, Sexuality and the UN's SDGs*, Sustainable Development Goals Series,
https://doi.org/10.1007/978-3-031-31046-1_1

global challenges, encourage growth and create a sustainable future for all (United Nations Development Programme, 2022a, 2022b). This leads to the stated aim to 'leave no-one behind'. These world leaders came from a wide selection of agencies, including governments, civil society organisations and donors. These new goals, the Sustainable Development Goals (SDGs) are the subject of the chapters in this book. The SDGs are interconnected and recognise that ending poverty and other deprivations go hand-in-hand with strategies that aim to reduce inequalities, improve health, education and stimulate economic growth (United Nations Development Programme, 2022a, 2022b). Agenda 2030 seeks to acknowledge the human rights of all and will stimulate action of the next ten years in areas that are crucially important for both humanity and the planet (UNSDG, 2022).

The Sustainable Development Goals

The 17 SDGs were set up with the aim to be as inclusive as possible, bringing an end to disease, poverty, hunger and other forms of inequality by 2030. Each goal has within it a series of targets, and in total there are 169 stated targets. The effects of the COVID-19 pandemic have been incorporated into each of these goals. For example, Goal 1: End poverty in all its forms everywhere, now includes the shocking fact that 119–124 million people have been pushed back into extreme poverty as a consequence of the pandemic. Goal 5: Achieve gender equality and empower all women and girls, now acknowledges that the pandemic has added to the drain of women and girls from the labour market by the added burden of unpaid domestic and care work that fell on them during that time. Additionally, there is acknowledgement as a result of the pandemic that an additional ten million girls are at risk of child marriage in the next decade (doubling the number from pre-pandemic estimates).

Goal 2: End hunger, achieve food security and improved nutrition, and promote sustainable agriculture might at first glance appear to be a goal for countries that have long-standing histories of food production problems caused by climate or conflict. However, the pandemic has exacerbated world hunger, and women and young children are at the greatest risk of malnutrition. In the UK, the leading provider of food bank parcels, the Trussell Trust, reported in the first year of the pandemic that they had experienced at 61% increase in food bank use in the last quarter of 2020 (Trussell Trust, 2020).

Goal 3: Ensure healthy lives and promote well-being for all at all ages, there is the obvious acknowledgement that the pandemic has halted or reversed progress in health generally, and shortened life expectancy. However, after decades of progress, it has also halted or reversed aspects of healthcare that relate more to females: reproductive health; maternal health; child health. This is something that Rosemary Morgan et al. (2022) have shown in respect of gender minorities, and Silverio et al. (2002) have shown in respect of its intersection with race. The pandemic affected all nations, irrespective of socio-economic standing, with gender disparity being revealed in research in Switzerland (Morgan, Cullati, et al., 2022) and also in Rosemary Morgan et al.'s report into gender disparity and COVID-19, with the largest gender gaps seen in North Africa and the Middle East.

Goal 4: Ensure inclusive and equitable quality education and promote lifelong learning opportunities for all. Education is seen as a route out of poverty, so it is positive to see that participation in pre-school learning has increased from 65% in 2010 to 73% in 2019, according to the UN's own statistics. However, COVID-19 is estimated to have wiped out 20 years of educational gains with an additional 101 million children falling behind in reading. UNESCO's report, *When Schools Shut: gendered impacts of COVID-19 school closures* (2021) showed that female and male pupils were negatively affected in different ways, globally. Girls were more likely to fall behind because of the increased pressure to engage in caring and domestic tasks in the home. In addition, the report highlights the rise in child marriages during the pandemic. Both factors led to fewer girls returning to school. Boys on the other hand also fell behind, but in their case, it was more often due to being engaged in paid work that took them out of the house and thus away from online and digital learning. Digital poverty is also an issue in Westernised countries.

Goal 5: Achieve gender quality and empower all women and girls, this might seem to be the most obvious SDG for this book to deal with. However, as we will show in the accompanying chapters, this is actually a central point to most of the other goals. It is also notable that the SDGs do not explicitly link this goal to sexuality. In the course of the pandemic, the paucity of women's voices at the decision-making levels of national and local government became much clearer in terms of daily press briefings that featured mostly male politicians. Globally, women represent just 25.6% in national parliaments, and 36.6% locally. In the UK, the 2019 General Election had seen a large number of high-profile female MPs retire from politics, the majority of them citing misogyny as the main cause. This form of exclusion of women from the public sphere through verbal violence is mirrored in the physical violence metered out in the domestic sphere. During the pandemic, violence against women was intensified, with the UK-based charity Refuge reporting a 61% increase in calls to its National Domestic Abuse Helpline in the first year of the pandemic (Refuge, 2021). As hinted at in relation to Goal 4, the pandemic also increased the burden of unpaid domestic and care work on women, squeezing them out of the paid workforce.

Goal 6: Ensure availability and sustainability management of water and sanitation for all, and Goal 7: Ensure access to affordable, reliable, sustainable and modern energy for all, both tie the climate crisis in with the equality for all that these goals push for.

Goal 8: Promote sustained, inclusive and sustainable economic growth, full and productive employment and decent work for all, can be closely tied with the aims of Goal 4 in terms of education being the basis for prosperity and inclusivity. The UN estimate that the pandemic will lead to an increase in youth unemployment in particular, with 31.1% of young women being negatively impacted, compared with 14% of young men. The pandemic caused catastrophic job losses through the world, with the UN estimating 255 million full-time jobs being permanently lost. Many of these jobs were occupied by females, as they relate to retail, tourism and hospitality. Several of the chapters in this book look at the notion of 'decent employment', and also the workplace environment. More particularly, the #MeToo hashtag was instigated to draw attention to the longstanding culture of sexual exploitation, harassment and assault in the film industry. The #MeToo movement and its consequences are covered in several chapters in this book.

Goal 9: Build resilient infrastructure, promote inclusive and sustainable industrialisation and foster innovation relates to manufacturing (which plummeted during the pandemic), and also the need to reduce rural poverty through connectivity. The means to do this stems from the requirement for research and development investment, which ties this goal very closely with the conduit from Goal 4 to get more people into education. Again, this is covered in several chapters, particularly in relation to the consequences of food production.

Goal 10: Reduce inequality within and among counties is a goal that highlights social and economic inequalities globally. It is a key motivation for people to move around the globe as refugees (the UN estimates that, in 2020, for every 10,000 people globally, 311 are refugees). These people are at high risk of death or disappearance when on a migratory route, with the UN reporting 4186 deaths and disappearances recorded on migratory routes worldwide in 2020. As the pandemic has exacerbated inequalities in all countries, the rise in right-wing politics has led to more stringent immigration policies being introduced, particularly by wealthier countries.

Goal 11: Make cities and human settlements inclusive, safe, resilient and sustainable, can be tied into Goal 1's aim to end poverty, and Goal 12: Ensure sustainable consumption and product patterns. Again, these are all issues that are touched upon in several chapters in this collection.

Goal 13: Take urgent action to combat climate change and its impacts, is continued in Goal 14: Conserve and sustainably use the oceans, seas and marine resources for sustainable development and Goal 14: Protect, restore and promote sustainable use of terrestrial ecosystems, sustainably managed forests, combat desertification, and halt and revere land degradation and halt biodiversity loss. It is well documented that women are most likely to be affected by the climate crisis, owing to their generally lower socio-economic status. The Paris Agreement, signed by all the major world leaders in 2016, set a five-year cycle of increasingly ambitious climate action to be carried out by the signatories. The goals of this agreement included limiting global warming to well below 2 °C through cutting greenhouse gas emissions. Just a year later, one of the first acts US President Donald Trump carried out was to announce the United States' withdrawal from this agreement. His rationale for this was based around the hypermasculine 'Make America Great Again' agenda that included expanding oil and coal industries, industries that are traditionally male dominated (Smith & Higgins, 2020). This act of hypermasculine bravado played to his right-wing followers, whilst at the same time Trump essentially scuppered the future of the planet in the long term. The link between gender, sexuality and environmentalism is one that crops up in several chapters in this book, highlighting its fundamental importance.

Goal 16: Promote peaceful and inclusive societies for sustainable development, provide access to justice for all and build effective, accountable and inclusive institutions at all levels. When Hillary Rodham Clinton gave a speech at the United National Fourth World Conference on Women in Beijing in September 1995, she drew on an existing feminist rally cry but brought it to a much wider audience: 'human rights are women's rights and women's rights are human rights'. Sixteen years later, she modified this slogan when she made a speech at the United Nations in New York on

International Human Rights Day, declaring 'gay rights are human rights and human rights are gay rights'. Human rights defenders run many risks in declaring their creed: in 2020, the UN reported 311 human rights defenders had been killed, in 32 countries: an increase of 18% from the previous year. As we will see below, human rights—particularly those of women and non-binary people—are increasingly under threat.

The final goal is one that links the other 16 together in terms of organisation: Strengthen the means of implementation and revitalise the global partnership for sustainable development. This relates to the need for investment, but also connectivity in the way that we see in Goal 9. It is also a goal that explores the need to gather more data: perhaps we can link this to Goal 5: Gender equality and speculate that the low number of women and other minorities who have voices of influence can be seen to be a problem for lack of representation. As the collection of essays in this book shows, the multidisciplinary approach we have taken to exploring the goals mirrors the multi-agency approach that Goal 17 aspires towards.

The slogan, 'leave no-one behind', appears to draw all of these goals together. However, if we look at the language used in these goals, it is clearly binary and omits any explicit reference to non-binary genders and sexualities. The very thing that makes the SDGs international—the adoption by all 193 United Nations Member States—can be seen as a weakness in that it omits reference to some of the most discriminated and disadvantaged people in the world: those who identify as LGBTQI+. Sixty-nine United Nations Member States criminalise same-sex relationships (as in January 2023), with six Member States legally imposing the death penalty for punishment of consensual same-sex sexual acts. LGBTQI+ people are continually discriminated against and marginalised in ways that negatively impacts their well-being, health and financial security (Dorey, 2018). It seems that to get the blanket agreement to those goals that the UN requires for them to work, the explicit reference to LGBTQI+ was omitted from all documentation relating to the Agenda for Sustainable Development.

Sexuality and the SDGs

International development has both reinforced and challenged inequalities relating to sexual orientation and gender identity, which has not only impacted the recognition of LGBTQI+ within the 2030 Agenda for Sustainable Development but also the Human Rights of individuals with a diverse sexual orientation and gender identity. Laws, programmes and policies that are discriminatory towards LGBTQI+ and do not acknowledge the specific needs of LGBTQI+ continue to hold individuals back (Stonewall, 2022). This impact is felt by LGBTQI+ individuals across the globe. Disparities in poverty, health, education, security and income cannot be addressed until the specific needs of LGBTQI+ are directly addressed by United Nation Member States. International organisations, programmes and actions associated with the development sector position heterosexuality as dominant and work to prioritise, support and benefit heterosexuality above other forms of sexuality (Browne, 2019). Development interventions are historically organised around a cisnormative binary, which privileges masculinity and straightness over femininity and queerness and assumes that individuals subjected to development are cisgender and heterosexual (Gosine, 2015; Schilt & Westbrook, 2009). Structural heterosexual norms create barriers regarding access to resources through a process which excludes LGBTQI+ (Gosine, 2015). For LGBTQI+, the non-conforming to society's regulation can lead to marginalisation, poor access to economic opportunities, healthcare, housing and an adequate standard of life. Binary understandings of gender and sexuality are embedded and woven through social institutions and everyday life in a way that is powerful, discriminatory and exclusionary towards LGBTQI+ people. Discriminatory laws, policies and developmental programmes which do not acknowledge the specific needs of LGBTQI+ are continuing to hold individuals back.

In the implementation of the Sustainable Development Goals, LGBTQI+ individuals have been left behind in a number of different ways. As international development programmes have failed to adequality take into account the specific needs of LGBTQI+, they are not upholding the principles to 'leave no one behind'. Social, cultural and legal discrimination is faced by LGBTQI+ people and it cannot be truly eradicated until development organisations and United Nations Member State governments account for and respond to the needs of LGBTQI+ people in their initiatives to address and achieve the 2030 Agenda for Sustainable Development.

The concept of development suggests that all should have access to healthcare, education and an adequate standard of living (Park, 2016), which clearly links with the SDGs. However, for LGBTQI+ individuals, exclusion and discrimination occurs and is often reinforced by law, policy and development practices that fail to take into account the need of SGMs or deliberately exclude individuals due to societal norms that underpin heterosexuality as dominant (Browne, 2019). Inequalities are at the heart of discrimination against individuals with diverse sexual orientation and gender identity.

Development programmes and policies reinforce inequalities for LGBTQI+ individuals as they mirror the views we have in society. Policy and development have evolved alongside society to reinforce the hetero-sexual and homosexual binary outlook. Development policies make binary assumptions around what development needs there are for women, girls, men and boys. The reality is much more complicated than the binary of men and women: it is important to shed light and explicitly question this.

Furthermore, LGBTQI+ people are often excluded by governments, charities and donors on the grounds of insensitive programme design, discriminatory policies and practices, lack of inclusive funding, and awareness and sensitivity training (Dorey, 2018). The 2030 Agenda for Sustainable Development endorses the principle of inclusiveness reaching the furthest behind first.

For LGBTQI+ issues to be acknowledged within international development it is important to engage and acknowledge issues LGBTQI+ face in all aspects of their lives and not just the impact of homophobia, transphobia, biphobia and interphobia (ReportOUT, 2022). Engaging with intersecting factors such as poverty, healthcare, education, social inequalities, gender equality, work and employment can help nations identify what factors are contributing to systematic oppression and discrimination experienced by LGBTQI+ individuals and how recognition within the SDGs can make a safer and more inclusive world for individuals of a diverse sexual orientation and gender identity (Davis, 2008; Trithart, 2021). No one single force is the cause of the injustices LGBTQI+ face. It is not only important to examine where the inequality and marginalisation of LGBTQI+ individuals is occurring but also consider the ways in which it can be challenged to ensure LGBTQI+ people have access to full participation within society regardless of their actual or perceived sexual orientation or gender identity.

The 2030 Agenda for Sustainable Development holds real potential for LGBTQI+ and is a step in the right direction. While more could have been done to specifically mention LGBTQI+ in the 2030 Agenda for Sustainable Development, the inclusive language used is a clear way to help make a positive change to the lives of LGBTQI+ people. The mandate of 'leave no one behind' has created a chance for the development sector to create an approach that is inclusive of individuals with a diverse sexual orientation and gender identity. To resist heteronormative discourse and have LGBTQI+ issues acknowledged by United Nations Member States, it is important to use and focus on the inclusive language that is presented within the 2030 Agenda for Sustainable Development. Within the Agenda 2030 for Sustainable Development, Clause 19 states that nations reaffirm their commitment to upholding the Universal Declaration of Human Rights as well as other international instruments relating to human rights and international law. The basis of the Sustainable Development Goals captures formal international treaties and resolutions and is grounded on the Universal Declaration of Human Rights which posits that 'all human beings are born free and equal in dignity and rights' (United Nations, 2022). United Nations Member States have the responsibility in conformity to the United Nations Charter to respect and promote the human rights and fundamental freedoms of all without distinction of any kind as to race, sex, religion, political or other status. Goal 10 of the Sustainable Development Goals focuses on reducing inequalities within and among nations. Target 10.2 states 'by 2030, to empower and promote social, political and economic inclusion of all, irrespective of age, sex...or other status', a classification that is interpreted as including LGBTQI+ people. While some nations may dispute linking LGBTQI+ people to 'other status', key international documents such as the Universal Declaration of Human Rights and legally binding international treaties including the International Covenant on Civil and Political Rights and the International Covenant on Economic, Social and Cultural Rights apply 'other status' as a flexible approach to capture the experience of social groups that are vulnerable, have suffered and continue to suffer marginalisation, discrimination and harassment due to their actual or perceived sexual orientation and gender identity (United Nations, 2022).

The adjective *all* within the goals and targets of the SDGs provides an opening for interpretation. When goals and targets use 'all men and women' this is an opening for organisations, groups and individuals to advocate for the rights and recognition of LGBTQI+. 'All men and women' includes everyone regardless of sexual orientation, gender identity. Agenda 2030 for Sustainable Development provides a unique opportunity for inclusiveness. Here, *all* is underestimated as this is the opening for heteronormative and binary thinking surrounding gender and sexuality to be resisted. The use of inclusive language in development policies, programmes and initiatives ensures dominant groups are not labelled as the 'norm' and minority groups as 'other'. It is about using the inclusive language that is presented to resist heteronormative assumptions, norms and hierarchies. Reducing systematic inequality, marginalisation, discrimination and ensuring transformative equality through the use of inclusive language and policy is a development imperative to guarantee the global mandate of 'leave no-one behind' is achieved.

SDGs and the Wider Picture When it Comes to Gender and Sexuality

The 17 SDGs commit these world leaders to eradicate inequality for all by 2030, and cover issues beyond the 'disease, poverty and hunger' of SDGs, to include environmental concerns, city design and education. There is a separate SDG for 'Gender equality' is Goal 5: Achieve gender equality and empower all women and girls. What the chapters in this book explore is how gender (and implicitly sexuality) cannot be treated as a separate goal, but instead is something that applies across the SDGs. As Elizabeth Mills has pointed out,

> If the global commitment to eradicate inequality for all people is truly unequivocal, as leaders claim it to be, the implementation of the Sustainable Development Goals (SDGs) needs to take into account the voices of those people who, because of their sexual orientation or gender identity and expression [...], have historically been excluded from the benefits of development policies and programmes. (Mills, 2015, p. 8)

Mills' observation, in 2015, became all the more relevant as the decade rolled on and globally we came to witness a retreat from equality laws that had seemed common sense in Westernised countries. The global financial crisis of 2008 unleashed a wave of right-wing populism that moved quickly through Westernised democracies. Whilst the election of Donald Trump in the United States in 2016 might have been seen as a zenith of this right-wing populism, some might have hoped that his defeat when seeking a second term would see the end of the threats to gender and sexuality rights that he had started to enact. However, what we have since seen is a more localised continuation of this right-wing populism aligned with Christian fundamentalism in the United States. By early 2022, several states had enacted bans on abortions after six weeks, a ban that would encourage friends, relatives, neighbours and the spouse of rapists to sue anyone who might provide or assist in an abortion enacted on his victim. The ban came with no exceptions, not even for victims of rape or incest. The ban also allowed 'investigators' to ask people who lose a pregnancy just how it was lost. In forcing by law to answer questions about miscarriage, this law is very close to the criminalisation of miscarriage that is found in El Salvador. It was no great surprise, but nevertheless a huge shock, when the US Supreme Court repealed the legislation known as Roe vs Wade in May 2022, thus removing the constitutional right for women to have abortions. The consequences of unwanted pregnancy in terms of poverty, health, education, employment and sustainable population growth are all linked by gender equality in this respect.

It is not just fertility rights that we find becoming the victim of right-wing, conservative populism. One of the acts that Trump did manage to get through when president related to trans rights for armed service personnel. More recently, in 2022, we find the freedoms and normalisation of gay rights, particularly in the Southern states, being rolled back by an alarming number of anti-LGBTQ+ bills. This is linked with rhetoric that seems to be inspired by misinformation about what it means to be trans, and hysteria over so-called grooming. In Florida, for example, state legislation has made it illegal to have instruction on gender identity and sexual orientation in schools between kindergarten and third grade; the so-called 'don't say gay law'. The raised awareness of health issues and the associated need to protect children caused by the COVID-19 pandemic became conflated with the perceived over-reaching of the state through the imposition of school closures and a derogatory sense of 'wokeness'. Florida governor Ron DeSantis positions the state as a last stronghold of liberty and 'American values', to such an extent that he uses the slur 'groomer' to refer to those who present LGBTQ+-positive arguments. To be gay, in the view of DeSantis and his followers, is to be inherently sexualised and therefore a threat to the innocence they argue is central to American values. This links back to national—and international—politics through QAnon, which frames Joe Biden as the 'groomer-in-chief', part of a mythical satanic child trafficking sect that is at the heart of the Democratic Party.

Populism has many forms, and perhaps one that is most devastating has been Russian president Vladimr Putin's decision to enhance his popularity by invading the neighbouring country of Ukraine. As a direct consequence of this, we can see two areas in which gender has been affected, both directly and indirectly.

Gender stereotypes, with the outdated insistence of female domesticity and fragility and masculine power and strength, was perhaps the first clear indication of how gender would become a vital part of this conflict. After Russia's invasion of Ukraine in March 2022, Ukrainian president, Volodymry Zelensky issued a decree making it unlawful for any men 'of fighting age' to leave the country. As a result, the millions of refugees who poured out of Ukraine were overwhelmingly women and children. In playing to these gendered stereotypes, Zelensky made real a gender division that feminism had sought hard to break down. Coupled with this, the women who stayed in Ukraine but ended up behind enemy lines are reported to have been subjected to rape and sexual assault: the ancient tools of war that again call us back to gender stereotypes at their most base and brutal form. Pramila Patten, the UN Secretary-General's special representative on sexual violence in conflict, reported in April 2022 that in addition to the rape and kidnap of women and girls by male Russian soldiers, there were also reports of the rape and sexual assault of Ukrainian men and boys by these same soldiers: rape as a deliberate strategy, a cheap, silent, and effective weapon against whole communities (Graham-Harrison, 2022; McKernan, 2022). The abhorrent use of sexual violence, or the threat of sexual violence, to gain control is one that will be played out in the criminal courts of the global community, led by the UN.

More indirectly, but more globally, gender has been affected by the wider implications of the war in Ukraine. As if the challenges to gender inequality produced by the pandemic were not enough, the fact that Ukraine is one of the world's largest producers of grain and sunflower oil has meant the cost of such products and those aligned with them has risen enormously. International sanctions against Russia, condoned by the UN, have led to fuel shortages or a huge increase in the cost of fuel. Thus, a global rise in the cost of living, already in place after the pandemic and, in the UK, adding to the effects of Brexit from January 2022, have meant a huge crisis. As governments race to help their citizens with the rise in fuel and food, the mantra in many households has been whether it is more important to heat or eat. As with the pandemic, it is women and those in the most vulnerable communities who suffer most from this cost-of-living crisis.

Structure of the Book

This book is multidisciplinary, therefore the chapters contain a variety of methodologies which allow each author to explore their theme to ultimately arrive at a conclusion that in turn links with the theme of the collection. Methodologies come from English Linguistics, Sociology, Media Studies and aligned subject areas. This diversity in approaches is a strength of the collection that allows us to explore areas of the SDGs in different ways, yet aligned conclusions relating to the need for the SDGs and the perceived deficiencies in them.

The book begins with a discussion of one of these areas of deficiency in the SDGS: sexualities. There is diversity of sexualities and gender identities that are integral to twenty-first-century life for many of us, yet these are actually missing from explicit mention in the SDGs. The chapters here show the relevance of sexuality in any discussion of the SDGs, and explore some of the consequences of omission.

The collection of essays opens with Dalton's chapter (Chap. 2) exploring the climate emergency as a global concern that disproportionately affects those from minority and marginalised communities. The climate emergency is just one of the factors leading to global migration, and in Chap. 3 Powell explores the experience of diverse sexuality in migrants attempting to negotiate their way through the UK immigration system.

In Chap. 4, Todd explores the climate emergency from the perspective of food production, with a discussion of the need to encourage more people to consume less animal produce and how this is a heavily gendered issue. Food poverty is also a factor in the barriers to education that Fairlamb explores in Chap. 5, where she presents case studies of secondary schools in the UK where they have been compelled to introduce imaginative strategies to ensure children have as good an experience as possible in the education system. These strategies are set amongst wider concerns to decolonise the curriculum, something which Fairlamb is able to link with the on-the-ground pastoral care offered in the schools in her study.

The concept of 'childhood' is explored in Chap. 6, where Weatherston looks at the barriers to health, education and life opportunities that are experienced by young girls forced into child marriage in India and Nepal. She explores how there is lack of consensus over just how to define what an 'adult' is, and how this is used to the detriment of young girls in particular.

The book then moves on to chapters that focus more on the concept of the 'safe' and 'decent' workplace, with Williams in Chap. 7 exploring the notion of 'decent' work when it comes to sex workers. Much of the Global North's engagement with gender equality issues in recent years has been influenced by the #MeToo movement. This emerged from the world of work: the Hollywood film industry and its entrenched system of sexual exploitation and assault that was normalised to such an extent that phrases such as 'the casting couch' fell into common usage beyond the confines of the studio system without being properly scrutinised. In Chap. 8, Thornborrow and Chartier look at the way the #MeToo hashtag was mobilised on social media. Following on from this, in Chap. 9 Chambers and Smith again draw on the concept of the 'safe' workplace, but explore gender-based violence in the context of higher education in the wake of the #MeToo movement. Their survey shows a long-standing, resilient culture of sexual harassment and violence for staff that is only now starting to be revealed more generally in the education context.

Another aspect of the shifts in gender relations seen in recent years can be found in the way it is represented in various forms of media. Diverse sexuality is approached through the voices of people in the trans community in Ward's chapter (Chap. 10), where she looks at the way trans people have been represented in print media, and in turn how this has affected trans people. In Chap. 11, Kristensen explores the way in which social media's attempts to present body-positive images is met with resistance, linking this with the gendering of food and the body that several of the SDGs cover. The collection concludes with two chapters that look at how popular culture has represented these shifts in gender relations towards greater gender equality through the medium of popular entertainment. In the first of these chapters, Chap. 12, Sadler explores how gender is represented through the retelling of the novel series *Poldark* in both the context of the 1970s and then the same characters reimagined in the twenty-first century, anchoring both dramatisations in a re-reading of the source materials. In particular, the treatment of sexual assault in these versions is explored in relation to how changes have been made in the light of gender equality issues in wider society. Finally, in Chap. 13, Gilligan's study focuses on another 'missing' element of the SDGs: explicit reference to men. By default, the SDGs focus on 'society' as being masculine with females and diverse identities being treated as add-ons. However, as Gilligan argues, there is much to be said still in terms of gender equality if we look at popular media representations of stay-at-home fathers. In turn, she argues of the consequences of our failure to engage critically with such mediated texts when it comes to teacher education.

Ultimately, the chapters in this book seek to shed light on the diversity of genders and sexualities that are largely hidden from view in the SDGs and show that, however well-intentioned these goals are, there is still some way to go.

References

Browne, E. (2019). *Gender Norms, LGBTQI Issues and Development*. ALIGN.

Davis, K. (2008). Intersectionality as Buzzword: A Sociology of Science Perspective on What Makes a Feminist Theory Successful. *Feminist Theory, 9*(1), 67–85.

Dorey, K. (2018). *"Leave No One Behind": LGBT Inclusion in Development*. [Online]. Retrieved May 21, 2022, from https://www.bond.org.uk/news/2018/02/leave-no-one-behind-lgbt inclusion-in-development.

Gosine, A. (2015). *Rescue, and Real Love: same-Sex Desire in International Development*. IDS.

Graham-Harrison, E. (2022). Men and Boys Among Alleged Rape Victims of Russian Soldiers in Ukraine. *The Guardian*, May 3. Retrieved May 29, 2022, from https://www.theguardian.com/world/2022/may/03/men-and-boys-among-alleged-victims-by-russian-soldiers-in-ukraine

McKernan, B. (2022, April 4). Rape as a Weapon: huge Scale of Sexual Violence Inflicted in Ukraine Emerges. *The Guardian*. Retrieved May 29, 2022, from https://www.theguardian.com/world/2022/apr/03/all-wars-are-like-this-used-as-a-weapon-of-war-in-ukraine.

Mills, E. (2015). *"Leave No-One Behind": Gender Sexuality and the Sustainable Development Goals*. Institute for Development Studies.

Morgan, D., Cullati, S., Kelly-Irving, M., Rosselet, M., Regard, S., & Courvoiser, D. (2022, March 28). Neighbourhood Socio-Economic Vulnerability and Access to COVID-19 Healthcare During the First Two Waves of the Pandemic in Geneva, Switzerland: a gender Perspective. *The Lancet*. https://doi.org/10.1016/j.eclinm.2022.101352

Morgan, R., PImenta, D. N., & Rashid, S. (2022, March 2). Gender Equality and COVID-19: Act Now Before It Is Too Late. *The Lancet*. https://doi.org/10.1016/S0140-6736(22)00278-1

Park, A. (2016). *A Development Agenda for Sexual and Gender Minorities*. Williams Institute.

Refuge. (2021, March 23). *A Year of Lockdown: Refuge Releases New Figures Showing Dramatic Increase in Activity*. Press Release. https://www.refuge.org.uk/a-year-of-lockdown/

ReportOUT. (2022). *Sustainable Development Goal Champions.* [Online] Retrieved April 7, 2022, from https://www.reportout.org/sdg-champions

Schilt, K., & Westbrook, L. (2009). Doing Gender, Doing Heteronormativity: "gender Normals", Transgender People, and the Social Maintenance of Heterosexuality. *Gender & Society, 23*(4), 440–464.

Silverio, S. A, de Backer, K., Dasgupta, T., Torres, O., Easter, A., Khazaezadeh, N., ... Magee, L. (2002, May 29). On Race and Ethnicity During a Global Pandemic: An "Imperfect Mosaic" of Maternal and Child Health Services in Ethnically-Diverse South London, United Kingdom. *The Lancet.* https://doi.org/10.1016/j.eclinm.2022.101433

Smith, A., & Higgins, M. (2020, May). Tough Guys and Little Rocket Men: @ Realdonaldtrump's Twitter Feed and the Normalisation of Banal Masculinity. *Social Semiotics*, pp. 547–562. https://doi.org/10.1080/10350330.2020.1763657

Stonewall. (2022). "Leave No One Behind": LGBT Inclusion and Development. [Online]. Retrieved May 23, 2022, from https://www.stonewall.org.uk/node/21899

Trithart, A. (2021). *A UN for All? UN Policy and Programming on Sexual Orientation, Gender Identity and Expression, and Sex Characteristics.* International Peace Institute.

Trussell Trust. (2020). *New Report Reveals How Coronovirus Has Affected Food Bank Use.* Retrieved May 31, 2022, from https://www.trusselltrust.org/2020/09/14/new-report-reveals-how-coronavirus-has-affected-food-bank-use/

UNESCO. (2021). *When Schools Shut: Gendered Impacts of COVID-19 School Closures.* Online Open Access. Retrieved May 31, 2022, from https://unesdoc.unesco.org/ark:/48223/pf0000379270

United Nations. (2022). The Universal Declaration of Human Rights. [Online]. Retrieved April 16, 2022, from https://www.un.org/en/about-us/universal-declaration-of-human-rights

United Nations Development Programme. (2022a). *What Are the Sustainable Development Goals?* [Online]. Retrieved March 23, 2022, from https://www.undp.org/sustainable development-goals

United Nations Development Programme. (2022b). *Working Together for a New Future.* [Online]. Retrieved May 27, 2022, from https://www.undp.org/

United Nations Sustainable Development Group. (2022). *Universal Values Principle Two: Leave No One Behind.* [Online]. Retrieved March 21, 2022, from https://unsdg.un.org/2030-agenda/universal-values/leave-no-one-behind

World Health Organisation. (2018). Millennium Development Goals (MDGs). [Online]. Retrieved March 2, 2022, from https://www.who.int/news-room/fact-sheets/detail/millennium-development-goals-(mdgs)

CHAPTER 2

Have We Left Behind the Rainbow Warriors? The Climate Emergency and Its Impact on Global Queer People and Their Communities

Drew Dalton

Introduction

In Kingston, Jamaica, a group of approximately 60 queer young homeless people have congregated together for safety. Self-titled as the 'Gully Queens' (Reuters, 2017) many have fled homophobia and transphobic violence from their communities, or fled family rejection from within their homes. Often resorting to petty crime, begging, or sex work to survive, and living in deep levels of poverty, these young people have assembled as a small queer community to live in precarious safety in the city's gullies. Walled in stone, these gullies are six to nine feet wide, and they lie below street level, draining rainwater and the city's refuse out to sea. Through

D. Dalton (✉)
Faculty of Education and Society, University of Sunderland, Sunderland, UK
e-mail: andrew.dalton@sunderland.ac.uk

D. Dalton, A. Smith (eds.), *Gender, Sexuality and the UN's SDGs*, Sustainable Development Goals Series,
https://doi.org/10.1007/978-3-031-31046-1_2

living in their open location, these queer young people face regular attacks from the public from being visible in the open gullies, are vilified by the press, and they face regular raids and confiscation of property by the police (The Independent, 2014). However, these young people also face a deeper and looming issue of climate change, whereby Jamaica's 2.93 million people are facing serious threats from hotter temperatures and droughts, but also floods linked to climate change (World Bank, 2022).

These waterways, as places of supposed refuge for the Gully Queens, have become a potential hazard, with a real risk of drowning as the gullies swell due to freak and sudden flooding, due to Extreme Weather Events (EWEs). With EWEs and flash flooding a serious and very real risk, compounded by the effects of state homo and transphobia and familial rejection, this presents these young people with few safer spaces left to go. The tangible links between institutional homophobia and transphobia, and the effects of the climate emergency on the lives of queer people have never been more pronounced, as evidenced by the lived experience of the Gully Queens. As such, this chapter will outline the multifaceted effects of the climate emergency and climate effects on the lives of queer people globally. It will argue that queer people are impacted by structural factors as set out by 'Giddens' Paradox' but with additional factors, as I expand upon the argument put forward by Giddens. Furthermore, it will outline some key recommendations to engage with queer people and their communities, if the United Nations Agenda 2030 and Sustainable Development Goal 13: Climate Action is to be met, to truly 'leave no one behind.'

Shifting from 'Climate Change' to 'Climate Emergency'

Climate change is characterised by changes to the global climate resulting from an enhanced greenhouse effect, which is caused by greenhouse gases, such as carbon dioxide which is produced predominantly by the burning and use of fossil fuels (McCormick, 2022). This has been felt significantly in some parts of the world where visible effects of it can be seen through melting glaciers, drought, forest fires, or extreme weather events (EWEs) such as tornadoes and hurricanes. In 2018, the Intergovernmental Panel on Climate Change (IPCC) launched a report on the impact of global warming if global temperatures reach higher than the 1.5 °C 'guard rail,' which could be exceeded in just 12 years, by 2030 (IPCC, 2018). Recognising the human-made impact of climate change, the IPCC (2018) report also outlined a series of catastrophic environmental disasters which would happen to life on earth should it rise above this level and stated that without global support and rapid changes from the carbon emissions of humans, the Earth will see a succession of harmful EWEs. Furthermore, the same report, forecasted a temperature rise of 2.5°–10 °C over the next century, which would lead to elimination of life, and significant changes to humans.

The planet has already been affected by climate change, which has seen some of the following impacts on ecosystems, communities, cities, and territories, as well as some future predictions, should climate change not be tackled. The following list sets out several impacts of climate change on the planet today (though this is not an exhaustive list):

- Changing weather patterns have seen an increased intensity, frequency, and duration of hurricanes, as well as the additional frequency of the strongest hurricanes (regarded as Category 4 and 5), all of which have increased since the early 1980s (NASA, 2022).
- Due to global warming, sea levels have risen by about 20 cm since reliable record keeping began in 1880 due to melting ice caps, glaciers, and floating ice, are already threatening coastal areas and island nations. It is projected to rise up between 30 and 243 cm by 2100, which will see additional storm surges and increased flooding for approximately 100 years, even if carbon emissions are stopped now. Worryingly, almost four in ten people (39%) live within 100 km from a shoreline and are at risk of flooding if sea levels continue to rise. In addition to this, 600 million of these people live in a 'low-level coastal zone,' and 200 million on a coastal flood plain (Met Office, 2022; NASA, 2022).
- Droughts, heatwaves, and desertification of areas are starting to happen, leading to increased poverty, agricultural failure, and environmental migrant movement (McCormick, 2022).
- Increased wildfires due to drought and record temperatures (US Geological Survey, 2022).
- The human impacts have seen increased conflict over resource scarcity ('water wars'), risks to water supplies, food insecurity, failing fisheries (due to ocean acidification), localised flooding, and heat stress (Met Office, 2022).

Reacting to the effects of climate change several nation states, such as the United Kingdom, alerted a state of 'climate emergency,' recognising the impact of climate change and pledging to become carbon neutral by 2030 (BBC News, 2019). The term 'Climate Emergency' recognises that the terminology of 'climate change' risks dulling down the significance of the change and intervention is needed. Reflecting this, in 2019 the Oxford Dictionaries declared 'Climate Emergency' their 'word of the year.' Though not broadly defined as a term beforehand, the Oxford Dictionaries has now defined it as, 'a situation in which urgent action is required to reduce or halt climate change and avoid potentially irreversible environmental damage resulting from it' (World Economic Forum, 2019b). This was recognised due to the growing use of this term, which had increased 100-fold over only a 12-month period, creating a sense of urgency and movement as evidenced by a series of strikes, social movement protests, and civil unrest in 2019 (World Economic Forum, 2019b). Due to the recognition of the urgency of the Climate Emergency itself and the institutional responses in using it, I have also decided to use this term throughout, to describe the process and effects of climate change, as well as the urgency in which to tackle it.

Amidst this, the relatively successful Paris Agreement adopted in 2015 gathered global agreement to keep the global temperature rise well below the 2 °C above pre-industrial levels (UN SDGs, 2022) and to strengthen the ability of countries to deal with the impacts of the Climate Emergency through finance, increased use of technology, and an enhanced capacity framework. As of April 2018, 175 parties had ratified the Paris Agreement and 168 parties had communicated their intentions to contribute towards reduced emissions and therefore, to the United Nations Framework Convention on Climate Change (1994) which is the underling intergovernmental forum with overall responsibility to this. Alongside this, the United Nations Sustainable Development Goals were also launched in 2015, with Goal 13: Climate Action, as one of the key goals (UN SDGs, 2022). SDG Goal 13, has specific targets which must be met by 2030, which are to include some of the following targets:

- **Target 13.1** Strengthen resilience and adaptive capacity to climate-related hazards and natural disasters in all countries.
- **Target 13.2** Integrate climate change measures into national policies, strategies, and planning.

- **Target 13.B** Promote mechanisms for raising capacity for effective climate change-related planning and management in least developed countries and small island developing states, including focusing on women, youth, and local and marginalised communities (UN SDGs, 2022).

Whilst the SGDs, and in particular Goal 13: Climate Action, were welcome additions to the international development agenda, not all actions on this goal have been successful by global governance. The 26th annual summit 'Conference of the Parties (COP26) in Glasgow, United Kingdom, saw some renewed success in nation state pledges to maintain the goal of 1.5 °C. However, COP26 also saw an intervention by delegates from China and India to change the agreement wording of 'phase down' rather than 'phase out' the use of coal, to the frustration of other nation states who wanted to phase out the use of fossil fuels entirely (BBC News, 2021). Significantly, Goal 13 of the SDGs has allowed for a significant open wording of 'marginalised communities' in Target 13.B to use, alongside the SDG statements to 'leave no one behind' and to 'reach the furthest behind first' (UN DESA, 2017). These statements are important to 'queer the SDGs,' as they provide access ports for queer organisations to engage with the SDG process, even if they are not named specifically (ReportOUT, 2021). The Climate Emergency narrative has been slow to acknowledge (if acknowledged at all) marginalised communities such as queer people globally, as the effect of its impact upon queer lives. However, this also links to a wider 'back of the mind issue,' which will be examined in the following section.

Giddens and the Climate Emergency as a 'Back of the Mind Issue'

Whilst the Climate Emergency has started to grow in prominence amongst global narratives and development circles, queer people have been left behind in these discussions and in key decision making. The Climate Emergency is an interesting paradox on the global stage, as it has entered mainstream debate and has touched upon global governance, but it is not felt to be a pressing issue amongst some of the world's population. This is due to it being presented as a 'back of the mind' issue, as set out by Giddens' (2009) work, which will be examined further now.

Giddens (2009) argued that at the very heart of Climate Emergency politics and action, there is a fundamental paradox. 'Giddens' Paradox' (Giddens, 2009) suggests three problematic areas which remain at the core of the narrative when tackling the Climate Emergency. Firstly, electorates of many nation states cannot grasp the significance of the Climate Emergency as it appears to be too abstract, not dramatic enough, and 'distant' from their lives. Giddens (2009) argues that many people will not understand the consequences of this until they see the most catastrophic results, yet by that time and if not tackled, humanity will experience freak weather systems, sea-level rises, higher temperatures, and weather-based disasters. At this point, Giddens (2009) argues, it will be too late.

Secondly, Giddens (2009) argues that another unique challenge in the Climate Emergency debate is that it is not a subject of debate which can be pushed away and dealt with later. Carbon emissions and greenhouse gases are within the atmosphere already and are here to stay. The notion of 'ecological temporality' is, 'the multiple, complex, contextual rhythms and processes of ecosystems' (Doyle, 2016, 26), arguing that humans have difficulty in conceptualising the expanse of ecological time which contributes to apathy and inaction in the face of the Climate Emergency (Doyle, 2016; Shotwell, 2016; Rush, 2018). Climate disasters have become a concern of the distant future and a 'back of the mind issue,' which means it is less attractive to act now. This 'creeping problem' is further reinforced by Western political discourse about climate change as a future-facing issue, which serves to also intentionally overlook the history of industrialisation, fossil fuel consumption, and land degradation that contribute to the Climate Emergency (Marshall, 2015). In this political landscape, the longer the issue is debated and fought over, the more pollution is happening, which is exacerbating the issue even further (Giddens, 2009).

A final, and linked point raised by Giddens (2009), is the problem with people as 'free riders,' who have ample opportunity to tackle climate change, but instead wait for others to do so. As Giddens (2009) goes on to say:

> Since the dangers posed by global warming aren't tangible, immediate, or visible in the course of day-to-day life, many will sit on their hands and do nothing of a concrete nature about them. Yet waiting until such dangers become visible and acute—in the shape of catastrophes that are irrefutably

> the result of climate change—before being stirred to serious action will be too late. (Giddens, 2009, p. 2)

Giddens' (2009) other central argument is that a strong state is needed to play a key role in averting future catastrophes, and this 'enabling state' is the only institution able to mould social behaviour, develop hard-hitting policies for re-shaping social behaviours, and establishing new energy investments. This is not a centralised state in Giddens' (2009) view, but an 'ensuring state,' which should be both an enabler and regulator, involving a cross-party consensus and full state capacity to reduce carbon emissions at a national and global level. Giddens' (2009) view of this state, and of global cooperation to ensure this, would involve a competitive site of innovation for ecological technological improvements, with climate change merging with all other political goals. Finally, he argues that a 'development imperative' is needed for poorer and developing countries to develop their economies, so they can take part in technological 'leap-frogging' to catch up, allowing greener development pathways for nation states to do this. Giddens (2009) has been accused of selling old wine in new bottles, with research in nation states such as Sweden showing that concern for climate change and climate action goes beyond simple self-interest as suggested by his work (Isenhour, 2013). Nonetheless, Giddens' (2009) notion of this paradox as a 'back of the mind issue' proves to be a useful framework in which to examine the position of queer populations. As global actors and nation states are beginning to talk about the Climate Emergency, are queer people and their communities still a 'back of the mind issue' in terms of state, institutional, and global leadership discussions, and narratives?

Whilst Giddens' Paradox (Giddens, 2009) becomes a useful theoretical framework to examine action (and inaction) regarding the Climate Emergency, this needs further development when considering queer populations, and so this will be expanded upon and theorised further. Queer people have been largely overlooked in many climate debates for three key reasons, namely: (1) Hetero/cisnormative structures and homogenised narratives, (2) the disconnect in climate justice movement representation, and; (3) queer people and communities as 'beyond the back of the mind.' These will be outlined now.

Hetero/cisnormative Structures and Homogenised Narratives—'It Effects All of Us Equally'

The climate justice conversation lacks sufficient representation and voices from marginalised groups, such as people living with disabilities; lesbian, gay, bisexual, transgender, intersex, and queer (LGBTIQ+) people; and migrants and refugees (Open Global Rights, 2022). When narratives around climate change have grown, they have tended to address populations as a homogenous whole, as a narrative of 'it effects all of us.' Whilst this is accurate in that the Climate Emergency does affect all aspects of the globe, it is and will be felt unevenly across places, spaces, and populations. The heteronormativity and cisnormativity of the SDGs have ensured that the language of international development remains firmly within cisgender normative binaries and heteronormative assumptions, which ensure that queer minorities are rarely considered.

In a review of the international development sector, Jolly (2011) found deeply heteronormative phrasing and categorisation in household models and family forms, work around HIV and AIDS, and efforts to combat violence against women. For example, when women's vulnerability is discussed in climate change literature, it is often generalised and reductive, which disregards intersectional privileges—instead, oversimplifying women's poverty as a cause without examining the unequal gendered power dynamics behind the poverty in the first place (Arora-Jonsson, 2011). Taking this further and applying this to climate action and its effects on women, often women are presented as a heteronormative and homogenous grouping, without accounting for the specific issues faced by lesbian, bisexual, and transgender women who are front facing in climate disasters. This process ensures that the homogenisation narrative of equally affected populations becomes not only problematic, but inaccurate.

Discussion about climate action and the SDGs, and the Climate Emergency at a United Nations levels, has not been forthcoming regarding queer people. Instead, it has remained focused on 'women and girls' as a homogenous grouping or the 'climate change/Emergency' is positioned as something which does have uneven impacts upon populations but has no focus on queer lives. It was interesting to note that at the time of writing this chapter, various keyword searches on the United Nations website for 'climate change and sexual and gender minorities' (the language of the UN for queer people) and 'climate change and LGBT' (and various iterations of this acronym), produced no relevant results (United

Nations, 2022). The narrative of climate change is deeply heteronormative and cisnormative at both global governance and at the development sector levels, with little to no acknowledgement of queer lives and communities as impacted by this. Behind this narrative sits many nation states, whereby colonial legacies of criminalisation feed into state, sector, and community-led homophobia, biphobia, and transphobia, making a 'dual burden' faced by queer people when linking their needs to the Climate Emergency, and accessing institutions to bring these needs to the forefront.

The Disconnect in Climate Justice Movement Representation

Interestingly, queer people are twice as likely to join climate causes and social movements than that of heterosexuals. This has been hypothesised as being due to specific community groups and online networks, which are essential for queer people to discuss ideas and reinforce a need for political engagement (Swank, 2018). Environmental and queer social movements both have their roots in tackling current oppressions, and so for many marginalised communities the realities and impacts of the Climate Emergency are keenly felt now, with the ability to speculate about climate change as a problem of tomorrow being inherently privileged (Rush, 2018).

Weder and Swastika (2021) noted from their research that environmentalism was stronger within queer communities than in heterosexual populations, noting that 'being green' is essentialised to being queer amongst their respondents. The perception of 'being revolutionary' within the green movement had similar echoes to that of the queer movement, which seeks to problematise the existing (heterosexual and cisgender) social order. However, whilst individuals may feel an embodied green identity, this does not always translate to a more engaged agenda on this issue within LGBTQI+ organisations. When social and political movements such as rights or legal-based movements around sexual and gender minorities overlook intersections of oppression, they lose political power as they foreground their 'first emergency,' whilst backgrounding other key issues such as the Climate Emergency (Gaard, 2011). It seems that climate politics and sexual rights politics, whilst both traditionally supported by queer people in different ways, tend not to connect with one another.

Queer Lives and Communities as 'Beyond the Back of the Mind'

The 'no one is left behind' slogan has been set out for the SDGs, however the engagement of queer people's communities and lives with Climate Emergency initiatives is obscured by two key forces. Firstly, the heteronormative and cisnormative forces which have underpinned the global governance and agenda setting of climate change, have also been present within social movements under the narrative of 'climate affects us all equally.' Queer people have been placed 'beyond the back of the mind' within the wider Climate Emergency discussions and have largely been overlooked by politicians, global bodies, development actors and institutions, but also by the climate movement itself. Some of these barriers to engagement are due to the perceived invisibility of queer people by the state, the criminalisation of their bodies, and hot and cold homophobia and transphobia (Martell, 2018). This means that both internally and externally, queer people have been side-lined from Climate Emergency master narratives, and their access to them.

The obfuscating nature of this wider climate narrative has yet to fully acknowledge the marginalised voices such as queer people, which are most at risk and instead, they have largely been positioned as internal 'LGBTQI+ concerns' when queer people live homeless or live in storm gullies as beggars and sex workers. The climate change movement has already been accused of being a predominantly White, middle-class social movement (Yaxley, 2021), and so it is imperative for the climate movement to give more focus on the most vulnerable groups internally, as well as external climate governance to do the same. Indeed:

> The climate movement will do a disservice to minorities if it doesn't centre their voices and experience in its activism. The ability to take climate action is a privilege. By centring minority groups in the climate movement, we improve everyone's lives and ensure that no one is left behind. (Yaxley, 2021)

A more intersectional approach to the impacts of the Climate Emergency is vital to highlight how different groups define and respond to their realities, with an under-reporting of those groups posing an issue for purposive and inclusive policy change, especially queer people of colour in the Global North and South, who often live in low-income livelihoods and who live on the frontlines of the Climate Emergency. The study of environmental justice has expanded to include women, indigeneity, citizenship, and more, but far less attention has been paid to sexual orientation and gender identity, including in the context of intersectionality (Goldsmith & Bell, 2022).

Yet despite significant queer membership of environmental social movements, there is a disconnect between the climate movements and traditional LGBTQI+ political movements. Messages have not flown readily between both groups and neither have substantial attempts at movement engagement between these organisations. The momentum of many queer organisations at a national level, and their engagement with the UN SDGs and climate discussions, have been slow to advance.

Giddens' (2009) notion of the 'Giddens' Paradox' gives a useful theoretical framework to begin to understand the slower progress in tackling the Climate Emergency from external organisations and actors, as well as within the queer movement. Despite more recent positive governmental shifts and pledges towards the Climate Emergency, more must be done. Yet Giddens' (2009) argument only takes us so far in understanding the ambivalence of tackling this problem and so it was important to add to this theoretical development, to bring queer issues under the Climate Emergency, to light. This chapter's advancement of Giddens (2009) work to include hetero/cisnormativity and the homogenising of population groups, alongside a disconnect of queer social movements feeding into the discussions about the SDGs and climate action, will both continue to ensure that the Climate Emergency and the impact on queer lives will remain beyond the back of the mind as an issue, unless firmly tackled and acknowledged.

Queer People and the Climate Emergency—Where Are the Links?

The Gully Queens mentioned in the introduction of this chapter are not the only ways in which the Climate Emergency has touched upon queer lives across the globe, and so with the advancement of the Climate Emergency, and the invisibilisation of queer lives in this climate narrative, it is important to examine how queer people have been impacted by it. It is increasingly clear that queer people are often facing the 'front line' of the Climate Emergency, and the associated climate effects and EWEs which come alongside it. Homelessness is a key factor in this increased vulnerability to a changing climate, and whilst globally it is estimated that 150 million people worldwide are homeless, which stands at around 2% of the global population, the numbers are likely to be much higher (World

Economic Forum, 2019a). However, certain groups such as queer people face over-representation in this area. Despite global homeless data being fragmented regarding queer populations, nation state reports tend to show that young queer people are more likely than many other societal demographics to live homeless, with an estimation of 20–40% of the homeless population being a sexual or gender minority (Fraser et al., 2019).

The cause of homelessness for queer people is due to a range of complex factors with a basis in homophobia, biphobia, or transphobia, including but not restricted to some of the following: family rejection, stigma, forced evictions, religious and conservative social attitudes, conversion practices, mental health, poverty, under-employment, and unemployment (World Economic Forum, 2016). Global homelessness leads to a precarity of existence for many queer people, with many finding spaces and sleeping in temporary shelters, or in unsafe open areas. Homeless people, and those with inadequate or temporary housing, will be strongly affected by any natural calamity and are clear victims of temperature rise and polluted air (Goldsmith & Bell, 2022). Further to this, the precarious economic and physical conditions that often affect homeless groups may also lead queer people to choose sex work and begging, despite the heightened risk of criminal prosecution, to meet their basic needs. This exposes them to hostility and abuse from police and municipal authorities, making it difficult for them to access government services should a climate disaster happen.

Compounding some of the vulnerabilities already faced by queer people are the scant regard to their needs in aid and reconstruction programmes provided by nation states and the international community. This lack of visibility allows queer people to be targeted by others, excluded from the allocation of resources, and little to no support offered after violations have happened. Human Dignity Trust (2019) notes that natural disasters and climate disasters 'unmake' queer homes, queer communities, and a wider sense of queer belonging in three important ways. Firstly, climate disasters ensure the destruction of residences belonging to queer people and their families; secondly, they elevate anxieties and concerns about privacy and discrimination for individuals and families in refuge shelters; and finally, they impact upon the loss of queer neighbourhoods or areas, and their accompanying community infrastructure (both visible networks such as safe houses or centres, and invisible or online networks, such as activist networks). Yet, despite homelessness figures showing an over-representation of queer people where they are documented, few links have been made to the effects of the Climate Emergency, and its effects, on this group.

Incidences showing the palpable and linked effects of the Climate Emergency on queer communities are therefore still emerging and are thus both under-researched and under-acknowledged within the climate, international development, and humanitarian aid literature (Human Dignity Trust, 2019). Despite not being directly related to the Climate Emergency, the fate of the Aravanis in Sri Lanka (a gender fluid category which may be regarded as transgender or intersex) provides a useful window in which to highlight the socio-historical invisibilisation of queer people from the state, humanitarian, and development organisations. After the 2004 Indian Ocean Tsunami in Sri Lanka, and subsequent disaster relief efforts and NGOs/INGOs moved in to provide support, many Aravanis were denied access to both social care and medical support because of entrenched discrimination from both the state, and from the NGOs/INGOs. This invisibilisation meant that they did not appear in damage assessments by either the government, or by other relief organisations working in post-disaster relief, meaning that they were denied bedding, shelter, and food. The Aravanis are already an oppressed minority in Sri Lanka, who often find employment in begging or dancing, and many who survived the Tsunami lost their small savings, make-up, dancing costumes and jewels, often their only tools for dancing employment in the future, with no recourse to funds (Humanitarian Practice Network, 2012). Furthermore, people needed to be registered as a resident of their municipality if they wished to access government food aid. This process involved sharing a permanent address with the police, which blocked some queer people from seeking support, in a nation state whereby homosexuality is illegal (The New Humanitarian, 2020). Echoing this, the process of invisibilisation is also replicated via external organisations and the state, in providing support to the public after climate-related incidents, where queer populations are often overlooked.

In parallel to the experiences of the Aravanis in Sri Lanka, the effects of the Climate Emergency are also a threat-multiplier in that they exacerbate existing social problems for queer populations and people. This was noted by research from Human Dignity Trust (2019), where they noted that in times of lawlessness after climate disasters and the increased pressure on more scarce resources, this leads homophobia, biphobia, and transphobia to 'rise to the surface.' Perpetrators of homophobia, biphobia, and transphobia use pre-existing stigma to gain resources or to enact violence or harm, with the perpetrators acting upon this without impunity or consequence. This is further compounded by international humanitarian law (IHL) which pays little head to queer people, their needs, and vulnerabilities. Where same-sex intimacy or gender identity and expression is no longer a crime and public attitudes are shifting favourably, homophobia, biphobia, and transphobia can also persist and surface in an extreme way in times of conflict or disaster (Human Dignity Trust, 2019). For example, despite Mozambique being regarded as one of the 'friendliest' nations in Africa for sexual and gender minorities (O'Donnell, 2016), the 2019 devastation of Cyclone Idai in the city of Beira, compounded existing issues of poverty, inadequate housing, and women's vulnerability to gender-based violence. Due to the devastation of Cyclone Idai, many poorly constructed shelters in which minority women lived were destroyed, leading to reports about the heightened visibility and therefore vulnerability, of lesbian and bisexual women to sexual violence and so-called corrective rape (The Ecologist, 2021).

In the wake of a climate disaster or EWE, many queer people often struggle to access government or institutional resources for fear of perceived, or real, persecution, particularly in countries where homosexuality or 'transgressive' gender expressions are criminalised. Instead of being understood as a relational concept which bestows roles and gender-based expectations on all people, gender is often narrowly equated with only cisgender women and girls in development and humanitarian organisations (Brody, 2021). This is significant as the United Nations Sustainable Development Goal 5, 'Gender Equality' to 'achieve gender equality and empower all women and girls' is problematic within its own defined binary version of gender (ReportOUT, 2021). This limitation means that specific vulnerabilities and needs of gender minorities are ignored, which is worrying in that social marginalisation, stigma, prejudice, and poverty commonly experienced by queer populations present increased susceptibility to climate-related incidents and shocks (Brody, 2021).

As an example of this, the aftermath of the 2013 Super Typhoon Yolanda in the Philippines saw gendered lines drawn in relief efforts. Queer people not only faced the shock of a super storm which destroyed households, belongings, and businesses (including loved ones), they also faced unique challenges due to their minority status. Despite a focus on gender in disaster relief and humanitarian rehabilitation in the Philippines, the recovery efforts were based around a cisgender man-woman binary (Nichols, 2019), reinforcing an essentialist and homogenising narrative, viewing all women as one group, rather than a group of diverse needs (Junio, 2018). Through this, many gender minorities were excluded from livelihood initiatives, unable to access housing benefits and sanitation facilities (UNDP et al., 2020). Existing state and international disaster policies and practices operate a compulsory heterosexuality (Rich, 1980) where the needs of queer people are either ostracised or disregarded on a social, economic, and institutional basis. This ensures that anyone perceived to be outside of the male-female binary and heteronormative grouping becomes more vulnerable when faced with the effects of natural disasters (Gaillard et al., 2016). Within post-disaster contexts, a pressing need for many people is livelihood and employment, which become significantly more difficult to achieve due to prejudice and discrimination, which was noted in the after-effects of Yolanda amongst queer Filipinos turned away from employment (Gaillard et al., 2016).

> [The after-effects of the Yolanda disaster] opened my eyes to the realities confronted by various LGBT people as they worked to rebuild after such unthinkable loss and devastation. [...] Meeting other LGBT people and hearing their stories taught me valuable lessons about intersectionality and how privilege works especially in times of disaster. For those advocating for the environment, we need to understand that climate justice is not separate from social justice. Everything is connected and all forms of oppression are systemic and linked. (Nichols, 2019)

Even within nation states with significant protective legislation and more open social attitudes, climate disasters can still be problematic as marginalised communities are rendered vulnerable when these climate disasters strike. Hurricane Katrina in 2005 devasted swathes of New Orleans in the USA, with deep-level floods and household destruction, leaving many people homeless, sanitation services swamped, and people forced to gather to live in football stadiums and temporary camps on dry ground. When seeking safety, transgender individuals were reportedly discriminated against, and even denied entry or access to emergency shelters, with two transgender individuals arrested for using the bathroom of their gender at a temporary emergency shelter (Goldsmith & Bell, 2022). Furthermore, stigmatising religious practices meant that queer people were also blamed as the cause of the hurricane by some religious leaders or denied aid from faith-based organisations for lacking identification that matched their name or gender. On a state level, queer people in relationships and families were further isolated from US state disaster relief policies and benefits for married (heterosexual) couples, in a nation state where same-sex marriage was not legalised until 2015. It was noted that the Federal Emergency Agency's lack of recognition of queer families led to an unequal distribution of aid resources, often to the detriment of the children of those families (Goldsmith & Bell, 2022).

Dominey-Howes et al. (2014) found that queer populations faced distinctive physical, sexual, and emotional violence from the impact of environmental disasters, finding both governmental and community support as discriminatory or prejudiced. Examples of these were evidenced in the 2020 Haitian Earthquake, as many queer people were denied access to emergency housing and relief, and in Nepal, a smallholder farmer who identified as a third gender was excluded from helping to build and take cover in shelter houses which are designed to protect the community from EWEs, which are often sex-segregated along a cisgender binary (Devex, 2020). In an example closely tied to the effects of the Climate Emergency, during the 2011 floods in Queensland, Australia, it was revealed that 43% of queer individuals felt afraid of the actual evacuation centres during the disaster and recovery process (Dominey-Howes, Gorman-Murray, & McKinnon, 2017).

There is a paucity of data on the specific health risks and issues faced by queer populations in the face of Climate Emergency induced disasters (Brody, 2021), and whilst shared vulnerabilities across all populations are clear, given the levels of social and economic exclusion faced by minority populations, this has impact on their ability to seek resilient outcomes (Knight, 2016; Outright International, 2020). Prior to a disaster, queer people may not have access to the same levels of resources, capital, information, restricted social networks, and assets as the general population, which affects resilience and how queer individuals (and communities) can experience a climate shock (Devex, 2020). The needs of queer people after climate-related disasters need better understanding, with the impact of food insecurity and malnutrition for those impacted by HIV and AIDS, being paramount. Globally, gay men, and men who have sex with men (MSM) are 27 times more likely to contract HIV, with rates of HIV 13 times higher amongst transgender people (UNAIDS, 2020). Amongst this group, pre-existing fears of seeking health care due to stigma and discrimination are heightened, which makes it significantly more difficult to seek urgent care after a climate-related event.

After climate disasters, some queer people may face unique health-related issues, especially those who do not have access to Anti-Retroviral

Therapies (ART) to control their HIV. During Hurricane Maria in the North-eastern Caribbean in 2017, many pharmacies were destroyed or lost electricity due to fallen powerlines or destroyed generators, meaning they were unable to get ART or hormone replacement therapy prescription refills to those who needed it (Melin et al., 2018). Similarly, during Hurricane Katrina, many queer people living with HIV were reluctant to disclose their HIV status to emergency relief doctors who were not familiar to them (Haskell, 2021). Whilst the Climate Emergency, and subsequent relief efforts at state and institutional level have been problematic for queer people and their communities, an emerging recognition of queer people and climate narratives has started to emerge, which will now be examined.

Resistance to This? Queer People and the Climate Emergency

Encouragingly, theoretical frameworks and climate action have begun to tackle the injustices of queer people left behind by environmental movements and wider narratives. Within queer theory, 'Queer Ecology' has emerged, to dismantle heteronormative ideals of nature and to redefine the Climate Emergency narrative as no longer a hetero-natural vision for the future, recognising that more specialised, diverse, and localised support is also needed (Mattson, 2020; The Ecologist, 2021). Mattson (2020) argues that when the present becomes uninhabitable due to the Climate Emergency, and the toxic mix of homophobia, biphobia, and transphobia, then thinking towards the future becomes a method necessary for survival. Queer bodies who have less social power in significant parts of the world, reimagine a future which is critical and affirmative. This 'queer futurism' becomes a technique in which to look forward to the future, when it is painful to examine the past and the present, to present a queer future of hopeful possibilities (Mattson, 2020).

This concept feeds into parallel 'ecological time' whereby we are reminded of the centuries-long impact of capitalist industries and the role of environmental degradation (Fitz-Henry, 2017), and takes us from a mindset of short-term and present rewards, into a conceptual future of what change needs to happen. Drawing from the concept of 'queer time' (Dinshaw et al., 2007) a queer ecological temporality has started to reclaim and expand the present to begin to recognise that the Climate Emergency is very much here, and will affect all affirmative models of the future, unless it is tackled (Mattson, 2020). This queering of climate change and its temporal nature has taken a mundane topic such as the weather and has used it to invoke a current crisis in queer lives, to distort the known into something familiar and strange (Chakrabarty, 2009). Queer ecologies and queer time are useful frameworks to engage with the Climate Emergency, with the effects of this leading many queer people to engage with environmental social movements. However, this has yet to feed into a wider queer discourse of rights and support, though there are promising signs of this, which will be discussed next.

As discussed, Giddens (2009) hoped for an 'ensuring state' and combination of global actors to tackle the Climate Emergency. Whilst this has mobilised in terms of a wider narrative within global relations and national-level politics, it has not mobilised in terms of supporting queer lives and the Climate Emergency, because of the hetero/cisnormative structures and homogenising wider narratives of it. Due to this, many queer organisations have begun the process of enabling resistance to the Climate Emergency and queer bodies as beyond the back of the mind factor.

As evidence of this, some queer movements have synthesised their lived experiences as queer people with that of climate action and the UN SDGs, as evidenced by a small but growing base of queer publications and news, as well as some wider representation on webpages such as Friends of the Earth (Friends of the Earth, 2020). Other actors have taken an economic lens to tackle queer lives and the Climate Emergency whereby in 2021 GiveOut launched the world's first 'LGBTQI Climate Fund' for individuals and businesses, stating that queer people are 'not sat at the table and are being excluded from government decision-making' (GiveOut, 2021; Reuters, 2021) with early recipients offering training to emergency shelters to include queer people, and campaigning for inclusion in climate change consultations. Other global organisations such as the queer human rights organisation ReportOUT have started to research the effects of the Climate Emergency as part of their 'Green in the Rainbow Project' (ReportOUT, 2021), and Queer X Climate, have developed a membership pledge of queer organisations and individuals to limit and account for their carbon emissions (Queer X Climate, 2022). A queering of ecological, environmental issues and the Climate Emergency has begun to emerge, though it is in its infancy, despite the looming issue of climate disasters.

What Needs to Happen Next? Some Recommendations

Time is running out for changes to be made to shift or mitigate against some of the harsher aspects of the Climate Emergency, and so it is vital that governments, global bodies, civil society, international development, and humanitarian organisations begin to involve queer populations into climate action as part of their ongoing and contingency planning. This section will outline key recommendations and some good practice to be taken forward to facilitate social change.

Firstly, environmental disaster preparedness and harm reduction for marginalised communities such as queer people are fundamental areas which require investment. Governments must ensure that queer communities are safe in times of crises and should implement laws and policies to tackle climate disasters inclusively, incorporating an intersectional approach from both governments and additional social actors.

Secondly, queer lives and communities need to be placed at the forefront as equals in the Climate Emergency debates and in climate action, as well as engaged in agenda setting and removing queer people from beyond the back of the mind as a population under threat. The Asia Pacific Forum for Women, Law, and Development (APWLD, 2015) has set an excellent example of women-led action to inform climate change policy planning, with the programme supporting the collective work of indigenous women and queer groups in eight communities in Asia-Pacific, including the Philippines, Nepal, India, Indonesia, Thailand, Papua New Guinea, Vietnam, and Bangladesh. The programme supported women and queer people to document their experiences, responses, and needs to ensure that those most affected by climate change can shape policies at the local, national, and international level. As a result of this work, a statement and set of recommendations aimed at ASEAN (Association of Southeast Asian Nations) policy makers was produced. There needs to be a much wider facilitation of space in bringing together queer movements, and climate and environmental movements, to ensure that there is no future disconnect and linkages between issues that can be made and fought for.

Thirdly, it is imperative that nation states decriminalise harmful, and often colonial laws, which seek to obstruct some of the world's most vulnerable queer populations from engaging in agenda setting at a nation state level, without fear of risk and harm. Localised issues facing queer people should be placed into wider global trends such as the Climate Emergency if populations are not to slip through the net and become isolated.

Finally, the very SDGs themselves and Agenda 2030 need to produce targeted action to ensure that queer people have clear representation and opportunities to engage with their own development. If we are to tackle the Climate Emergency, we should be reaching the furthest behind first, to ensure that the lives of people such as the young 'Gully Queens' are not overlooked in our development of humanity.

References

APWLD. (2015). *Statement from LGBTI and Indigenous Women Affected by Climate Change*. [Online] https://apwld.org/statement-from-lgbti-and-indigenous-women-affected-by-climate-change/

Arora-Jonsson, S. (2011). Virtue and Vulnerability: Discourses on Women, Gender, and Climate Change. *Global Environmental Change, 21*, 744–751.

BBC News. (2019). *UK Parliament Declares Climate Change Emergency*. [Online] https://www.bbc.co.uk/news/uk-politics-48126677

BBC News. (2021). *COP26: What Was Agreed at the Glasgow Climate Conference?* [Online] https://www.bbc.co.uk/news/science-environment-56901261

Brody, A. (2021). *Mapping the Linkages Between Climate Change, Health, Gender and SOGIESC for the Asia-Pacific Region*. [Online] https://www.sparkblue.org/system/files/2021-02/Desk%20review_climate%20change_gender_health_Feb2021.pdf

Chakrabarty, D. (2009). The Climate of History: Four Theses. *Critical Inquiry, 35*(2), 197–222.

Devex. (2020). *Responses to Climate Change Must Be LGBTQ-Inclusive, Experts Say*. [Online] https://www.devex.com/news/responses-to-climate-disasters-must-be-lgbtq-inclusive-experts-say-98062

Dinshaw, C., Edelman, L., Ferguson, R. A., Freccero, C., Freeman, E., Halberstam, J., et al. (2007). Theorizing Queer Temporalities: A Roundtable Discussion. *GLQ: A Journal of Lesbian and Gay Studies, 13*(2), 177–195.

Dominey-Howes, D., Gorman-Murray, A., & McKinnon, S. (2014). Queering Disasters: On the Need to Account for LGBTI Experiences in Natural Disaster Contexts. *Gender, Place and Culture, 21*(7), 905–918.

Dominey-Howes, D., Gorman-Murray, A., & McKinnon, S. (2017). Problems and Possibilities on the Margins: LGBT Experiences in the 2011 Queensland Floods. *Gender, Place and Culture, 24*(1), 37–51.

Doyle, J. (2016). *Mediating Climate Change*. Routledge.

Fitz-Henry, E. (2017). Multiple Temporalities and the Nonhuman Other. *Environmental Humanities, 9*(1), 1–17.

Fraser, B., Pierse, N., Chisholm, E., & Cook, H. (2019). LGBTIQ+ Homelessness: A Review of the Literature. *International Journal of Environmental Research and Public Health, 16*(15), 26–77.

Friends of the Earth (FOE). (2020). *Why Climate Change is an LGBTQ+ Issue.* [Online] https://foe.scot/why-climate-change-is-an-lgbtq-issue/

Gaard, G. (2011). Green, Pink, and Lavender: Banishing Ecophobia Through Queer Ecologies. *Ethics and the Environment, 16*(2), 115–126.

Gaillard, J. C., Sanz, K., Balgos, B. C., Dalisay, S. N. M., Gorman-Murray, A., Smith, F., & Toelupe, V. A. (2016). Beyond Men and Women: A Critical Perspective on Gender and Disaster. *Disasters, 41*(3), 429–447.

Giddens, A. (2009). *The Politics of Climate Change.* Polity Press.

GiveOut. (2021). *Why Climate Change Is an LGBT Issue.* [Online] https://give-out.org/why-climate-change-is-a-lgbt-issue

Goldsmith, L., & Bell, M. (2022). Queering Environmental Justice: Unequal Environmental Health Burden on the LGBTQ+ Community. *American Journal of Public Health, 112*(1), 79–87.

Haskell, B. (2021). *Sexuality and Natural Disaster: Challenges of LGBT Communities Facing Hurricane Katrina.* [Online] https://papers.ssrn.com/sol3/papers.cfm?abstract_id=2513650

Human Dignity Trust. (2019). *Criminalising Homosexuality and LGBT Rights in Times of Conflict, Violence and Natural Disasters.* [Online] https://www.humandignitytrust.org/wp-content/uploads/resources/8.-Criminalisation-Conflict-and-Natural-Disasters-March-2019-1.pdf

Humanitarian Practice Network. (2012). *Making Disaster Relief and Reduction Programmes LGBTI-Inclusive: Examples from Nepal.* [Online] https://odihpn.org/publication/making-disaster-risk-reduction-and-relief-programmes-lgbti-inclusive-examples-from-nepal/

IPCC. (2018). *Global Warming of 1.5°C. An IPCC Special Report on the Impacts of Global Warming of 1.5°C Above Pre-industrial Levels and Related Global Greenhouse Gas Emission Pathways, in the Context of Strengthening the Global Response to the Threat of Climate Change, Sustainable Development, and Efforts to Eradicate Poverty.* [Online] https://www.ipcc.ch/sr15/chapter/spm/

Isenhour, C. (2013). The Politics of Climate Knowledge: Sir Giddens, Sweden and the Paradox of Climate (in)justice. *Local Environment, 18*(2), 201–216.

Jolly, S. (2011). Why Is Development Work So Straight? Heteronormativity in the International Development Industry. *Development in Practice, 21*(1), 18–28.

Junio, A. (2018). *KFAW. The 27th Foreign Correspondent Report: Sexual Minorities and Disasters in the Philippines: Where Are They*? [Online] http://www.kfaw.or.jp/correspondents/docs/27-2_Philippines_E.pdf

Knight, K. (2016). *LGBT People in Emergencies – Risks and Service Gaps.* [Online] https://www.hrw.org/news/2016/05/20/lgbt-people-emergencies-risks-and-service-gaps

Marshall, G. (2015). *Don't Even Think About It: Why Our Brains Are Wired to Ignore Climate Change*. Bloomsbury.

Martell, F. (2018). *Global Gay: How Gay Culture Is Changing the World*. MIT Press.

Mattson, L. (2020). *Elemental Climate Disaster Texts and Queer Ecological Temporality*. Graduate Theses and Dissertations. [Online] https://scholarcommons.usf.edu/etd/8252

McCormick, J. (2022). *Introduction to Global Studies* (2nd ed.). Bloomsbury.

Melin, K., Maldonado, W. T., & López-Candales, A. (2018). Lessons Learned from Hurricane Maria: Pharmacists' Perspective. *The Annals of Pharmacotherapy, 52*(5), 493–494.

Met Office. (2022). *Effects of Climate Change*. [Online] https://www.metoffice.gov.uk/weather/climate-change/effects-of-climate-change

NASA. (2022). *The Effects of Climate Change*. [Online] https://climate.nasa.gov/effects/

Nichols, E. (2019). *What the Impact of Stonewall Has Taught Me About Environmental Rights*. [Online] https://www.greenpeace.org/international/story/22806/what-the-impact-of-stonewall-has-taught-me-about-environmental-rights/

O'Donnell, B. (2016). *Here Are the Most and Least Tolerant Countries in Africa*. [Online] https://www.undispatch.com/here-are-the-most-and-least-tolerant-countries-in-africa/

Open Global Rights. (2022). *Facing Intersecting Crises: LGBTIQ+ Resilience in Fiji*. [Online] https://www.openglobalrights.org/facing-intersecting-crises-lgbtiq-plus-resilience-in-fiji/

Outright International. (2020). *Vulnerability Amplified: The Impact of the COVID-19 Pandemic on LGBTIQ People*. [Online] https://outrightinternational.org/content/vulnerability-amplified-impact-covid-19-pandemic-lgbtiq-people

Queer X Climate. (2022). *Pledge*. [Online] https://www.queersxclimate.org/pledge

ReportOUT. (2021). *Queering the Sustainable Development Goals*. [Online] https://www.reportout.org/post/queering-the-sustainable-development-goals

Reuters. (2017). *Jamaican LGBTQ Youths Escape Persecution in City Storm Drains*. [Online] https://www.reuters.com/article/us-jamaica-lgbt-homeless-idUSKBN1685AY

Reuters. (2021). *UK Charity Launches World's First LGBT+ Climate Fund*. [Online] https://www.reuters.com/article/us-climate-change-lgbt-trfn-idUSKBN2B32YD

Rich, A. (1980). Compulsory Heterosexuality and Lesbian Existence. *Journal of Women's History, 15*(3), 11–48.

Rush, E. A. (2018). *Rising: Dispatches from the New American Shore.* Milkweed Editions.

Shotwell, A. (2016). *Against Purity: Living Ethically in Compromised Times.* University of Minnesota Press.

Swank, E. (2018). Sexual Identities and Participation in Liberal and Conservative Social Movements. *Social Science Research, 74*, 176–186.

The Ecologist. (2021). *Queer African Voices Call for Climate Justice.* [Online] https://theecologist.org/2021/jul/08/queer-african-voices-call-climate-justice

The Independent. (2014). *Pipe Dreams in Jamaica: The LGBT Teens Who Refuse to Conform.* [Online] https://www.independent.co.uk/arts-entertainment/films/features/pipe-dreams-in-jamaica-the-lgbt-teens-who-refuse-to-conform-9661601.html

The New Humanitarian. (2020). *LGBTQ+ People Left Out by Exclusionary COVID-19 Aid Practices.* [Online] https://www.thenewhumanitarian.org/news-feature/2020/06/24/LGBTQ-gender-coronavirus-discrimination-aid

UN DESA. (2017). *Reaching the Furthest Behind First Is the Answer to Leaving No One Behind.* [Online] https://www.un.org/development/desa/en/news/sustainable/reaching-furthest-behind.html

UN SDGs. (2022). *Homepage.* [Online] https://sdgs.un.org/

UNDP, ODI, & Galang. (2020). *Making It Work: Lesbian, Bisexual and Transgender Women's Economic Empowerment in the Philippines.* [Online] https://www.undp.org/philippines/publications/making-it-work-lesbian-bisexual-and-transgender-women%E2%80%99s-economic-empowerment-philippines

UNAIDS. (2020). *Relative Risk of Acquiring HIV Infection Compared to the Rest of the Population.* [Online] https://www.unaids.org/en/resources/presscentre/featurestories/2020/september/20200928_new-hiv-infections-increasingly-among-key-populations

United Nations. (1994). *Framework Convention on Climate Change.* [Online] https://unfccc.int/process-and-meetings/what-is-the-united-nations-framework-convention-on-climate-change

United Nations. (2022). *Homepage.* [Online] https://www.un.org/en/

US Geological Survey. (2022). *Wildfire and Climate Change.* [Online] https://www.usgs.gov/science-explorer/climate/wildfire

Weder, F., & Swastika, S. (2021). Advocacy for Sustainability Communication: Unseen Potential of Queer Communicators in Environmental, Climate Change and Sustainability Science. *Sustainability, 13*(24), 138–171.

World Bank Climate Knowledge Portal. (2022). *Country: Jamaica.* [Online] https://climateknowledgeportal.worldbank.org/country/jamaica

World Economic Forum. (2016). *The Real Cost of LGBT Discrimination*. [Online] https://www.weforum.org/agenda/2016/01/the-real-cost-of-lgbt-discrimination/

World Economic Forum. (2019a). *How to Solve Homelessness – Lessons from Around the World*. [Online] https://www.weforum.org/agenda/2019/12/how-to-solve-homelessness-poverty-cities-urbanization/

World Economic Forum. (2019b). *Oxford Dictionaries' Word of the Year for 2019 Is 'climate emergency.'* [Online] https://www.weforum.org/agenda/2019/12/word-of-the-year-oxford-dictionaries-climate-emergency/

Yaxley, D. (2021). *Queer Activism and the Fight for Our Climate*. [Online] https://www.2050.scot/blog/queer-climate-activism

CHAPTER 3

'Developed': Administrative Violence in Sexual Diversity Asylum Claims at the UK Home Office

Alex Powell

The UN Sustainable Development Goals are intended to be framed in terms consistent with a set of universal values. The second of these universal values is the idea of 'no person left behind'. This idea

> represents the unequivocal commitment of all UN member states to eradicate poverty in all its forms, end discrimination and exclusion, and reduce the inequalities and vulnerabilities that leave people behind and undermine the potential of individuals and of humanity as a whole. (United Nations Sustainable Development Group, 2022)

Despite this, the International Rescue Committee noted the existence of a 'Refugee Gap' in their 2019 report (Rescue.Org, 2019). In 2020, attempts were made to remedy this with the introduction of a refugee

A. Powell (✉)
Oxford Brookes University, Oxford, UK
e-mail: a.powell@brookes.ac.uk

D. Dalton, A. Smith (eds.), *Gender, Sexuality and the UN's SDGs*, Sustainable Development Goals Series,
https://doi.org/10.1007/978-3-031-31046-1_3

specific target at 10.7, which requires states to 'facilitate orderly, safe, regular and responsible migration and mobility of people, including through the implementation of planned and well-managed migration policies'. This alongside, the introduction of some specific indictors in relation to refugees demonstrates attention has been directed towards the refugee gap. However, as Denaro and Giuffre (2022) show, major issues around taking account of the lived experiences of refugees remain. By looking at the experiences of sexually diverse refugees (see for example: Dustin, 2018; Dustin & Ferreira, 2021; Powell, 2021b), this chapter seeks to add qualitative detail to the concept of the refugee gap and, in so doing, to Evaluate the practice of the Uk, a state traditionally regarded as highly developed, through the framework of the Sustainable Development Goals (SDGs). Further, the chapter offers space to devote critical attention to the way in which the SGDs are themselves framed.

Sustainable Development Goal 16 calls for states to provide 'access to justice for all and build, effective, accountable and inclusive institutions at all levels'. While refugees are not generally framed as being the subject of this goal, with their experiences instead linked to Goal 10, as discussed above, Denaro and Giuffre (2022) present extensive evidence that indicator 10.7 was originally developed to form a part of the Goal 16 framework. Under this conceptualisation, a state that was responsible for generating a large number of refugees could be viewed as having an issue with regard to the rule of law. This is because, a fear of persecution from the state, or the inability/unwillingness of a state to protect a given claimant from third party persecution, is often strong evidence of an inadequate, arbitrary, or discriminatory legal system. However, as the participants in Denaro and Giuffre's research point out, the change to fit the refugee specific indicator under the Goal 10 framework came somewhat at the last minute, with the result that there is relatively poor synthesis between the indicator and the issue it seeks to address (Denaro & Giuffre, 2022, pp. 95–100).

In particular, Denaro and Giuffre draw attention to methodological issues which arise as a result of the indictor being linked to Goal 10 and the focus of 'well-managed migration' therefore being applied to refugee receiving nations. Specifically, they address the fact that this results in a government-centred approach to understanding migration and asylum (Denaro & Giuffre, 2022, p. 100; Mayblin, 2019). They also argue this focus may not be appropriately respectful of the need for asylum seekers to leave their countries of origin and travel by means which may necessarily be irregular (Denaro & Giuffre, 2022, p. 95), and that 'future research could explore the importance of evaluating the main impact of migration policies in terms of access to rights and integration of the target population' (Denaro & Giuffre, 2022, p. 103). In agreement with these three issues, this chapter explores the narratives of sexually diverse refugees residing in the UK to draw attention to the importance of evaluating policy around refugees and migrants with regard to the abilities of these groups to access their rights and integrate into the receiving country. Through doing this, the chapter proposes to add substantive depth to the refugee gap concept.

Often it is assumed that states located in the global north have attained a substantial level of development. However, recent policy changes such as the Nationality and Borders Act 2022 in the UK limit the ability of people to claim legal rights. As such, it can be seen that the focus on development can lead to complacency. By drawing on the author's research with sexually diverse[1] refugees (interviews undertaken 2018–2020), this chapter seeks to explore how forms of administrative violence (Powell, 2021a, 2022) and administrative lawlessness (Juss, 1994, 1997) occurring within UK institutions such as the Home Office raise challenges to the idea that countries such as the UK comply with the SDGs, as well as adding conceptual detail to the refugee gap.

Sexual Diversity Asylum Claims in Theory and Practice

As mentioned above, the Nationality and Borders Act 2022 has recently led to sweeping changes within the UK asylum system. As identified by the United Nations High Commissioner for Refugees, it is likely the new framework will lead to increased arbitrariness, unjustifiable distinctions between claimants, and the UK acting in a manner incompatible with its international obligations (United Nations High Commissioner for Refugees, 2022a, 2022b). However, as the research on which this chapter is based was undertaken between 2018 and 2020 the reflections offered are addressed towards the policy framework at that time. This is because, while analysis of the new framework is necessary and urgent, it is argued that it is most appropriate to analyse the experiences of participants with regard to the system as it existed at the time of their claim. Further, given that the purpose of this exploration is to show the flawed processes

[1] This research was supported by a City, University of London doctoral studentship between September 2017 and September 2020. The study was approved by the City Law School Research Ethics Committee at City, University of London. Ethical approval was granted on 23 September 2018 under Application ID: ETH1819-0040.

existing within states widely considered to be highly developed, it is argued that analysis of the previous system offers a useful way to identify issues with both UK practice and the goals themselves.

The research on which this chapter draws consisted of eight semi-structured interviews with self-identified sexually diverse refugees sometimes referred to as LGBTQ+ or SOGI. The interviews were conducted in semi-private locations (such as cafes) between 2018 and 2020. In the interviews, participants were invited to explore how they understood their own sexual diversities and to reflect upon how these had been (mis)understood by the Home Office. While the central findings of this research related to an overreliance on identity politics within the decision-making processes (Dustin, 2018; Lewis, 2014; Powell, 2021b), other findings have drawn attention to how shortcomings in the process led to enactments of violence against claimants (Powell, 2023). Departing from these projects somewhat, this chapter offers reflections on how these policy-based issues speak to the extent to which the UK can be said to have achieved Goals 10 and 16.

Elsewhere, I have defined a framework of administrative violence, this term draws on the work of Hannah Arendt (1970, pp. 38–81) to conceptualise,

> Injury sustained through the implementation of instrumental, formal processes which are justified as a social necessity, and operating at a level of abstraction, where attribution of individual responsibility is obscured or entirely denied. (Powell, 2021a, p. 301)

This has relevance to sustainable development Goal 16, particularly in relation to target 16.3 'Access to civil justice'. Further, it has implications for Goal 10; for example, it can be argued to impact the Uk's ability to comply with target 10.7 'Facilitate orderly, safe, regular and responsible migration and mobility of people', including through the implementation of planned and well-managed migration policies. This impact can be particularly seen in relation to 10.7.4 'Proportion of the population who are refugees, by country of origin' due to the fact that policies that would be identified as meeting the definition of administrative violence are likely to result in a lower number of refugees being accepted. Further effects can also be identified in respect of indicator 10.7.2, with regard to the UK having 'migration policies that facilitate orderly, safe, regular and responsible migration and mobility of people'. This is because, in the context of the hostile environment, a well-managed policy could actually be one that limits the ability of asylum seekers to enter a country (see Hathaway, 1992).

Other literature raises issues with the extent to which the Home Office complies with the terms set out in Sustainable Development Goal 16. For example, Juss (1994, p. 84) has developed the concept of administrative lawlessness to describe situations in which administrative agencies step outside of their legal powers. This, alongside other noted UK practices in relation to immigration and asylum, such as government criticism of human rights lawyers, is problematic in regard to target 16.3, which calls on states to 'promote the rule of law at the national and international levels and ensure equal access to justice for all'. This target is challenged because in conditions of administrative lawlessness challenges arise in relation to the UK's compliance with the rule of law.

The drafting process of the refugee specific target and associated indicators makes clear these were originally intended to fall under the Goal 16 umbrella and were, as such, directly intended to offer a framework through which states correspondence and compliance to the rule of law could be assessed (Denaro & Giuffre, 2022). As such, it is argued that this constitutes a fruitful ground against which compliance with Goal 16 might be measured, even if this is not a formal part of the SDG framework.

The UK legal framework, as it existed prior to the Nationality and Borders Act 2022, was made up of a complex framework of primary and secondary legislation (UK Visas and Immigration, 2016). This framework, in its broadest sense saw the body of asylum law existing within part 11 of the Immigration Rules.[2] This body of rules, in turn, is created and amended by the Secretary of State for the Home Department pursuant to the powers given to them under Section 3(2) of the Immigration Act 1971. The legal framework is intended to give practical implementation to the Refugee Convention 1951[3] and its 1967 optional protocol,[4] to which the UK is a signatory. Crucially, the convention and the protocol offer a definition of a refugee at Article 1A(2). Specifically, they define a refugee as,

[2] The rules can be accessed online. See: https://www.gov.uk/guidance/immigration-rules/immigration-rules-part-11-asylum (accessed 05/08/2022).

[3] Convention Relating to the Status of Refugees, 28 July 1951, 189 UNTS 137 Article 1A(2).

[4] Protocol Relating to the Status of Refugees (adopted 31 January 1967, entered into force 4 October 1967) 606 UNTS 267.

> A person who owing to a well-founded fear of being persecuted for reasons of race, religion, nationality, membership of a particular social group or political opinion, is outside the country of his nationality and is unable, or owing to such fear, is unwilling to avail himself of the protection of that country; or who, not having a nationality and being outside the country of his former habitual residence as a result of such events, is unable or, owing to such fear, is unwilling to return to it.

As such, signatories to the convention have agreed to recognise as refugees all people fleeing a well-founded fear of persecution where that fear is based on their race, religion, nationality, membership of a particular social group, or political opinion.

Despite the above, there is no international body empowered to undertake binding action to enforce this definition. This makes forms of international monitoring such as the Sustainable Development Goals highly important. Since 1999, UK law has recognised that sexually diverse people, or in the wording of the courts, 'homosexuals' can for a particular social group for the purposes of Article 1A(2).[5] However, this marked a start, rather than an end, in the journey towards sexually diverse people being protected under the Refugee Convention. Following the decision in Jain, a practice called 'discretion reasoning' started being applied.[6] Indeed, Chelvan (2011, p. 57) argued that 'The effect of Jain was that the court's understanding of the lives of gay men resulted in a purely "conduct-driven approach" reducing their lives to the engagement of the sexual act … in the so-called "privacy" of the bedroom'. This approach saw courts effectively articulating a 'reasonable expectation that persons should to the extent that it is possible, co-operate in their own protection'.[7] To do this, claimants would need to keep their sexual diversity a secret from those around them. The idea here being that there was no well-founded fear of persecution if, through non-disclosure, a risk of persecution would not arise. Dustin (2018, pp. 109–112) argued that discretion reasoning formed a catch-all excuse for rejection. This appears to be reflected in the staggering 98% rejection rate for sexual diversity claimants found prior to 2010 (UK Lesbian and Gay Immigration Group, 2013).

[5] Islam v Secretary of State for the Home Department and R v Immigration Appeals Tribunal Ex p Shah [1999] UKHL 20, [1999] 2 AC 629.

[6] Jain v. Secretary of State for the Home Department [1999] EWCA Civ 300.

[7] V95/03567 [1996] RRTA 246.

In 2010, the UK Supreme Court found that the policy of discretion reasoning was incompatible with the UK's obligations under the convention.[8] In doing so, the court set out a new test that decision-makers tasked with determining refugee status in sexual diversity claims should use. This requires that a decision-maker should 'ask itself on the evidence whether it is satisfied that ... [the claimant] is gay' [82]. If this stage is satisfied, then the decision-maker should 'ask itself whether it is satisfied on the available evidence that gay people who lived openly would be liable to persecution in the applicant's country of nationality' [82]. Finally, the decision-maker should 'consider what the applicant would do if he were returned to that country' [82]. If the applicant would either be open regarding their sexual diversity or hide it to avoid the threat of persecution they are a refugee. This new test was regarded as a 'key factor in the improvement of first decisions' (UK Lesbian and Gay Immigration Group, 2013).

However, problems continued in the wake of this decision. In particular, the decision has been attributed as having caused a shift from 'discretion to disbelief' (Millbank, 2009). The issue here being that decision-makers now deny claims on the basis that the claimant is not a sexually diverse person. This, at least prior to the passing of the Nationality and Borders Act, constituted the key issue in sexual diversity asylum claims.

To an extent, these evidential issues could be regarded as obvious because, as Lewis has argued, 'decision-makers still have no idea what claimants need to do to prove their sexual orientation' (Lewis, 2014, p. 963). Indeed, as I have argued, even the issue of what counts as evidence relies on the ways in which sexual diversity is constructed by decision-makers (Powell, 2020, 2021a).

Broadly speaking, policy and much academic literature has supported a greater focus on sexual identity (Dustin & Ferreira, 2021; Powell, 2021b). For example, Chelvan's Difference, Shame, Stigma, Harm model, which has been partially adopted by the Home Office, has been directly framed as part of a push to assess the credibility of sexual diversity asylum claims on the basis of identities rather than sexual practices (Chelvan, 2011, pp. 60–62). This model is one among many that seek to assist decision-makers. Chelvan's approach seeks examples of difference from surrounding society within the lived experiences of claimants (Chelvan, 2014).

[8] HJ (Iran) and HT (Cameroon) [2010] UKSC 31.

However, it has been criticised for its overly simplistic and overly identarian qualities (Dawson & Gerber, 2017; Dustin & Ferreira, 2021).

The Lived Experiences of Sexually Diverse Refugees

As Dustin and Ferreira (2021, p. 318) noted, there is a 'growing concern ... that decision-making in sexual orientation and gender identity (SOGI) asylum claims in Europe is often unfair ... and fails to comply with the spirit if not the letter of the Refugee Convention'. Indeed, this goes beyond the mere question of whether or not a claim is granted. Attention should also be given to the potential duration, cost, and emotional impact that the processes of refugee status determination can lead to (Dustin 2018; Powell, 2023). Claims are often granted following a process of appeal. However, to simply say that, therefore, the system works and can be considered 'well-managed' in accordance with Goal 10 or 'delivering justice for all' in accordance with Goal 16 would be to elide and ignore the unfairness and harm these experiences subject sexually diverse asylum seekers to (Dustin & Ferreira, 2021, p. 318). As such, this section provides further qualitative details regarding the actual experiences of asylum claimants.

Turning firstly to Goal 16, which includes targets 16.3 '[to] promote the rule of law at the national and international levels and ensure equal access to justice for all', 16.6 '[to] develop effective, accountable and transparent institutions at all levels', 16.7 '[to] ensure responsive, inclusive, participatory and representative decision-making at all levels' and 16.B '[to] promote and enforce non-discriminatory laws and policies for sustainable development', it is argued that participant narratives suggest that the UK continues to fall short in a multitude of ways that cannot be accounted when the focus is only on state centred indicators of success.

Firstly, several participants noted the impact of delays on their wellbeing. For example, Abasi told me,

> It took a long time, a long time, until I got my second interview. So, I claimed asylum in January, the second interview was in July and waiting is the hardest part because I wasn't sure what was going to happen. At any point they could just tell me okay, you're not welcome to stay so just take your stuff and go home. (Abasi, Egyptian refugee to author)

The issue here is that the system is not adequately responsive to claims, with delays being a frequent experience. Indeed, in 2019 the Home Office scrapped the six-month target for asylum decisions to be made after an increasing number of cases failed to be decided within the timeframe (Right to Remain, 2019). This clearly suggests a system which is not well managed and leads to claimants being subjected to serious distress by delays.

Abasi also said that [I] had to wait another two months for them to make a decision after the interview. That was the worst bit. That was like literally after I have finished everything and I am just waiting for them to make a decision.' As this suggests, the issues are exacerbated by the fact that these processes carry high individual stakes.

Putting aside the issue of delays, participants noted practical issues that limited their ability to engage comfortably with the process. For example, despite being based in London at the time of his claim, Abasi recounted how,

> The interview was in Newcastle which was one of the most stressful things. They did send me the interview three days, the letter just before the interview and they are expecting me to be in Newcastle ... I am a person who your government did see I was entitled to legal aid so that means that financially I am not going to be able to do this. So, you're putting me in a very tight position.

In stating this, it should be borne in mind that those seeking asylum generally face a bar on employment and receive little financial support (Powell, 2019b; Refugee Action, 2018). As such, a process that necessitates expensive travel is not accessible.

Other forms of exclusion, such as difficulties in obtaining clear information and guidance were also noted by participants. For example, Abdullah told me: 'When I applied, of course, I was very confused about what to do because everywhere online said something different' (Abdullah, Omani refugee to author). This is problematic in terms of Goal 16 because a lack of clear information is a significant barrier to asylum seekers actively participating in the systems design to determine their claims, particularly in the context of limited access to legal aid. Similar issues were also reported by Abeo, who told me, 'To be honest, before I claimed asylum in the UK ... I have to say, I didn't know I could claim asylum on that basis and I think that says a lot ... I had never heard of asylum before (Abeo, Nigerian refugee to author). These issues should again be regarded in a context where the Home Office views a prompt application as a hallmark of personal credibility (UK Visas and Immigration, 2015). Indeed, under the provisions off the Nationality and Borders Act 2022, failure to make a prompt application is now groups for a claim to be placed into group 2 with the results that even successful claims lead to reduced rights as per Section 12(2)B.

Indeed, Abdullah went on to note further issues such as the Home Office's reliance on poorly maintained computer equipment which limited his ability to respond clearly and fully to questions. Specifically, he identified,

> I had problems in the interview process. The computers were very old and the keyboard was so bad that I was forced to give very short answers because something as short as a yes would take him like a few second to type down because the keyboard was so stuck to some letters, to almost all letters … He had to … bang the keyboard. This did make me feel uncomfortable because now I am forced to give either very slow or very short answers. If I give long answers, comfortably, like I am doing now, he is going to take ages to write it down and in fact he is going to forget what I said halfway down the line … sometimes it took minutes to write a sentence. That was really bad. That was the worst part of it.

These kinds of problems are significant because of the central role that the idea of coherent and plausible narrative plays in the success and failure of asylum claims, particularly when there is limited objective evidence regarding the claim (Dustin, 2018; Millbank, 2009; Powell, 2021b). Further, as Masani's narrative makes clear, it can be extremely distressing for refugees to recount potentially traumatic experiences while feeling that they are not being listened to. Masani set out how,

> It also kind of felt like they weren't listening to me, like they were asking me questions but the whole time she is just typing and not really responding like a human being or recognising that talking about some of these things might be difficult for me. (Masani, Ugandan refugee to author)

The above reflects both on the architecture of the encounter—in terms of the Home Office decision-makers typing notes during the interview—and on the attitude of the decision-makers themselves, in terms of leading claimants to feel that they are not being believed or listened to. As I have argued elsewhere, these experiences can be regarded as forms of administrative violence (Powell, 2023).

The issues noted in this regard extended beyond just the provision of IT equipment or the conduct of the interviews to also reflect on the nature of the spaces in which refugee status determination is conducted. For example, Adroa told me,

> One of the most challenging things was the lack of privacy. It was just like an open building, there was no kind of little space where you could speak to anybody. You could just speak to someone behind a screen with a microphone and you just have to shout. I'm apply for asylum ... WHAT ... on the grounds ... What? And they just read everything, 'Is it political?' No. 'Is it religious?' No ... There was no tick for sexuality. And then I have to say it is because I am a gay man and there are people there that are listening, because you have to shout so that you can be heard. (Adroa, Ugandan refugee to author)

One of the key elements of an asylum claim is that a Refugee needs to demonstrate a 'well-founded' fear of persecution. Often, though it need not, such a fear will relate to historic experiences of persecution. As such, asking claimants to offer information in non-private spaces can constitute a significant barrier to inclusion and participation within the process.

In my previous work, I have drawn attention to the problematic, specific, and essentialised ways in which sexuality is constructed for the purposes of refugee status determination (Powell, 2020, 2021b). This can also be seen as an issue which reflects on inclusion and participation, because it requires claimants to articulate themselves in specific ways which may not align with their self-conceptions. As this suggestion, even policies which superficially present as 'well-managed' in the terms called for by Goal 10 can fail to account for the diversity of experiences among asylum claimants. For example, Chataluka reflected on how his practice of saving screenshots and details of conversations had significantly enhanced his ability to put forward his claim. Specifically, he identified,

> I build up a case properly and I think we went about it in a very professional way. So, chats with people on gay applications, screenshots and that, choosing which to put and others to be deleted. Because if you take a screenshot of all your chats, it doesn't say anything so just like take one here and three or four. You don't take all the pages and put them together in one page. That was my job, because I like technical things. [I had] pictures and chats

which was like from 2002 and 2004 and 2005. I was lucky to have that because no one has that. (Chataluka, Egyptian refugee to author)

Two issues that arise in this context are the fact that Chataluka felt that it was necessary to prepare his case in a professional way. While it is good that he has been able to do this and secure status, an asylum system that relies on professionalism on the part of claimants built up systematically over a number of years cannot be said to be operating in a manner commensurate with the Refugee Convention. In stating this, note should be taken that the convention is intended to cover those fleeing persecution, even when that persecution requires them to suddenly flee.

Building on the above, another issue that arises in respect of Goal 16 is what Juss has termed administrative lawlessness (Juss, 1994, 1997, pp. 42–60). That is, moments in which the institutions tasked with administrating refugee status determination in the UK. Act outside of their legal power. Indeed, taking a wider view of the idea of the rule of law, as proposed under target Goal 16, it can be seen that Chataluka's experiences above could be viewed as incompatible with the rule of law. An example of this issue that came up in my interviews were situations where claimants felt like they were being asked to supply sexually explicit evidence. For example, when asked whether he felt that his interviewer was seeking sexually explicit evidence Abasi told me, 'Yes ... It did make me feel uncomfortable. Because there is a person that I completely don't know who is judging me. He is there to judge me. Having to just expose myself like that did make me feel vulnerable at some points which wasn't nice' (Abasi, Egyptian refugee to author). This is despite the 2013 decision of the European Court of Justice—implemented into UK law because the UK was at the time an EU member state—in A, B, and C, which ruled that sexually explicit evidence was on a blacklist that should not be accepted.[9]

Another well-documented practice which has been specifically prohibited by with the Asylum Policy Instructions, is the practice known as 'discrepancy systems' (Juss, 1997, pp. 62–67; UK Visas and Immigration, 2016). This involves decision-makers repeatedly asking similar questions and trying to catch out claimants. For example, Abeo told me about how they felt their interviewer had been trying to create contradictions in order to refuse their claim, stating,

[9] *Cases C-148 to C-150, ABC v Staatssecretaris van Veiligheid en Justitie* [2014] ECRI-2406.

> I think it is a deliberate attempt by the Home Office to find any excuse whatsoever to ridicule people who are claiming asylum and you have to understand, there is a quota and the government is much more concerned with rejecting more people than accepting more people and in that context you will look for any reason, excuse, given by anyone to remove them from that system and that creates a lot of anxiety among refugees. (Abeo, Nigerian refugee to author)

However, he went on to place this in the context of the wider system, instead of attributing individual blame to the decision-maker they had engaged with. Specifically, they told me,

> So, I am equally a victim of the system as much as my interviewer is a victim of the system … and this is how I see my interviewer, they lack the knowledge to deal with the stories they are being told. Because they have their own trauma. They sit down to hear those stories over and over, some of the stories are gory, they are painful and they have to disconnect from those stories and I want to imagine that there will be times where interviewers will go to a room after hearing a story and break down and I wonder if they ever give them any psychological support as well.

As the above suggests, issues arising in interviews can be attributed to poor training or the impact of decision-makers own lived experiences on how they interpret events. These are issues I have expanded on elsewhere (Powell, 2021a, 2021b).

One final issue that is important in regard to the wider focus of the Sustainable Development Goals on 'No person left behind', as well as in support of the underlying principles of non-discrimination is the treatment of asylum claimants within immigration detention. The UK is one of the only states to maintain a practice of indefinite detention and there has been extensive critique of the standards and utilisation of immigration detention facilities within the UK (Bosworth, 2019; Gerlach, 2022). Obviously, as a form of indefinite detention given for an administrative purpose not inherently related to the commission of an offence, the widespread use of immigration detention is again problematic in regard to the rule of law. Further, note should be taken of the additional vulnerability sexually diverse people face within the context of immigration detention. For example, Babu told me,

> You're basically put in detention centre with people who are like terrorists, people from the Taliban. People who are like from these terrorist group. Of

> course, being gay that puts you at like you're very vulnerable to this kind of like … I was harassed a few times in there. I reported it, but nothing. (Babu, Egyptian refugee to author)

As this suggests, there is a general lack of protection for sexually diverse claimants within the detention facilities (Zitsch, 2015). Indeed, some participants even described their experiences of detention in similar terms to the persecution that had caused them to leave their countries of origin. For example, Babu went on to tell me that,

> I have to say, it was a massive shock to me because this was not what I expected from claiming asylum. And, of course, like, you have no contact with your family, you have no contact with anyone. Because they give you a phone but you have to pay for it. You can work inside the detention centre, they pay you £1 an hour … But I think it was the reality of being like, regardless of where you are, it is discrimination. Like regardless. And I felt like I ran away from being persecuted for being gay and now I am being persecuted here just for claiming asylum. (Babu, Egyptian refugee to author)

At a superficial level, the use of administrative detention may appear consistent with the idea of a well-managed migration policy, at least where this is utilised in a manner consistent with the legal framework which states that detention should only be utilised where deportation is imminent. However, this again outlines the importance of taking note of the lived experiences of refugees in evaluating both the actions of states and the utility of the SDG framework as a metric through which to consider the extent to which states are properly protecting the rights of refugees and asylum seekers.

Implications for States and the Sustainable Development Goal Framework

Countries such as the UK regularly call on other countries to alter their behaviour in regard to issues of human rights or the treatment of individuals or groups within their borders. Despite this, government agencies and representatives themselves regularly reject similar calls when they are levied against the UK. For example, the UK government directly rejected the findings of the UN special Rapporteur on Poverty.[10] Similarly, the UK did not step back from the memorandum of Understanding with Rwanda even when this policy was sharply criticised by the United Nations High Commissioner for Refugees (United Nations High Commissioner for Refugees, 2022a, 2022b).

Given the above, it might legitimately be asked what value the above analysis of UK asylum practice with regard to sexually diverse people as interpreted through the framework of the Sustainable Development Goals has. However, it is argued that such critique serves three core purposes: firstly, it allows attention to be drawn to the experiences those most vulnerable may continue to endure, even when engaging with a state that is commonly regarded as highly developed in relation to most international metrics. Secondly, this analysis allows consideration to be given to how the misplacement of indictors, such as the association with the refugee specific indicators to Goal 10, may undermine the effectiveness of the Sustainable Development Goals as a metric against which states practice can be assessed. Finally, such an analysis brings to the fore examples of how issues that are often regarded as marginal to the majority of the population can be ignored within frameworks such as the Sustainable Development Goals. As such, the analysis helps to draw attention to the continued refugee gap and the human cost this leads to.

In addition to the above, the analysis also normatively reinforces the importance of understanding the Sustainable Development Goals in the context of the universal values. For example, the experiences charted here and the continued existence of the refugee gap within the Sustainable Development Goals themselves raises the question of the extent to which the goals are properly cognisant of the idea of 'no person left behind'. As such, it is hoped that this chapter serves as a critical challenge to reaffirm belief in such values both within the operation and monitoring of the goals and within states' practices.

Despite the criticisms levelled within this chapter, note should be taken that I would strongly refute the idea that there are simple answers to the multitude of questions raised by sexual diversity asylum claims. Indeed, as Dustin and Ferreira set out, issues exist with all of the major proposals for how these issues might be addressed (Dustin & Ferreira, 2021). However, the purpose of this chapter was to draw attention to how practices in relation to certain groups, particularly those who are stigmatised or

[10] UN Doc A/HRC/41/39Add.3.

marginalised, call into question the extent to which even those nations commonly regarded as being highly developed are able to fully meet the targets and indicators under the Sustainable Development Goals framework.

One area of particular concern that this chapter has sought to draw attention to are the issues which the systems of refugee determination, particularly but not exclusively in relation to sexual diversity, pose for the rule of law. Of course, there are, first and foremost, concerns regarding the extent to which the UK's practice in regard to refugee status determination is consistent with the Refugee Convention. This issue has only been exacerbated by the recent Nationality and Borders Act which, in purporting to distinguish between asylum seekers on the basis of their mode of entry being unlawful, can be argued to show relatively unambiguous incompatibility with Article 31 of the Convention which exempts refugees from penalty for illegal entry (Prabhat et al., 2022). It is noted that this section limits that protection to those who are 'coming directly from' the country where they face persecution. However, it can still be argued that the present drafting of the Nationality and Borders Bill is overly broad in nature and seemingly punishes all asylum seekers entering the UK unlawfully without regard to the directness of their journey. Indeed, the United Nations High Commissioner for Refugees noted that 'wide-ranging inadmissibility rules have the potential to deny refugees their right to seek asylum in the UK. Such provisions are potentially at variance with the Refugee Convention' (United Nations High Commissioner for Refugees, 2022a, 2022b).

Further concerns regarding the UK's present trajectory around the rule of law have arisen and these give further colour to how matters regarding the experiences of refugees provide a useful context for understanding the state's performance in relation to Goal 16. For example, the repeated suggestions by UK government ministers that 'activist lawyers' (Grierson & Taylor, 2020), 'left-wing lawyers' (Forrest, 2021), and 'do-gooders' (Woodcock, 2020) were seeking to undermine their attempts to deal with the number of people claiming asylum in the UK—or worse that lawyers representing migrants and asylum seekers were 'abetting the work of criminal gangs' (Scholfield, 2022)—can be viewed as challenging both the independence of the judiciary and the important role that legal professionals play in the protection of rights in regard to both domestic and international law (International Bar Association, 2021). These concerns are clearly shared by the bodies representing legal professionals in the UK with the Law Society and the Bar council issuing a relatively unprecedented press release on 14 June 2022 that reminded the government,

> Legal challenges ensure government is acting lawfully, following laws agreed by parliament.
>
> It is misleading and dangerous for the Prime Minister to suggest lawyers who bring such legal challenges are doing anything other than their job and upholding the law. Anyone at risk of a life-changing order has a right to challenge its legality with the assistance of a lawyer, who has a duty to advise their client on their rights.
>
> The Bar Council and Law Society of England and Wales together call on the Prime Minister to stop attacks on legal professionals who are simply doing their jobs. (Law Society and Bar Council UK, 2022)

I reproduce this quote in full because it very plainly speaks to how issues, such as those around refugee status, can signify and draw attention to fundamental deficiencies in regard to compliance with the Sustainable Development Goals. For example, attempts to change refugee policy in the UK—which could arguably be viewed as fitting with the 'well-managed' framing provided under Goal 10—lead on to even more fundamental issues such as government attacks on the legal profession, which constitute a relatively clear-cut assault on the rule of law (Law Society and Bar Council UK, 2022).

Indeed, note should be taken that often, where government ministers have challenged the legitimacy of lawyers and, perhaps more implicitly, judges, this has often been justified on the basis that the UK needs to 'take back control of its borders' (Walters, 2022). This is, of course, on one level, an attempt to capitalise on the political utility and popularity of certain narratives that underlaid the vote to leave the European Union (Powell, 2019a). However, such a narrative also links to the idea of managed migration. Indeed, as Denaro and Giuffre (2022, pp. 100–102) argue, the framework under Goal 10 leaves open the potential that a highly restrictive asylum police could nonetheless be regarded to be well-managed. As such, note should be taken that the inclusion of the refugee specific indicator actually risks legitimising punitive and restrictive policies with regard to migration and asylum.

In accordance with the above, further reflections and research should be considered over the relationship between the refugee indicators and Goal 10. This is because, in framing the focus as being related to the extent to which processes are well managed, the goal excludes, or at least limits, its ability to engage with the concrete experiences of refugees, the barriers they are forced to content with in claiming their rights, and even leaves open the possibility that limitations to their rights—such as the previously mentioned right to arrive irregularly—could even be framed as being done in service of the very indicators which have been intended to address the failure of the original Sustainable Development Goals to capture and protect this highly vulnerable group.

The above is particularly exacerbated when contextual factors, such as high levels of anti-refugee and migration discourse in the UK are accounted for. For example, asylum in the UK is often framed by media sources as vexatious and expensive. As such, indicators which open pathways that can be presented to the general population as issues of well-managed migration, but which in fact fairly fundamentally undermine the rights of certain groups should be viewed as relatively poor indicators of sustainable development, at least when this is framed in view of the universal values, such as the idea of no person left behind (Barrett, 2020).

Conclusion

This chapter has explored the experiences of sexually diverse refugees as a case study through which to consider UK practice in relation to Sustainable Development Goals 10 and 16. In so doing, the chapter has sought to reflect on and contribute to the continued 'refugee gap' under the Sustainable Development Goals framework. While offering critical reflections on this gap, particularly in terms of the lack of focus on the qualitative experiences of claimants, the chapter has also considered issues within the UK's practice, thus showing how a more qualitative approach to the Sustainable Development Goals could provide a far stronger metric by which state conduct might be assessed.

The chapter developed over three sections. Section 1 focused on setting the scene with a particular focus on presenting the framework of refugee protection in the UK prior to May 2022. Section 2 then explored the experiences of sexually diverse refugees directly and placed these into conversation with Goals 16 and 10. In doing so, this section also reflected on the importance of individual experiences to understanding the extent to which states have achieved the compliance with the indicators and targets under the Sustainable Development Goals framework. Finally, section 3 considered the implications of this chapter for the wider idea of 'developed' nations and presents a call for the treatment of marginalised groups to be given greater weight under the Sustainable Development Goals framework in accordance with the second universal value of 'no person left behind'.

References

Arendt, H. (1970). *On violence*. Harcourt.

Barrett, D. (2020, September 1). Cost of Britain's Asylum System DOUBLES in Five Years to £1billion, New Figures Reveal. *Daily Mail*. Retrieved July 27, 2022, from https://www.dailymail.co.uk/news/article-8683503/Cost-Britains-asylum-DOUBLES-five-years-1billion-new-figures-reveal.html

Bosworth, M. (2018). Affect and Authority in Immigration Detention. *Punishment & Society, 21*(5), 542.

Chelvan, S. (2011). Put Your Hands Up (If You Feel Love). *Immigration, Asylum and nationality Law, 25*, 56.

Chelvan, S. (2014, August 7). LGBTI Asylum Claims – The Difference, Stigma, Shame, Harm Model. *Right to Remain*. Retrieved July 5, 2022, from http://www.righttoremain.org.uk/legal/lgbti-asylum-claims-the-difference-shame-stigma-harm-model/

Dawson, J., & Gerber, P. (2017). Assessing the Refugee Claims of LGBTI People: Is the DSSH Model Useful for Determining Claims by Women for Asylum Based on Sexual Orientation. *International Journal of Refugee Law, 29*(2), 292–322.

Denaro, C., & Giuffre, M. (2022). UN Sustainable Development Goals and the 'Refugee Gap': Leaving Refugees Behind? *Refugee Survey Quarterly, 41*(1), 79.

Dustin, M. (2018). Many Rivers to Cross: The Recognition of LGBTQI Asylum in the UK. *International Journal of Refugee Law, 30*(1), 104.

Dustin, M., & Ferreira, N. (2021). Improving SOGI Asylum Adjudication: Putting Persecution Ahead of Identity. *Refugee Survey Quarterly, 40*(3), 315.

Forrest, A. (2021, July 29). Boris Johnson Accused of Damaging Rule of Law After Renewed Attack on 'Left-Wing Lawyers'. *The Independent*. Retrieved July 31, 2022, from https://www.independent.co.uk/news/uk/politics/boris-johnson-left-wing-lawyers-b1893121.html

Grierson, J., & Taylor, D. (2020, August 27). Home Office Wrong to Refer to Activist Lawyers, Top Official Admits. *The Guardian*. Retrieved July 2022, from https://www.theguardian.com/politics/2020/aug/27/home-office-wrong-to-refer-to-activist-lawyers-top-official-admits&gt

Hathaway, J. (1992). Emerging Politics of Non-Entrée. *Refugees, 91*, 40.

International Bar Association. (2021, February 4). *UK Government Ministers Condemned for Anti-Lawyer Rhetoric*. International Bar Association. Retrieved August 5, 2022, from https://www.ibanet.org/article/DE8B1F7B-1658-4BBA-B6EF-431DCAB5C0B3

Juss, S. (1994). *Immigration, Nationality and Citizenship*. Continuum International Publishing.

Juss, S. (1997). *Discretion and Deviation in the Administration of Immigration Control*. Sweet and Maxwell.

Law Society and Bar Council UK. (2022). *Prime Minister Must Stop Attacks on Legal Professions, Say Bar Council and Law Society*. Retrieved August 7, 2022, from https://www.barcouncil.org.uk/resource/prime-minister-must-stopattacks.html#:~:text=Following%20the%20Prime%20Minister's%20comments,following%20laws%20agreed%20by%20parliament

Lewis, R. (2014). 'Gay? Prove It': The Politics of Queer Anti-deportation Activism. *Sexualities, 17*(8), 958.

Mayblin, L. (2019). Imagining Asylum, Governing Asylum Seekers: Complexity Reduction and Policy Making in the UK Home Office. *Migration Studies, 7*(1), 1.

Millbank, J. (2009). From Discretion to Disbelief: Recent Trends in Refugee Determinations on the Basis of Sexual Orientation in Australia and the United Kingdom. *International Journal of Human Rights, 13*(2–3), 1.

Powell, A. (2019a). The Will of the People: The UK Constitution, (Parliamentary) Sovereignty, and Brexit. In T. Ahmed & E. Fahey (Eds.), *On Brexit: Law, Justices and Injustices*. Edward Elgar.

Powell, A. (2019b). *Work Ban Forces Asylum Seekers into Destitution – But We Now Have a Chance to Change This Policy*. Retrieved August 4, 2022, from https://theconversation.com/work-ban-forces-asylum-seekers-into-destitution-but-we-now-have-a-chance-to-change-this-policy-112254

Powell, A. (2020). Normative Understandings: Sexual Identity, Stereotypes, and Asylum Seeking. In C. Ashford & A. Maine (Eds.), *Research Handbook on Gender, Sexuality and the Law*. Edward Elgar.

Powell, A. (2021a). *Queering Refugee Law: A Study of Sexual Diversity in Asylum Policy and Practice in the United Kingdom*, Unpublished PhD Thesis, School of Law, City University of London.

Powell, A. (2021b). "Sexuality" Through the Kaleidoscope: Sexual Orientation, Identity and Behaviour in Asylum Claims in the United Kingdom. *Laws, 10*, 90.

Powell, A. (2023). Administrative Violence: First Instance Decision-Making in Sexual Diversity Asylum Claims. In E. O'Loughlin & S. Wheatle (Eds.), *Diverse Voices in Public Law*. Bristol University Press.

Prabhat, D., Rifath, R., Singleton, A., Ziegler, R., Powell, A., & Sedacca, N. (2022). *Reconsidering Asylum: Is It for Those Who Need Protection*. Retrieved July 21, 2022, from https://blogs.law.ox.ac.uk/research-subject-groups/centre-criminology/centreborder-criminologies/blog/2022/05/reconsidering

Rescue.Org. (2019). *Missing Persons: Refugees Left Out and Left Behind in the Sustainable Development Goals*. International Rescue Committee Report.

Right to Remain. (2019). *Home Office Abandons Six-Month Target for Asylum Decisions*. Retrieved September 8, 2022, from https://righttoremain.org.uk/home-office-abandons-six-month-target-for-asylum-decisions/

Scholfield, K. (2022, June 16). Boris Johnson Told to Apologise for Suggesting Lawyers are 'Abetting' People Traffickers. *Huffington Post*. Retrieved August 22, 2022, from https://www.huffingtonpost.co.uk/entry/boris-johnson-urged-apologise-lawyers-criminal-gangs_uk_62ab2bbae4b06169ca957e08

UK Lesbian and Gay Immigration Group (UKLGIG). (2013). *Missing the Mark: Decision Making on Lesbian, Gay (Bisexual, Trans and Intersex) Asylum Claims (Unison, 2013)*. Retrieved July 25, 2022, from https://www.rainbowmigration.org.uk/sites/default/files/2021-03/Missing-the-Mark-Oct-13_0.pdf

UK Visas and Immigration. (2015). *Asylum Policy Instruction: Assessing Credibility and Refugee Status*. Retrieved August 5, 2022, from https://assets.publishing.service.gov.uk/government/uploads/system/uploads/attachment_data/file/397778/ASSESSING_CREDIBILITY_AND_REFUGEE_STATUS_V9_0.pdf

United National Sustainable Development Group (2022). *Leave No One Behind*. https://unsdg.un.org/2030-agenda/universal-values/leave-no-one-behind#:~:text=Universal%20Values,-Principle%20Two%3A%20Leave&text=It%20represents%20the%20unequivocal%20commitment,of%20humanity%20as%20a%20whole

United Nations High Commissioner for Refugees. (2022a). *UNHCR Observations on the Nationality and Borders Bill, Bill 141, 2021–2022*. Retrieved August 5, 2022, from https://www.unhcr.org/uk/615ff04d4.pdf

United Nations High Commissioner for Refugees. (2022b). *News Comment: UNHCR's Grandi Fears UK Legislation Will Dramatically Weaken Refugee Protection*. Retrieved July 26, 2022, from https://www.unhcr.org/en-us/news/press/2022/4/626975e14/news-comment-unhcrs-grandi-fears-uk-legislation-dramatically-weaken-refugee.html

Walters, J. (2022, May 10). Priti Patel Says Rwanda Asylum Plan 'Will Take Time' as She Vows to 'Take Back Control'. *Daily Express*. Retrieved July 27, 2022, from https://www.express.co.uk/news/uk/1607851/priti-patel-rwanda-immigration-vote-leave-brexit-latest-news-ont

Woodcock, A. (2020, October 6). Priti Patel Accused of Putting Lawyers at Risk by Branding Them 'Lefty Do-Gooders'. *The Independent*. Retrieved July 27, 2022, from https://www.independent.co.uk/news/uk/politics/priti-patel-immigration-lawyers-migrants-law-society-bar-council-b832856.html

Zitsch, L. (2015). Where the American Dream Becomes a Nightmare: LGBT Detainees in Immigration Detention Facilities. *William and Mary Journal of Race, Gender, and Social Justice, 22*, 105.

CHAPTER 4

Vegansexuality: Troubling Gender and Sexuality Norms to Combat Climate Change

Megan Todd

Introduction

The COVID-19 pandemic has driven many to consider our relationship with the planet and the other sentient beings we share it with. Many are of the opinion that we are in the midst of the Anthropocene and Sixth Mass Extinction (Moore, 2016; Wagner et al., 2021), meaning that finding a way to sustainable development, which meets our political and economic needs without harming the environment, has never been more urgent. The case for climate veganism has been made convincingly, with various studies showing that adopting a plant-based diet is the single biggest way to reduce our environmental impact. Vegan feminists have argued that there is a link between eating meat and gender inequality; that the exploitation and objectification of animals as 'meat', parallels the oppression of

M. Todd (✉)
University of Central Lancashire, Preston, UK

D. Dalton, A. Smith (eds.), *Gender, Sexuality and the UN's SDGs*, Sustainable Development Goals Series,
https://doi.org/10.1007/978-3-031-31046-1_4

women by men (Adams, 2010). More recently, debates have extended to engage men in such debates (Lockwood, 2021).

Drawing on the work of Carol J. Adams (1990) and others, this chapter will locate the sexualised and embodied relationship between masculinity and meat, in order to highlight the 'carno-phallogocentrism' (Derrida, 1992) inherent in hegemonic (and heteronormative) masculinity. Using feminist scholarship, the chapter will suggest a move to a vegan identity or ethic based on shared vulnerabilities, in which the suffering of an-Other is foregrounded. There are many reasons that a vegan diet might be adopted, but here the emphasis is placed on veganism as a practice of non-violence (Francione, 2015). An understanding of hegemonic masculinity recognises that whilst people navigate a multitude of masculinities, there remains a dominant way of being, and thinking, in the Global North. Hegemony is understood as a dominant and dominating mode of thought which operates through control and consent, being at once economic and cultural (Gramsci, 1972). This power is, in the Foucauldian sense, not simply executed through apparatuses of the state but is exercised through the social body, producing subjectivity. Thus, hegemonic masculinity acts as a normalising gaze. The notion of a vegan sexual identity (Potts & Parry, 2010)—or 'vegansexuality'—has been posited as a way to challenge the prevailing associations between meat-eating and heteronormative masculinity in Western societies (Cole & Stewart, 2017). Less has, to date, been made of the ways in which meat-free sex or intimate relationships can combat environmental devastation. This chapter, therefore, looks at the ways in which challenges to normative gendered sexualities can pave a way towards the UN's SDGs, specifically Goal 13 Climate Action (though this also links directly to Goals 2 Zero Hunger, 5 Gender Equality and 15 Life on Land, among others). To begin with, it provides a discussion of the current climate crisis and looks at the role of the meat and dairy industry. There follows a focus on the ways in which a carnist hegemonic masculinity relies on an Othering of marginalised groups in society, in order to allow/enable their subjugation and the assault of our planet. Finally, the chapter outlines ways in which vegan identities and praxis offer a counter to violent suppression and climate devastation.

Global Catastrophe

The science is clear: unless decisive action is taken now, we will be party to the destruction of all we know: our nations, our ecosystems, our ways of living. Back in December 2018, the Intergovernmental Panel on Climate Change (IPCC), whose climate predications have consistently underestimated both the scale and speed of climate change, stated that we must limit global warming in the next 12 years or irrevocably harm the ecosystem essential for life on earth. At that summit, David Attenborough warned that 'right now we are facing a manmade disaster of global scale, our greatest threat in thousands of years: climate change. If we don't take action, the collapse of our civilisations and the extinction of much of the natural world is on the horizon' (McGrath, 2018).

The world's poorest populations and indigenous communities are on the frontline, with the Global South taking the brunt of climate change: the struggle for climate justice here, as in the Global North, is also a fight for gender, racial, sexual and economic equality. Seventy per cent of the food consumed around the world is produced by small-holders and subsistence farmers in Africa and Asia whose ability to farm (and live) is impacted by climate change; most of these farmers are women (Wolfenson, 2013). Yet we are already getting a taste of the future in the UK. In July and August of 2022, we experienced two heatwaves, the first of which, at a conservative estimate caused, over 1000 excess deaths in the UK alone (Vaughan, 2022).

Extreme weather events are becoming increasingly familiar in these unprecedented times. Globally, devastating wildfires rip through swathes of land, while destructive storms and catastrophic floods now frequently destroy buildings and forests, often rendering land uninhabitable and unproductive. Our seas, too, are poisoned (Jamieson et al., 2019); topsoil is being lost 10–40 times faster than it can be replenished by nature, resulting in 30% of the world's arable land becoming unproductive because of soil erosion (Pimentel, 2006). The world's insect populations have fallen drastically since the 1970s, in excess of 60% in many places; many mammalian and bird species are on the brink of extinction (Wagner et al., 2021). The statistics are shocking, all the more so because these are disasters driven by our actions.

That our economy is destroying our ecology is not news. Long before Carson's *Silent Spring* (Carson, 1962), which evidenced the devastating effects of DDT and other pesticides, in the nineteenth century, scholars such as the suffragette Eunice Foote, John Tyndall and the Swedish scientist Svante Arrhenius, were aware of the potential for human impact on climate change (Thompson, 2019). Karl Marx—now seen by scholars as the first ecosocialist—having studied Justus von Liebig's work on soil metabolism, warned of how capitalism was creating a dangerous 'metabolic rift' between humans and the rest of the natural world (Foster, 2020, p. 15).

In 2017, research showed that 100 contemporary fossil fuel producers, which included ExxonMobil BP and Shell were responsible for 71% of industrial greenhouse gas emissions since 1988, releasing more emissions in the last 28 years than in the 237 years prior to 1988 (Griffin, 2017). We also know that these major corporations have suppressed such damaging knowledge (Supran & Oreskes, 2017), supported, in part, by our governments who continue to pursue short-term gain in exchange for long-term catastrophe. Migration, conflict, famine, economic instability, collapse of social systems, mass rape and torture become inevitable in such circumstances. Many of these impact women and girls in particular, exacerbating already deep-rooted gendered inequality. According to the UN, 80% of people displaced by climate change are women, leaving them at heightened risk of violence (BMJ, 2022). No wonder, then, that for many scholars and activists, the twenty-first-century zeitgeist is characterised by an increasing sense of anxiety and urgency (Klein, 2014).

The Role of Individuals

While, ultimately, nothing short of a system change will solve these interlocking crises permanently, it is vital not to lose hope—for one thing, to do so would mean no significant pressures are put on those corporations most responsible for this massive catalogue of harms. It is not yet clear whether crucial ecological tipping points have already been breached. Thus, it makes sense to reduce what harms we can, and to save what can still be saved. Whilst individual actions, on their own, are not going to solve these escalating problems, it is nonetheless possible for individuals to make changes that can help mitigate some of them.

One significant choice for individuals—in fact, the second most important way for individuals to reduce their carbon footprint (a convenient neoliberal construct of BP)—is to adopt a vegan lifestyle. As Al Gore (2006) has argued, it makes absolute sense in the current situation for individuals to have regard to their personal impact on the planet—by, for instance, using public transport more instead of individual car journeys, flying less frequently, and eating less fish and meat. Even better, of course, would be for such aware and concerned individuals to follow the logical progression of their actions by going on to demand *collective* action—both governmental and corporate—as well. To do so is in no way to be 'well-meaning' or 'moralistic' (Thornett, 2019, p. 193).

Meat and Dairy Feed the Crisis

Whilst not solely responsible for the Climate Crisis, the meat and dairy industries are certainly fuelling this global crisis: in fact, globally, animal agriculture is responsible for more greenhouse gas (GHG) emissions than all forms of transport combined.

As early as 2006, the UN's Food and Agriculture Organisation (FAO) raised serious concerns about the vast quantity of GHG emissions caused by meat production. In 2016, another report concluded that a global shift to a plant-based diet could reduce mortality and greenhouse gases caused by food production by 10% and 70%, respectively, by 2050 (Springmann et al., 2016). In 2019, a special IPCC study, on climate change and land use, warned that efforts to curb greenhouse gas emissions and the impacts of global warming will fall significantly short without drastic changes in global land use, agriculture and human diets. The study estimated that a shift by the world's population to a diet containing no animal-source food would save GHG emissions the equivalent of 18 billion tonnes of CO2. In the same year, a report published in *The Lancet* concluded that a dietary shift towards plant foods and away from animal products is vital for promoting the health of our planet. The report states that projections for the future show that 'vegan and vegetarian diets were associated with the greatest reductions in greenhouse-gas emissions' (Willett, 2019, p. 470). While in 2021, a study by the UN's FAO estimated that 34% of GHG emissions caused by human activity can be attributed to how we produce, process and package food. R.K. Pachari—who, whilst Chair of the IPCC, was awarded the Nobel Peace Prize in 2007 for his climate work—has argued that vegetarianism should be the diet of everyone in developed world, purely on environmental grounds.

Most recently, the IPCC report *Climate Change 2022: Mitigation of Climate Change* concluded that 'studies demonstrate that a shift to plant-based diets rich in pulses, nuts, fruits, and vegetables could lead to substantial reduction of greenhouse gas emissions as compared to current dietary patterns in most industrialised countries'. The report says that other co-benefits include lowering the risk of cardiovascular disease, type 2 diabetes, and reducing mortality from diet-related non-communicable diseases. This came with a stark warning, however. The very narrow window we have to mitigate against this disaster is rapidly closing.

Industrialised Animal Agriculture

Overall, the impact of modern agriculture on the planet is gigantic: it uses 70% of all available freshwater and is directly responsible for 60% of global biodiversity loss. However, the biggest climate and ecological challenge is that posed by the current global level of meat consumption—which is arguably 'totally unsustainable'. Currently, over 70 billion land animals are slaughtered every year for human consumption—a figure which has doubled in the last 50 years, and which is expected to double again by 2050. The crucial aspect of all this is that two-thirds of these animals are 'farmed' by intensive methods, known as 'concentrated animal feeding operations' (CAFOs) (Thornett, 2019, p. 182).

This massive number of animals are fed by the production of vast quantities of cereals and soya that could otherwise be eaten directly by humans—including the billions of people who go hungry every year. Over one-third of the world's cereal output is dedicated to farm-animal feed. By far the biggest source of 'food waste' is feeding human-edible grain to industrially reared farm animals. In fact, doing so makes no sense—economic or otherwise—as we get far less protein and calories from animals than from the grains we feed to them. One study by the University of Minnesota showed that for every 100 calories fed to cattle (which actually have the worst calorie-conversion rate of all farmed animals), as little as 3% of those calories are obtained by humans from the resulting meat. The research also revealed that, as regards protein, for every 100 g fed to animals, humans only receive 43 g from milk, 35 g from eggs, 40 g from chicken, 10 g from pork—and only 5 g from beef (Lymbery, 2017, p. 52). If one person eats beef one to two times a week for one year, this contributes 604 kg of emissions to their carbon footprint. Eating beans one to two times a week contributes just 7 kg. Eating tofu for the same amount of time contributes 12 kg. This form of intensive animal agriculture is most marked in the US—which now has over 50,000 CAFOs, along with over 250,000 industrial-scale 'facilities' that fall just below the CAFO threshold.

According to BCG's report, investments in plant-based alternatives result in 11 times more greenhouse gas reductions than those in zero-emission cars. In other words, the industrialised farming of animals is simply inefficient: converting carbohydrates and protein that could be eaten directly by humans into much smaller quantities of energy and protein. Though eating non-factory farmed meat cannot be the answer, for organic meat, dairy and eggs are frequently even more unsustainable (Simon, 2013). Raising one animal to feed another is simply inefficient.

Nature's Revenge?

However, as well as driving the climate crisis, intensive animal farming is also leading to multiple human-health crises and global wildlife extinction. This is via land usage: a 2006 report by the UN's FAO, *Livestock's Long Shadow: Environmental Issues and Options* (Steinfeld, 2006), found that livestock was the biggest single user of land, taking up 26% of the ice-free surface of the planet, while a further 33% of arable land was given over to the production of feed stuff for the livestock. Since then, one estimate is that livestock now occupy 20% of terrestrial-animal biomass, and 80% of anthropogenic land use overall (Bar-On et al., 2018). In addition, 70% of the world's freshwater is used for agriculture, the majority of which is for animal feed. The World Wildlife Fund estimates that 2.7 billion people already experience freshwater shortages at least once a month; but, by 2025, two-thirds of the world's population could face water scarcity, if we continue to farm animals on the present scale (UN-Water, 2021). Fishing and aquaculture is also part of this problem, being inefficient, inhumane, a source of disease and significant contributor to carbon emissions (Sala et al., 2021).

All this means there is fierce competition for land between wildlife and people, which will be intensified by climate change and the associated loss of land as sea levels rise, forcing millions inland, to areas previously used for agriculture. Even if we manage to restrict the rise in global average temperatures to two degrees, there will still be a one-metre rise in sea levels. When we also take into account the growing appetite for meat in developing countries, we will have a doubling of current global livestock numbers. This will need more land—more or less the same amount as will be lost via rising sea levels if there is a rise of two degrees (Stern, 2007).

One result of the destruction of the natural world via intensive animal agriculture and climate change is the increase in devastating pandemics, involving zoonotic viruses and pathogens which cross over to humans from the dwindling number of wild animal species, either directly, or indirectly via farmed animals (and fish). In 2009, Jonathan Safran Foer stated that 'humans are setting the condition for the creation of the superpathogen of all superpathogens, a hybrid virus that could cause a repeat, more or less, of the Spanish 'flu epidemic of 1918' (138)—a predication which sadly came true. Apart from COVID-19, this century has experienced three other coronavirus epidemics: SARS in 2002 and 2004; and MERS in 2012. In addition, from 2013–16, there was the Ebola epidemic, caused by a filovirus. All of these were zoonotic pathogens which crossed over from wildlife species to humans. A 2008 study, *Global trends in emerging infectious diseases*, concluded that of the 335 new diseases that emerged between 1960 and 2004, at least 60% originated with non-human species (Jones et al., 2008).

Much of the increasing appearance and spread of such zoonotic viruses is associated with deforestation, including in the Amazon rainforest;the majority of this being associated with intensive animal agriculture, whether for grazing or for growing animal feed. The international beef and leather industries have been responsible for about 80% of all deforestation in the Amazon region—around 14% of the world's total annual deforestation (Thornett, 2019, p. 183). Yet, even at the height of the COVID-19 pandemic, Bolsonaro, President of Brazil, actually *increased* the rate of the destruction of Brazil's tropical rainforest, leading some experts to predict that the next could well originate from there (Borges & Branford, 2020).

Since the end of 2021, just as some were thinking that Covid was on the way out, there has been a devastating outbreak of avian (bird) 'flu in Europe, which began in farmed geese, and then crossed over to chickens raised for their flesh and eggs. This is already causing the death of tens of thousands of wild birds in the UK and there are fears that the annual release of reared game birds this October could lead to a totally catastrophic avian 'flu epidemic this winter. Some experts predict that it is only a matter of time before a strain of bird 'flu causes a widespread human outbreak. The H5N1 strain, which is confirmed as being present in the UK, is particularly deadly, with a 60% mortality rate for infected humans. An additional concern is that various communicable diseases are becoming resistant to antibiotics, as a result of their widespread use in animal agriculture. Leading Jonathan Safran Foer to observe that 'our sustenance comes from misery…when we eat factory-farmed meat we live, literally, on tortured flesh. Increasingly, that tortured flesh is becoming our own' (Foer, 2009, p. 143).

Meat and the Other

There is a rich coalescence between the histories of the feminist and animal-rights movements. Activists such as Margaret Sibthorp and Edith Ward in the nineteenth century recognised the connections between the subjugation, the tortured flesh, of women and non-humans. The 1990s saw a resurgence of vegetarian ecofeminism, an ideology which is intensifying today.

A key aspect of this thinking is a recognition of the ways in which the ideology of carnism (meat-eating) contributes to the Othering of those on the margins of society and the destruction of the planet. Merchant (1989), argues that since the eighteenth century, with the rise of industrialisation and urbanisation, nature came to be viewed in mechanistic terms as passive, inert and, crucially, to be plundered, Derrida's (Derrida, 1988) 'constitutive outside'. Through this process, nature was relocated to the female body, which was also constructed as submissive, irrational and plunderable. The Western (heterosexual) male subject becomes the defined norm, a de-natured being where 'the animal' is suppressed (Elias, 1978). As Plumwood (1993) posits, such dualisms (culture/nature, human/animal, mind/body, man/woman, straight/queer) are crucial to the ways in which notions such as hegemonic masculinity derive their power. Thus, hegemonic masculinity is fundamentally anti-ecological (Gaard, 2014). The Western subject emerges as not only phallocentric (Smart, 1989) in its notions of virility and phallic symbolism but carnophallogocentric, according to Derrida (1992). Patriarchy and carnism are both ideologies which rely on differential power relations between groups, where axes of oppressions, (racism, colonialism, sexism, heterosexism, classism, ableism, ageism, speciesism), coalesce and intersect.

For Adams (1990), who traces the history of Western meat-eating with the objectification of women, any attempt to reconceptualise the feminine must recognise the intersections of meat, masculinity, sexuality and colonialism. Animal flesh became a consummate male food, and a man eating meat is an exemplar of maleness (Sobal, 2005, p. 137). Thus, meat is considered a better food; women, children, and the working classes, were left with 'poor substitutes' fruit, vegetables, grains. This is very much still the case. In 2021, when I holidayed on the Isle of Man, one café offered a 'Daddy's breakfast' meat-feast of sausage, bacon, black pudding, white pudding. Mothers were offered no such feast!

Adams utilises the concept of the absent referent to highlight the processes whereby any presence of embodied animal is vanished in the consumption of meat. As such, she highlights the ways in which violence against women and other animals is invisibilised in contemporary culture, a culture which consumes women and animals both symbolically and literally—they are there to serve or be served up. Thus, the consumption of meat becomes a re-articulation of (heteronormative) masculinity, a rationalising of capitalist accumulation and a display of carnivorous virility (Derrida, 1992). As Mary Douglas (1970) notes, what enters into and leaves the body is heavily regulated and highly gendered. Women (and by extension other marginalised groups, animals and the planet) exist for men or not at all (Pharr, 1988). Recognition of patriarchal control over women's and animals' bodies within the meat and dairy industry, is pathologised as hysteria (Beers, 2006). This is connected to the claims of climate paranoia and the obloquy directed at environmental campaigners and activists by denialists (Goodman, 2021). Voices of dissent are minimised, trivialised, invisibilised. As Ahmed (2010) noted, feminism is made to be the problem, not sexism, similarly, vegans become the problem, not animal consumption (Twine, 2014). Describing the violence of factory farming, Derrida (2008, p. 26) states that 'such a subjection…can be called violence in the most morally neutral sense of the term […] No one can deny seriously, or for very long, that men do all they can in order to dissimulate this cruelty or to hide it from themselves, in order to organise on a global-scale the forgetting or misunderstanding of this violence'. This psychic numbing applies equally to climate breakdown, violence against women and so on, allowing otherwise compassionate humans to engage in behaviours which cause harm and death to other sentient beings, harm which is entirely unnecessary. Cohen's (Cohen, 2001) recognition of the difference between knowing and acknowledgement is important here; certain ideologies allow us to, or insist that we, bury unpalatable truths or look the other way. To engage in veganism therefore becomes an act of non-violence, not just towards animals but anyone, and anything, deemed the 'Other' of hegemonic masculinity.

Feminist Recognition of Shared Suffering

The environmental and economic impacts of meat-eating make it very much a feminist issue but one which should concern us all (Martin, 1994). Malnutrition and starvation affect women and girls more globally; in times of scarcity, males take precedence. Water shortage, too, is an issue for women and girls as they still, overwhelmingly, have to walk for it and carry it. In the UK, Government subsidies for the meat industry means there is less availability for those living in poverty (impacting particularly on women and children) (Campbell, 2013; Stevenson, 2018). In 1789, Bentham (1996) argued that the capacity to suffer was a fundamental criterion for ethical consideration. Like non-human animals, women, LGBT+ people and ethnic minority people throughout much of history have been denied the official right to suffer. Our shared outsider status, the cognitive estrangement from social norms whether as feminists, vegans, environmental activists and so on, provides a radical position from which change can arise. Here, therefore, is another opportunity to make the shifts in behaviour needed. Philip K. Dick's (Dick, 1968) *Do Androids Dream Electric Sheep?* shows a veganism that comes as a result of mass extinction and ecological catastrophe (nuclear). It is not a veganism which comes from animal rights ethics but a sudden, shared awareness of vulnerabilities. Atwood's MaddAddam trilogy (2003, p. 13) also links carnism to the Anthropocene, symbolic of humanity's destructiveness and greed.

We have had a glimpse of a possible dystopian future. During the heatwaves of 2022, the UK experienced the hottest night on record, with daytime temperatures of 40 °C. Unprecedented health warnings were issued across the UK and in the rest of Europe. Our favourite holiday destinations across the channel witnessed what was called a 'heat apocalypse' as wildfires raged (Henley & Jones, 2022), with many south European nations, such as France, experiencing their fourth heatwave this summer. The 20 hottest years ever have all been in this century, of which the warmest seven have been since 2015. Following the driest July in England since 1935, official droughts (the first since 2018) have been declared in eight of England's 14 areas, with water rationing likely. Unlike the drought of 2012, when many areas of the UK had a hosepipe ban, swiftly followed by the wettest few days since 2010, further dry conditions are expected as a result of climate breakdown. We do not yet know the full impact on crops, let alone wildlife, but the outcome looks bleak (Hess & Holman, 2022)—with reduced crop-yields and higher food prices already being predicted. Expectation of drought has led to many countries—the UK, US, and Spain, to name just a few—turning to desalination plants, at huge financial, environmental and ecological costs (Fountain, 2019).

Even if we have no empathy for animals, perhaps it is possible to move towards eating to protect ourselves. The precarious position the ruthlessness of human actions puts us all in, as we witness mass extinction, the Anthropocene, might be the nudge we need (Kolbert, 2016). As Meyerding (1982, pp. 22–3) has argued, we can't 'strengthen our feminist struggles against one aspect of patriarchy by ignoring or accepting other aspects'. What is needed, is a deep respect for difference.

Vegan Identity: Creating a Climate for Change

A vegan identity offers both respect for difference and a challenge to environmental degradation. Just as Mulvey's (1975) violent male gaze is also a carnist gaze, the vegan gaze picks out a route for change. Indeed, in the past decade, veganism seems to have become more mainstream and recognised as an acceptable dietary choice. In 2020, it was acknowledged as a philosophical belief protected by the 2010 Equality Act (McKeowan & Dunn, 2021). Not only has it largely disassociated itself from perceptions of disordered, pathological, eating, it also seems to be 'sexy' (Wright, 2019). However, though numbers of vegans in the UK have risen quickly, meat consumption globally continues to rise, especially in those nations once known for their primarily plant-based diets, such as India (Potts, 2016).

Whilst veganism is often constructed as being about what individual vegans refuse to eat, there is more to being a vegan than being a fussy eater. As a political ideology which challenges the commodification of animals (Pedersen & Stanescu, 2014) and/or is part of an environmentally sustainable philosophy (Buttny & Kinefuchi, 2020; Hudepohl, 2021), it paves the way for positive change. Whilst scholarship on the political or collective dimensions of veganism is limited, it is useful to understand these shared ideological or ethical aspects of veganism when arguing for its role in environmentally sustainable lifestyles. The social and political dimensions of a vegan identity as counter to compulsory carnism, are as potentially powerful as political lesbianism was/is in terms of challenging violent heteronormative relations and behaviours (Rich, 1980). For instance, Cherry (2015) found that members of the punk movement changed their diet to become vegan. The shift in diet emerged with their changing identity, as a result of intragroup interaction. The reconstruction of the identity was related to the political, moral and ethical issues at the heart of the punk movement.

Food is not just based on taste buds but on tastes (Bourdieu, 1982). What others are eating in our social milieu, can have a profound impact on what we see as 'normal'. Food is habit, culture, identity (Elias, 1978). The cultural and moral arenas in which social norms, including food choice, are adopted and communicated are far from static. Whilst conformity bias may make people more likely to accept the norm most common among their perceived peers, there are many other influences on the uptake of social norms, including prestige, success and notions of moral right (Witt, 2012). As many have highlighted, emotions play a big role in dictating food norms, disgust in particular (Elias, 1978; Witt, 2012). One question, therefore, is whether cultivating widespread feelings of disgust towards meat-eating (though not meat-eaters), for instance, would be an ethically justifiable social tool for activists to employ in order to bring about a morally and socially desirable result (Kelly & Morar, 2018). Other emotions, like shame and guilt also need to be acknowledged and perhaps harnessed. Walter Benjamin's (Benjamin, 1969) reading of Kafka's *Animal Stories* reveals the role of shame when we forget our obligations to others for immediate gratification. Just as we have 'forgotten' the lives of women, People of Colour, LGBT+ people, disabled people, we have also forgotten the lives of animals. Shame can mobilise our ability to respond to sentient life—our own animal being. The gnawing horror/grief which is so frequently the central experience of vegan subjectivity, of recognising injustice and violence, is another potential uniting point, a grief shared by feminist, LGBT+ and environmentalist activists (Quinn, 2021).

Love, attraction and friendship might also be starting points for social shifts. The intentional choice of vegan partners (vegansexuality), to avoid conflict or to construct a safe and understanding space as observed by Potts (2008), offers a route to change. This vegansexuality can be understood as an embodied ethical form of sexuality which forms a spectrum, at one end vegans experience a likelihood of sexual attraction towards those who do not consume animals or other animal products. At the other end, vegansexuality can be expressed as physical aversion to the bodies of those who consume animals and animal products. Potts' study can be understood, from a Foucauldian perspective, in terms of the invention of new sexualities and identities, via power and resistance, discourse and confession. There was a global backlash against the idea of vegans 'rejecting' meat-eating partners; at the same time self-identified 'vegansexuals' began 'coming out'. These choices in relationships, reflecting a dedication to cruelty-free lifestyles, revealed a fear at the heart of carnism. In the backlash Potts and Parry (2010) describe, the denunciation of meat ('real food') was equated with a refusal of sex (or 'real sex' i.e., heterosex with a meat-eating man). Just as feminists have been constructed as joyless deniers of male pleasure (Smart, 1989), vegans were also depicted in this way. Vegansexuality counters the cultural link between meat-eating and heteronormative masculinity and undermines phallocentric myths of consent: to rape women, to slaughter animals, to plunder the environment. A vegan imagination, much like a feminist or sociological imagination, enables an alternative vision understating of our past and vision of the future. More and more celebrity vegans 'come out', we are seeing a growth in vegan cultural events—Veganuary, festivals, concerts and camp outs. From these, spring communities or families of choice (Weeks et al., 2001). We are seeing towns and cities (e.g. Nagpur, Haywoods Heath, Buenos Aires), organisations and businesses sign the Plant Based Treaty. History shows that systemic change movements can come from almost nothing to a critical mass big enough to force change, in a very short time. Perhaps we are reaching the social tipping point for veganism, where the beliefs and behaviours spread from minority tendency to majority practice.

Through vegansexuality, communities, or families of choice, hegemonic masculinity's dependence on a constitutive Other is revealed, rendering it highly unstable. The vegan ethic situates a recognition of embodied precarity at the heart of our existence. Butler's (Butler, 2009) 'grievability' of the animal, of the planet, is recognised. There is an emphasis on shared vulnerability, shared suffering, reason is coextensive with emotion. The vegan ethic thus resists hegemonic masculinity and the ways in which it derives its illusory coherence.

Conclusion

Given the urgent need to transform our (diet) practices, veganism forms part of a developing nexus of practices associated with sustainable development and green consumerism. Ways of thinking, just like ways of production, and ways of being are hard to change but change we must if we want to live in thriving communities, with enough energy, in a relatively climate-safe environment. Such change clearly has to happen from above. But we must not ignore the power of change from below. To combat the climate crisis we need to focus on both individual and collective solutions. As we have seen from some of the examples given earlier in this chapter, individual acts can lead to collective action. Veganism as mode of thinking (like feminism and queer theory), as an orientation, as well as goal-orientated activist practice, offers a path to change. As a pessimist, I no longer hope for a better future but I do hope for a less dreadful one. The time has come for planet over palette, to turn away from our (dis)comfort food. No daily choice we make has greater impact on the environment. The transformation necessitates individual and communal change. Identities are not stable, they vary depending on social context and are influenced by the intersectionality of other identities. These elements, variability and intersectionality, need to be further explored to advance the fight against prejudice, climate crisis and inequalities. Climate devastation is not just an animal rights and environmental disaster, it is about workers' rights, women's rights, declining rural communities, public health and global poverty. We must start today, if we want any chance of living in kinder, regenerative, sustainable communities. Gandhi said, 'be the change you wish to see in the world'. This will require rationing of basic foodstuffs, seasonal eating, local eating but above all, drastic reduction in meat and dairy consumption, such changes can be contagious. It is time to put the land wasted for animal farming to feed the privileged few to better use, before many more lives are destroyed—human and animal.

We must acknowledge and confront our collective failure to confront capitalism's power—political and economic. Its determination to continue mass consumption charged by carbon is having disastrous consequences. The UN's Goal 2.I—Food for all—is failing. From 2019 to 2022, the number of undernourished people grew by 150 million, a crisis driven largely by climate change, conflict and the COVID-19 pandemic. The current crisis in food and fuel price spikes is related to this. Veganism offers a solution. Our understanding of sustainability has to change; it is not about keeping life as it is, with a few more solar panels, wind turbines and electric cars.

The media's current romance with veganism reflects widespread cultural anxiety surrounding the meat and dairy industries in recent years. Together with the growing voice given to activist discourses revealing the cruel and environmentally catastrophic consequences of modern factory farming, it is taking its toll on the traditional prestige that meat has been afforded in Western society (Fiddes, 1991). Where veganism was once seen as a radical step, to continue to consume meat, dairy and fish as we currently do, is surely the more perilous one. The climate for consumption change is being created and affluent societies have a moral obligation to lead this shift. Ending unnecessary suffering requires a relatively easy act; limited cost to the self, reduces violence, exploitation and suffering for the many and may foster a conscious empathy for those most affected by (and least responsible for) climate change. Even if we have little regard for others and only ourselves, if we believe humans come first, then the case for veganism has never been stronger. It is necessary in order for us to continue living and breathing on what is left of this earth.

References

Adams, C. J. (1990). *The Sexual Politics of Meat*. Bloomsbury Press.

Adams, C. J. (2010). Why Feminist-Vegan Now? *Feminism & Psychology, 20*(3), 302–317.

Ahmed, S. (2010). *Feminist Killjoys (and Other Willful Subjects)*. http://sfonline.barnard.edu/polyphonic/ahmed_01.htm

Atwood, M. (2003). *Oryx and Crake*. London: Virago.

Bar-On, Y. M., Phillips, R., & Milo, R. (2018). The Biomass Distribution on Earth. *PNAS Proceedings of the National Academy of Sciences of the United States of America, 115*(25), 6506–6511.

Beers, D. L. (2006). *For the Prevention of Cruelty: The History and Legacy of Animal Rights Activism in the United States*. Swallow Press.

Benjamin, W. (1969). *Illuminations: Essays and Reflections*. Schocken.

Bentham, J. (1789/1996). In J. H. Burns & H. L. A. Hart (Eds.), *An Introduction to the Principles of Morals and Legislation*. Clarendon Press.

Borges, T., & Branford, S. (2020). *Rapid Deforestation of Brazilian Amazon Could Bring Next Pandemic: Experts, in Mongabay Series: Amazon Conservation*. https://news.mongabay.com/2020/04/rapid-deforestation-of-brazilian-amazon-could-bring-next-pandemic-experts/

Bourdieu, P. (1982). *Distinction: A Social Critique of the Judgement of Taste*. Routledge and Kegan Paul.

British Medical Journal. (2022). Conflict, Climate Change, and Covid-19 Combine to Create a Breeding Ground for Sexual and Gender Based Violence. *British Medical Journal, 378*, o2093. https://doi.org/10.1136/bmj.o2093

Butler, J. (2009). *Frames of War*. Verso.

Buttny, R., & Kinefuchi, E. (2020). Vegans' Problem Stories: Negotiating Vegan Identity in Dealing with Omnivores. *Discourse and Society, 31*(6). https://doi.org/10.1177/0957926520939689

Campbell, B. (2013). *End of Equality?* Seagull Books.

Carson, R. (1962). *Silent Spring*. Houghton Mifflin Company.

Cherry, E. (2015). I Was a Teenage Vegan: Motivation and Maintenance of Lifestyle Movements. *Sociological Inquiry, 85*(1), 55–57.
Cohen, S. (2001). *States of Denial: Knowing About Atrocities and Suffering of Others*. Polity Press.
Cole, M., & Stewart, K. (2017). Speciesism Party: A Vegan Critique of Sausage Party. *Interdisciplinary Studies in Literature and Environment, 24*(4), 767–786.
Derrida, J. (1988). *Limited, Inc.* (S. Weber, Trans.). Northwestern University Press.
Derrida, J. (1992). Force of Law: The "Mystical Foundation of Authority". In *Deconstruction and the Possibility of Justice* (M. Quaintance, Trans. and D. Cornell et al., Eds.). Routledge.
Derrida, J. (2008). *The Animal That Therefore I Am*. Fordham University Press.
Dick, P. K. (1968). *Do Androids Dream of Electric Sheep?* Del Ray.
Douglas, M. (1970). *Purity and Danger: An Analysis of Concepts of Pollution and Taboo*. Praeger.
Elias, N. (1978). *The Civilizing Process: Sociogenic and Psychogenic Investigations*. Urizen Books.
Fiddes, N. (1991). *Meat: A Natural Symbol*. Routledge.
Foer, J. S. (2009). *Eating Animals*. Hamish Hamilton.
Foster, J. B. (2020). *Socialism and Ecology: The Return of Nature*. Monthly Review Press.
Fountain, H. (2019, October 22). The World Can Make More Water From the Sea, But at What Cost? *New York Times*. https://www.nytimes.com/2019/10/22/climate/desalination-water-climate-change.html
Francione, G. (2015). *Animal Rights: The Abolitionist Approach*. Exempla Press.
Gaard, G. (2014). Toward New Masculinities, EcoGenders and Ecosexualities. In C. J. Adams & L. Gruen (Eds.), *Ecofeminism: Feminist Intersections with Other Animals and The Earth*. Bloomsbury.
Goodman, R. T. (2021). What Is the Matter with Politics? Paranoia, Precarity, Climate Change. *symploke, 29*(1), 217–234. Project MUSE. https://doi.org/10.1353/sym.2021.0012
Gore, A. (2006). *An Inconvenient Truth: The Planetary Emergency of Global Warming and What We Can Do About It*. Rodale.
Gramsci, A. (1972). *Selections from the Prison Notebooks of Antonio Gramsci*. International Publishers.
Griffin, P. (2017). The Carbon Majors Database, CDP Carbon Majors Report. *CDP Worldwide*. https://cdn.cdp.net/cdp-production/cms/reports/documents/000/002/327/original/Carbon-Majors-Report-2017.pdf?1501833772
Henley, S., & Jones, S. (2022, July 18). 'Heat Apocalypse' Warning in Western France as Thousands Flee Wildfire. *The Guardian*. https://www.theguardian.com/world/2022/jul/18/heat-apocalypse-warning-western-france-thousands-flee-wildfire

Hess, T., & Holman, I. (2022, August 5). UK Drought: Are Farmers Facing the Crop Failures of 1976 All Over Again? *The Week*. https://theconversation.com/uk-drought-are-farmers-facing-the-crop-failures-of-1976-all-over-again-188175

Hudepohl, D. (2021). Why Going Vegan Is One of the Best Things You Can Do for the Environment. *Fork Over Knives*. https://www.forksoverknives.com/wellness/vegan-diet-helps-environmental-sustainability/

IPCC. (2018). Global Warming of 1.5°C. An IPCC Special Report on the Impacts of Global Warming of 1.5°C Above Pre-industrial Levels and Related Global Greenhouse Gas Emission Pathways, in the Context of Strengthening the Global Response to the Threat of Climate Change, Sustainable Development, and Efforts to Eradicate Poverty. V. Masson-Delmotte, P. Zhai, H. O. Pörtner, D. Roberts, J. Skea, P.R. Shukla, ..., T. Waterfield (eds.). Cambridge University Press.

IPCC. (2019). In P. R. Shukla, J. Skea, E. C. Buendia, V. Masson-Delmotte, H.-O. Pörtner, D. C. Roberts, et al. (Eds.), *Climate Change and Land: An IPCC Special Report on Climate Change, Desertification, Land Degradation, Sustainable Land Management, Food Security, and Greenhouse Gas Fluxes in Terrestrial Ecosystems*. https://www.ipcc.ch/srccl/

IPCC. (2022). In P. R. Shukla, J. Skea, R. Slade, A. Al Khourdajie, R. van Diemen, D. McCollum, et al. (Eds.), *Climate Change 2022: Mitigation of Climate Change: Contribution of Working Group III to the Sixth Assessment Report of the Intergovernmental Panel on Climate Change*. Cambridge University Press. https://doi.org/10.1017/9781009157926

Jamieson, A. J., Brooks, L. S. R., Reid, W. D. K., Piertney, S. B., & Narayanaswamy, B. E. (2019). Microplastics and Synthetic Particles Ingested by Deep-Sea Amphipods in Six of the Deepest Marine Ecosystems on Earth. *Royal Society Open Science, 6*(2), 180667.

Jones, K., Patel, N., Levy, M., et al. (2008). Global Trends in Emerging Infectious Diseases. *Nature, 451*, 990–993. https://doi.org/10.1038/nature06536

Kelly, D., & Morar, N. (2018). I Eat, Therefore I Am: Disgust and the Intersection of Food and Identity. In T. Doggett, A. Barnhill, & M. Budolfson (Eds.), *The Oxford Handbook of Food Ethics*. Oxford University Press.

Klein, N. (2014). *This Changes Everything: Capitalism vs the Climate*. Simon & Schuster.

Kolbert, E. (2016). *Summary of the Sixth Extinction*. Bloomsbury Publishing.

Lockwood, A. (2021). Vegan Studies and Gender Studies. In *The Routledge Handbook of Vegan Studies*. Routledge.

Lymbery, P. (2017). *Dead Zone: Where the Wild Things Were*. Bloomsbury.

Martin, L. (1994). Feminism and Vegetarianism. In A. Jaggar (Ed.), *Living with Contradictions: Controversies in Feminist Social Ethics*. Routledge.

McGrath, M. (2018). *Sir David Attenborough: Climate Change 'Our Greatest Threat'*. https://www.bbc.co.uk/news/science-environment-46398057

McKeowan, P., & Dunn, R. (2021). A 'Life-Style Choice' Or a Philosophical Belief?: The Argument for Veganism and Vegetarianism to be a Protected Philosophical Belief and the Position in England and Wales. *Liverpool Law Review, 42*, 207–241.

Merchant, C. (1989). *The Death of Nature*. Harper.

Meyerding, J. (1982). Feminist Criticisms and Cultural Imperialism. *Agenda, 2*(6), 22–23.

Moore, J. W. (2016). *Anthropocene Or Capitalocene?: Nature, History, and The Crisis of Capitalism*. PM Press.

Mulvey, L. (1975). Visual Pleasure and Narrative Cinema. *Screen, 16*(3), 6–18.

Pedersen, H., & Stanescu, V. (2014). Conclusion: Future Directions for Critical Animal Studies. In N. Taylor & R. Twine (Eds.), *The Rise of Critical Animal Studies*. Routledge.

Pharr, S. (1988). *Homophobia a Weapon of Sexism*. The Women's Project.

Pimentel, D. (2006). Soil Erosion: A Food and Environmental Threat. *Journal of the Environment, Development and Sustainability, 8*, 119–137.

Plumwood, V. (1993). *Feminism and the Mastery of Nature*. Routledge.

Potts, A. (2008). *Exploring Vegansexuality: An Embodied Ethics of Intimacy*. The Practical Ethics Blog. http://practicalethics.net/blog/author/anniepotts

Potts, A. (2016). *Meat Culture*. Leiden.

Potts, A., & Parry, J. (2010). Vegan Sexuality: Challenging Heteronormative Masculinity through Meat-free Sex. *Feminism & Psychology, 20*(1), 53–72.

Quinn, E. (2021). Vegan Studies and Queer Theory. In L. Wright (Ed.), *The Routledge Handbook of Vegan Studies*. Routledge.

Rich, A. (1980). Compulsory Heterosexuality and Lesbian Existence. *Signs: Journal of Women in Culture and Society, 5*(4), 631–660.

Sala, E., Mayorga, J., Bradley, D., et al. (2021). Protecting the Global Ocean for Biodiversity, Food and Climate. *Nature, 592*, 397–409.

Simon, D. (2013). *Can Animal Foods Be Produced Sustainably? (Part Two – Organic Follies)*. https://meatonomics.com/2013/09/03/can-animal-foods-be-produced-sustainably-part-two-organic-follies/

Smart, C. (1989). *Feminism and the Power of Law*. Routledge.

Sobal, J. (2005). Men, Meat and Marriage: Models of Masculinity. *Food and Foodways, 13*(1–2), 135–158. https://doi.org/10.1080/07409710590915409

Springmann, M., Godfray, H. C. J., Rayner, M., & Scarborough, P. (2016). Analysis and Valuation of the Health and Climate Change Cobenefits of Dietary Change. *PNAS Proceedings of the National Academy of Sciences of the United States of America, 113*(15), 4146–4151.

Steinfeld, H. (2006). *Livestock's Long Shadow: Environmental Issues and Options*. Food and Agriculture Organization of the United Nations.

Stern, N. H. (2007). *The Economics of Climate Change: The Stern Review*. Cambridge University Press.
Stevenson, P. (2018). Paying for the True Costs of Our Meat, Eggs and Dairy. In J. D'Silva & C. McKenna (Eds.), *Farming, Food and Nature*. Routledge.
Supran, G., & Oreskes, N. (2017). Assessing ExxonMobil's Climate Change Communications (1977–2014). *Environmental Research Letters, 12*(08), 084019.
Thompson, C. (2019). How 19th Century Scientists Predicted Global Warming. *JSTOR Daily*. https://daily.jstor.org/how-19th-century-scientists-predicted-global-warming/
Thornett, A. (2019). *Facing the Apocalypse: Arguments for Ecosocialism*. Resistance Books.
Twine, R. (2014). Vegan Killjoys at the Table – Contesting Happiness and Negotiating Relationships with Food Practices. *Societies, 4*(4), 623–639.
UN-Water. (2021). *The United Nations World Water Development Report: Valuing Water*. UNESCO. https://unesdoc.unesco.org/ark:/48223/pf0000375724
Vaughan, A. (2022, July 28). 40°C Heatwave May Have Killed 1000 People in England and Wales. *New Scientist*. https://www.newscientist.com/article/2331349-40c-heatwave-may-have-killed-1000-people-in-england-and-wales/#:~:text=That%20study%20calculated%20the%20risk,1141%20in%20the%20worst%20case
Wagner, D., Garmes, E., Forister, M., Berenbaum, M., & Stopak, D. (2021). Insect Decline in the Anthropocene: Death by a Thousand Cuts. *PNAS Proceedings of the National Academy of Sciences of the United States of America, 118*(2). https://doi.org/10.1073/pnas.2023989118
Weeks, J., Heaphy, B., & Donovan, C. (2001). *Families of Choice and Other Life Experiments*. Routledge.
Willett, W. (2019). Food in the Anthropocene: The EAT–Lancet Commission on Healthy Diets from Sustainable Food Systems. *The Lancet Commissions, 393*(10170), 447–492. https://www.thelancet.com/commissions/EAT
Witt, C. (2012). *The Metaphysics of Gender*. Oxford University Press.
Wolfenson, K. (2013). *Coping with the Food and Agriculture Challenge: Smallholders' Agenda*. Preparations and Outcomes of the 2012 United Nations Conference on Sustainable Development (Rio+20), Natural Resources Management and Environment Department Food and Agriculture Organization of the United Nations, Rome.
Wright, L. (2019). *Through a Vegan Studies Lens*. Press.

CHAPTER 5

Ensuring Equitable, Equal, Empowering Education

Alex Fairlamb

This chapter will examine ways that two different schools in the North-East have sought to identify the barriers that young girls face in the current educational system and the strategies that they have put into place in order to try and remove these. This is important because, as the UN Sustainable Development Goals identify (United Nations, 2016), education is not yet equitable and equal for all genders (particularly vulnerable and disadvantaged children) and as such greater work must be done to ensure that educational provision is inclusive and to ensure educational outcomes of not only academic attainment but also personal development by 2030. Through the lens of these two schools, this chapter will explore literacy and the curriculum, Pupil Premium strategies and organisations who alongside schools provide further opportunities to demolish disadvantage and gender issues within schools.

Education is a multi-faceted and complex beast. Virtuous in its intentions and its attempts to ensure equity for all in society and globally, it is often the poor relative of government policy and can be fraught with

A. Fairlamb (✉)
King's Priory Academy, Tynemouth, UK

D. Dalton, A. Smith (eds.), *Gender, Sexuality and the UN's SDGs*, Sustainable Development Goals Series,
https://doi.org/10.1007/978-3-031-31046-1_5

inadequacies. Universally, education is regarded as one of the greatest levellers in society, enabling people to grow their knowledge and skills in the hope of betterment and achieving their desired end goals. However, education is also frequently underfunded and as such, the far-reaching effects of a chronic lack of required investment, has meant issues in terms of ensuring that educational provision is inclusive, equal for all and meets the needs of the learners it serves.

A school is more than a centre of learning, it is also a centre of support and pastoral care for the most vulnerable in society (both students and other stakeholders, such as parents and carers). This includes those who live in, or experience, poverty and/or discrimination on the basis of basic human rights, linking to the protected nine characteristics such as race, gender and/or socio-economic status (Equality and Human Rights Commission, 2010). It is where many will access basic provision which they are not able to within their home or community environment, such as food and health resources. Therefore, as the nucleus of a person's development emotionally, physically and mentally, it is our duty of care to ensure that education meets the needs of all and is representative of all those within the communities which it serves.

Why This, Why Now?

The basic and brutal truth that we have to acknowledge, in order to learn lessons and to improve educational provision, is that our current institutions, systems and policies are not addressing the disadvantage or gender gap as we had hoped they would. Whilst many involved in education have been doing their utmost to ensure education is equal and equitable, there are still significant gaps in outcomes and opportunities for our more disadvantaged and vulnerable children. For young girls and trans-girls, compounding this with additional barriers due to their gender, means that there is still much work to be done to ensure equity. Rowland (2017, p. 9) outlines the statistics in Britain, even prior to the impact of Covid-19:

Vulnerable Learners: Why We Need to Do Better

- Just 14% of looked-after children achieved five good GCSEs, including English and Maths (2015).
- 6% of 16–64-year olds with learning disabilities are in work. The figure is 5.2% for females.

- 46% of people entering the prison system have literacy skills no higher than an 11-year-old.
- Fewer than 44% disadvantaged pupils achieved five good GCSEs, including English and Maths, in 2016.
- 12% of children in secure training centres said they were Gypsy, Roma or Traveller, nearly 100 times greater than the estimated proportion in the general population.

Such statistics highlight how already there was already much work to be done to eradicate disparities and barriers within education prior to the COVID-19 pandemic, beginning in late 2019. With the implementation of lockdown in various countries during 2020, the educational landscape changed dramatically within a rapid period of time. Whilst one of the more obvious, visible disruptions was the move from traditional in-school learning changing to educational provision being online (with cohorts of key worker and vulnerable children able to attend school), the social, mental and economic impact of the pandemic upon children and education has been equally palpable, even if it is not always immediately visible to those beyond the education sector.

Looking globally at the impact, girls were disproportionately more negatively affected by the pandemic when looking at access to education. This has been due to double labour, with girls expected to do additional chores and childcare at home during the pandemic, an increase in pregnancy and isolation from safeguarding provision to help tackle gender-based violence and autonomy over their own actions (Kwauk et al., 2021). In the UK, the government has stated that 'the impact of the COVID-19 pandemic on women and girls has been disproportionate and profound. We, the G7, share a commitment to placing gender equality and the empowerment of all women and girls at the heart of our work to build back better' (Department for Foreign Affairs, 2021). Added to this, the United Nations (UN) has stated that 'COVID-19 has wiped out 20 years of educational gains', with 'an additional 101 million children in grades 1–8 falling below minimum reading proficiency levels in 2020' (United Nations, 2021). Consequently, even though the UN Sustainable Development Goals were launched in 2016, the argument as to the need for such targets as improving education for all, has been bolstered further. In 2022, two years into the ripple effects of the pandemic, we need to recalibrate and refocus, and explore effective programmes and strategies that have helped to drive inclusivity and equity, in order to make progress towards achieving the ambitious targets set out in the UN Sustainable Development Goals to tackle inequality, such as 4.6 'Ensuring all young people achieve literacy and numeracy' (United Nations, 2016).

Literacy as a Bedrock for Equity

As mentioned, ensuring that all children are literate and numerate is an essential part of ensuring equity. As Rowland (2017, p. 9) argues:

> [L]anguage comprehension facilitates independent learning. It helps to ensure pupils do not opt out and contributes to belonging. It can help all aspects of school life. It is important for leaders to consider the impact of underdeveloped language comprehension on disadvantaged pupils.

Consequently, the fundamental bedrock of an educational policy and institution should be ensuring that students are able to become fluent readers and writers, that they can use vocabulary accurately and in varying contexts. This has been recognised as a matter of importance as a strategy to close the gender gap in education, which has been exacerbated by the pandemic, 'scale up early literacy and maths programmes to help ensure all girls secure foundational learning' (Department for Foreign Affairs, 2021).

Recent research has highlighted the extent and impact of disadvantage within literacy, with the National Literacy Trust determining that '1 in 8 of the most disadvantaged children in the North East [of England] do not have a reading book', with the result being that '[c]hildren who say they own a book are 15 times more likely to read above the level expected for their age than their peers who don't own a book (28.8% vs 1.9%)', and added to this, they 'are four times less likely to read below the expected level (12.9% vs 48.1%)' (Clark & Teravainen, 2017, pp. 1–2). Consequently, a key focus of school inspection bodies such as Ofsted and Education Scotland, has been to embed within their new frameworks the importance of determining the efficacy of literacy strategies and programmes implemented within educational settings. Their rationale states: 'If pupils are not able to read to an age-appropriate level and fluency, they will be incapable of accessing the rest of the curriculum, and they will rapidly fall behind their peers' (Ofsted, 2022), resulting in them evaluating literacy provision through deep dives and strategies to support weaker readers to catch up with peers.

'The Golden Five'

A secondary school example of a whole-school strategy to help close the literacy gap is a strategy known as 'The Golden Five', which contains five evidence-informed methods to support the explicit teaching of fluent reading, the development of tier 2–3 vocabulary acquisition and techniques to ensure that students can improve their ability to write well-constructed paragraphs.

The key intent of the 'The Golden Five' is to create a teaching culture of 'We are ALL teachers of literacy', challenging the misconception that the responsibility of developing literate students is the job of the English department alone. The importance of disciplinary reading and vocabulary instruction is at the forefront of this strategy. Additionally, it aims to develop the literacy skills of students through five whole school strategies which are adapted for subject specific purposes and for registration programmes so that the reading gap is closed and the students' ability to use a wide range of tier 2–3 vocabulary accurately improves, thereby helping to close the literacy gap for disadvantaged and Special Educational Needs (SEN) students. Such a focused literacy strategy therefore aims to support the scaling up of reading and writing, to ensure that girls develop the core skills to be able to access wider curriculums.

The five strategies are as follows:

- Directed reading—teacher-led and modelling reading of text.
- Frayer models—teacher-led, explicit pre-teaching of tier 2–3 vocabulary.
- Single paragraph outline, a strategy taken from The Writing Revolution (Hochman et al., 2017)—teachers explicitly model how to construct a paragraph by returning to a sentence-level construction approach, rather than ploughing into the production of a full paragraph without careful planning.
- Kernel sentences, a strategy taken from The Writing Revolution (Hochman et al., 2017)—this strategy empowers students to break down the key aspects of a paragraph. By plotting out and pre-planning these aspects, students can then combine these aspects to use to construct either expanded sentences or a paragraph.
- *Because*, *but*, *so*, a strategy taken from The Writing Revolution—teachers provide students with the beginning of a sentence and ask them to turn it into three separate complex sentences, using each conjunction in turn.

Naturally, staff training is fundamental in the success of such initiatives. Primary practitioners receive training on varying models of reading, such as phonics, decoding and fluency. However, this is not a typical part of a secondary teacher or further education teacher's training, which has created disconnect in supporting the development of reading skills from novice to mastery. The impact of not ensuring secondary practitioners are trained in literacy techniques is evidenced by research in 2020 that over 120,000 disadvantaged students made the transition from primary to secondary school below the expected standard for reading. The educational prospects for this group are grave. If their progress mirrors previous cohorts, 'we would expect one in ten to achieve passes in English and Maths at GCSE, and fewer than 2% to achieve the English Baccalaureate'.

Consequently, considered and carefully structured literacy strategies which are consistent across a secondary skill and are rooted in evidence, which help to continue a child's reading development are vital. Woolley (2020, p. 47) argues that an increase in disciplinary literacy is needed to help to close the gender gap for girls in education as at present there is an unequal balance of girls in industries such as screenwriting, so therefore they need to develop a real life understanding of writing. Done well, it can build confidence, provide space for exploring that all-important identity and personal voice, and encourage girls to think about the kinds of writing they might experience in different careers, thus opening up the careers conversation in a tangible way.

As aforementioned, the role of ensuring that teachers and learning assistants are given substantial training in teaching children how to read and write accurately and confidently is key, which is why more secondary schools are now buying in companies to deliver phonics training to their practitioners.

A whole-school literacy strategy can really strengthen reading, but it cannot be considered to be the silver-bullet and that it works in isolation, as the EEF identifies in their 'Improving Literacy in Secondary Schools' report (Coleman & Quigley, 2021). In tandem with the whole school literacy strategy, there needs to be targeted intervention for below-average readers and additional bespoke support, including training and supporting parents and carers with helping their child to read. Through a multi-faceted and consistent approach, these strategies can help to reduce the literacy gap and ensure that all children are proficient with literacy.

A Diverse Curriculum

The importance of having a diverse curriculum cannot be overstated. Unless the children see themselves represented in the curriculum, and unless the curriculum is constructed into a progression model which builds upon prior learning so that students can 'know more and do more', the curriculum offer is not diverse. As Reid (2020, pp. 45–46) states:

> [W]e have a duty to offer a curriculum that allows students to access what I have termed the 'broader picture': learning about the canon (or the facts or the dominant discourse) but also how it came to be that way. In order to achieve this, there needs to be a conversation in the curriculum between what the traditional canon is made of and what has often been excluded. Considerable thought needs to be given to how this weaves together as a whole narrative, as I believe it is in this whole that the transformative potential for students and their communities lies.

When deconstructed, this means:

1. It is the duty of care of educators and educational policy makers to ensure that as architects of the curriculum, that what we select from the domain of our subject disciplines to teach is representative and diverse. This must include challenging examination boards to ensure that their courses of study are diverse too. We need to see all genders represented, all ethnicities and cultures, people with disabilities and ensure that we have a global approach to representation in the curriculum. There have been recent developments, with the introduction of migration courses in History. However, as Criado-Perez identified, an analysis in 2015 of an A Level Music course by a popular English examination board highlighted that the study included no women at all (Criado-Perez, 2019, p. 18). This will have a significant and positive impact on our children, who want and need to see themselves within our curricula. As Reid (2020, p. 45) further argues:

   > I believe it is a matter of intellectual integrity to insist on reading these voices together. By understanding how the world works, they also get to have a stake in it. They can see that the world is not something done to them but something that they are part of.

The canon is there but it excludes much. As practitioners, we need to fully audit and evaluate what we teach and ensure that we develop the curriculum beyond the canon. That is not to say that we throw the baby out with the bathwater and reject the canon completely. It means taking this as part of the curriculum, and then enriching it beyond this. Just as we may continue to teach Charles Dickens and Jane Austen in English Literature, this should be part of a broader set of texts and authors such as Naoki Higashida, Maya Angelou, Malorie Blackman, Kazuo Ishiguro and Malala Yousafzai. Included with this should be an open discussion of what the traditional canon is and why more diverse texts have been threaded into the curriculum. In 2016, Criado-Perez organised a group of activists to challenge the Bank of England's decision to remove Jane Austen from the £10 bank note. The campaign was won, and Austen remained. As an English teacher, this provides an opportunity for debate and discourse around the importance of this campaign and keeping Jane Austen on the note given her works, but it also enables children to propose alternatives for future notes such as Malorie Blackman or Bernadine Evaristo, based on their understanding of who would traditionally be considered for a note due to an outdated canon and who should now be considered for a note.

2. As we audit our curriculums, this might result in experiencing some uncomfortable truths as we realise that what we have taught previously has perhaps not met the needs of *ALL* of our students. However, we need to get comfortable with being uncomfortable when evaluating our curriculums in the vein of Angelou's 'when we know better, we do better'. Just as once upon a time we used VAK (Visual, Audio, Kinaesthetic) principles within teaching and learning, we now look back uncomfortably and woefully knowing that this pedagogy is incorrect and yielded no benefits to the children. So, once we know something isn't meeting the needs and we have educated ourselves, we then have a great responsibility to action in.
3. That a diverse curriculum helps us to ensure that we move further towards an inclusive society that is rooted in mutual tolerance. To do this, we need to ensure that we educate children about *all* members of our world, not just dead, white English men.
4. Cultural capital. This has been thee big phrase of the past year in education. There has been a renaissance in Bourdieu's concept that access to arts and literature can enhance a person's power and posi-

tion within society (Cairns, 2019). The 'canon' is too often seen as the key criteria for ensuring that children have cultural capital—that they know classical composers such as Mozart and authors such as Dickens. However, as Criado-Perez (Criado-Perez, 2019) identifies, the canon ignores the social and cultural constructs that prevented the canon to be beyond what it came. Mendelssohn's work was sometimes written by his sister Fanny, for which he lays claim as the patriarchal society at the time did not permit women to become composers. Dr. James Barry, a trans person, was an incredible army surgeon in the nineteenth century who performed the first caesarean where mother and child lived, however does not feature in examination boards' courses on the 'History of Medicine' as, at the time, society rejected and persecuted trans people. What makes it such that we should learn about the work of Pare (a fourteenth-century male French army surgeon who first used ointment on wounds) but not Barry? GCSE and A Level specification are very guilty of not being diverse, but as mentioned earlier, conversations are beginning to happen led by organisations such as the Historical Association. The curriculum and 'canon' needs rethinking and updating.

As target 4.7 in the UN Sustainable Development Goals identifies, in order to ensure inclusive and equitable quality education, our curriculums need to include learning about and discussing 'human rights, gender equality, promotion of a culture of peace and non-violence, global citizenship and appreciation of cultural diversity' (United Nations, 2016). National data can prove useful in further understanding the need for this as it demonstrates how the population is becoming increasingly diverse, and add weight to arguments for why therefore curriculums need to reflect this. National statistics figures show that Muslim, Hindu and Jewish populations are rising and that the number of the 'UK population identifying as lesbian, gay or bisexual increased from 1.6% in 2014 to 2.2% in 2018. Younger people, aged 16–24 years, were most likely to identify as LGB in 2018 (4.4%)' (Government Office of Science, 2021). Clearly, in order to achieve gender equality in education and to dismantle cultural barriers, equal and accurate representation within the curriculum is a given. For example, in Teesside—are the Gypsy Roma Traveller communities represented and how so? In Bolton, are the increasing number of Polish students represented in the curriculum and how so?

The next step should be to look at your curriculum vision. Does it need changing? Why and how? The key to this is to avoid trying to fast-track changes which can result in accidentally adopting a tokenistic approach. Curriculum evaluation needs careful consideration, meaningful construction and several 'let's look at this again, have we met our vision and the needs of our communities?' moments. The approach to it should be 'blended, not binary'. Diversity should not be a bolt on to the curriculum where it is shoehorned into a scheme of learning to tick a box, nor should it be confined to calendar days alone. Hamer (2016) identifies clear stages whereby we can determine how we are ensuring that our curriculums have diversity meaningfully woven through and how we can avoid 'diversity drops' as I call them (where diversity is just dropped in and the mainstream curriculum has bolt-ons added to it) (Table 5.1).

Table 5.1 Example of a History topic which is 'blended, not binary' after having reviewed it (Fairlamb, 2020)

Causes of WW1: Main	*Building upon Year 8 Studies*
Recruitment	**What I used to teach:** recruitment of British, white men. Local study focus **What I now teach**: recruitment of British men, recruitment of Empire troops, recruitment of women, local study focus. Compare and contrast differing propaganda techniques **Homework**: Black Poppies, recruitment in the West Indies
Life in the trenches	**What I used to teach**: British men's experiences of the Western Front and the key battles on the Western Front **What I now teach**: British and Empire troops' experiences of the Western Front, warfare pre-1914 comparison, comparing conflict in Africa and the Middle East **Homework (flipped reading):** directed reading, conflict in North Africa and the Mediterranean
Weaponry	**What I used to teach**: four new weapons introduced and their impact **What I now teach**: four weapons introduced and their impact, where and who created them, including women and local Belgian refugees **Homework (flipped reading):** directed reading, conflict in North Africa and the Mediterranean
Medicine and injury	**What I used to teach:** not included **What I now teach**: common injuries, linking to weaponry in the previous lesson and the treatment of soldier by the RAMC, FANY, VAD
Home front	**What I used to teach:** role of women, DORA **What I now teach**: DORA, role of women, contract workers, Belgian refugees (local), anti-German sentiment and propaganda.

(*continued*)

Table 5.1 (continued)

Causes of WW1: Main	*Building upon Year 8 Studies*
Total war?	**What I used to teach**: Zeppelins and barrage balloons **What I now teach**: local history, female sources
A war to end all wars?	**What I used to teach**: not included **What I now teach**: the Big Three and their aims, Paris Peace Conference, Wilson
Treaty of Versailles	**What I used to teach**: not included **What I now teach**: build-up to the signing, the terms, differing opinions at the time—linking to Hitler, American isolationism, link to Russia and the Treaty of Brest-Litovsk as a comparison
Britain post-WW1 suffrage	**What I used to teach**: not included **What I now teach**: long-term big picture of growing calls for suffrage from the late 1700s, including involvement in Chartism and the emergence of the Suffragists and Suffragettes. Link to women's role in the war. The impact of the war on women—jobs, society, politics etc.
Britain 1920s	**What I used to teach**: not included **What I now teach**: economic problems of Britain after the war and the downturn in industries such as coal, growth of trade unionism, fear of communism (linking to the Russian Revolution homework) and the General Strike. This helps us understand during Year 11 the Cold War and the attitude of Churchill and Britain. This will help us at 'A Level' to understand Anglo-Soviet relations such as the Civil War, Zinoviev Letter, Acros Raid and Munich Conference
American: Dark side	**What I used to teach**: not included **What I now teach:** increasing laws against immigration, Black people and minorities over the course of the late 1800s (building on Year 8 content), linking in American attitudes after the First World War in terms of rejection of increasing isolationism and fear of communism. Limits on immigration. Link to race riots in Britain, for example, Liverpool

Removing Barriers to Inclusivity

A key, ambitious target of the UN Sustainability Goals is their aim to 'remove gender disparities and ensure equal access to all levels of education and vocational training for the vulnerable, including persons with disabilities, indigenous peoples and children in vulnerable situations' (United Nations, 2016). As earlier identified, there is a great disparity in access to education in the UK. Whilst every child legally has the right to education, and protocols are put into place in order to ensure that children attend, current legislation and governmental policy does not always take into account the visible and invisible barriers that can prevent a child from making it across the threshold of an educational establishment. Whilst schools will often have in place attendance officers, and local authorities will issue fines to parents and carers who do not ensure their child attends school, greater work needs to be done to ensure that a supportive, rather than penal, approach is taken to increasing attendance and ensuring more inclusivity. Careful analysis of the reasons why children do not attend need to be looked at. For example, with girls, those assigned female at birth and trans-boys, this can include absence due to menstruation (pain, stigma, confidence, lack of access to sanitary products). Additionally, the barriers they could face might include being young carers, looking after younger siblings and fear of sexual harassment within school settings. The Department for Education (DfE) has focused in significantly on the issue of 'peer on peer' abuse from 2021, including upskirting, texting and misogynistic language and behaviour within schools. All of this can affect attendance, and therefore adversely affect not only attainment but also mental health and social development.

Case Study 1: Shane Elsworth, Vice Principal Academic at Bede Academy, Blyth, Northumberland, UK

In Barnsley in 1999 it was acutely obvious to see which children were in receipt of free school meals. Each morning, during the daily registration routine, children were handed a token clearly identifying them as the poorest children in the room. Whilst most teachers will cringe at the idea of this daily ritual of highlighting poverty, there are hidden indicators of poverty embedded in school systems and routines which need to be uncovered and understood.

The Uniform Act 2021 (DfE, 2021) has shone a light on school uniform as one of the most significant costs for families and it highlighted the need for affordability. This legislation requires that schools carry out due diligence to ensure that the total cost of a whole school uniform per child is affordable for all families. This is a welcome change to alleviate some of the demands of purchasing uniform. Purchasing new uniform is an obvious pressure point for families and at Bede Academy, in Blyth, families in need of support are given a uniform voucher each year equal to the cost of uniform for their child. Interestingly though, the support for uniform doesn't stop there. Poverty Proofing at Bede Academy identified some other, more subtle, indicators of poverty associated with uniform which students were acutely aware of, but teachers had missed. These included a faded blazer, where uniform which has been passed on multiple times has fading around the straps of the school bags and the length of time it takes to get uniform replaced when it no longer fits. The pastoral team at Bede Academy now look out for these indicators that a family might need financial support.

By introducing initiatives such as uniform banks, listing affordable locations and sites for uniform staples (such as skirts and shirts) and by removing the need for 'school branded' items, this can help to significantly reduce costs. This is important as a child might feel embarrassed about attending in well-worn items, or fear being punished for not wearing all of the correct items of uniform. Given that girls are still disproportionately affected by the 'pink tax' with uniform costs for girls being 11.8% higher than for boys, uniform subsidy and support should be an integral part of a school's pastoral provision.

Case Study 2: Rosanna Hume, Lead Practitioner for Intervention and Pupil Premium at St Wilfrid's RC College, South Shields, UK

The effective identification of barriers, and the removal of them, is integral to the success of creating an equal society in schools. Barriers faced by young pupils at a large inner-city comprehensive in central London will often be different to those faced by rural communities in Yorkshire or coastal communities in the North-East of England. Knowing the school context and the problems the community faces is essential. By forensically identifying the needs of the school community, identifying the barriers they face in equally accessing all aspects of the school day and removing these barriers, we can create a more equal society within the four walls of our school building and extend the impact of these measures into our wider community too.

One such barrier identified has been the attendance of more vulnerable girls. It was reported by Plan UK in 2021 that 'nearly two million girls (64%) aged 14–21 in the UK have missed a part day or full day of school because of their period, with 13% of girls missing an entire school day at least once a month'. Good school attendance is vital for all pupils but especially for our more vulnerable pupils, so the initiative below set up by one North-East England secondary school has helped to remove the barrier of attendance for some disadvantaged pupils.

SDG target 4.5 refers to the need to 'eliminate gender disparities in education and ensure equal access to all levels of education and vocational training for the vulnerable, including persons with disabilities, indigenous peoples and children in vulnerable situations' (United Nations, 2016). At a local secondary school and sixth form college in the North-East of England, the school Student Council highlighted a problem they felt their peers were affected by and, by working together with staff, they have been able to tackle the issue of hygiene poverty. In 2018, the school launched their 'Canny Clean' hygiene bank (*canny* means *really* in the local Geordie dialect). The use of this word helped to personalise it to the students and reduce the chance of stigma with the hope of making it more welcoming. The scheme gave free access for all students in a bid to not only tackle stigma and embarrassment around periods, but also support students of all genders in accessing hygiene products. This included items such as deodorants, soap, shampoo, tights, sun cream, underwear and so on. They wanted to ensure that all pupils could have full access to the school day, including Physical Education lessons and external trips, so they made sure to include overnight packs in the Canny Clean hygiene bank too. By providing such supplies, this provided support for girls and trans-boys during menstruation, as well as encouraged them to attend school as the hygiene items, such as deodorant, helped to minimise fears of odours. The hygiene bank is funded through donations as well as through the school Pupil Premium funding and is organised and promoted by the students themselves. The voice was central in the proposal of creating a hygiene bank, furthering Reid's earlier argument about empowering students to be empowered to bring down the master's house; in essence, tackling the long-standing class and male-dominated narratives in education, which do not take into account the barriers that disadvantaged children face nor the barriers that young women, LGBTQ+ and people of colour experience in accessing fair educational provision.

Pupil Premium Strategies

A fundamental aspect of school funding, is the allocation of Pupil Premium (PP) funding. Each school and academy trust are allocated funding based on the number of PP students on their roll, and each are given autonomy as to how to use this spending to support disadvantaged students to engage in education equitably.

Case Study 1 Continued It is easy to assume that since access to education in the UK is comprehensive and free, it does not cost, but if all children are to experience the fullness of life that comes from a rich and inspiring curriculum offer, they must be able to access all of it. The curriculum in its entirety, including the co-curriculum, is the right of every child and we must work hard to eradicate barriers to access. Failure to do so results in entrenched lack of access and disadvantage. 'If all of your friends or people you know go to the after-school clubs, school trips, that kind of isolates you from them. You're singled out, you're not with them, just a spare person'—15-year-old boy (CPAG, 2022).

According to the Education Endowment Fund's Teaching and Learning Toolkit, arts participation results in gains of three months' progress each year. However, in 2014 research into the costs of going to school, from young people's perspectives (Farthing, 2014), Farthing found that 14% of low-income children chose not to study music or art due to the costs associated with these subjects. About 57% of low-income children had missed out on at least one school trip. In addition to this, there are significant advantages in sport if a child's parents are able to purchase equipment, pay for club membership and pay for transport between sporting fixtures.

It takes courage and significant financial commitment to create a truly equitable curriculum offer. At Bede Academy in Blyth children (and their families) are reminded every time a financial contribution is requested that equity is at the heart of the curriculum offer and financial assistance is available. Practically, this has resulted in around £20,000 (just 5% of the Pupil Premium) being committed to subsidising the cost of the wider curriculum. It has enabled the school to take record numbers of students on visits to the theatre to support the English curriculum, to take almost an entire secondary year group on a residential experience, to pay for music and LAMDA lessons for children who cannot afford peripatetic lessons and to provide necessary resources to enable children to continue their art and revision at home.

Ensuring that curriculum provision is both equitable and free is not as straightforward as it appears. Removing the barrier of cost is a step in the right direction but it does not overcome a reluctance to participate in all the curriculum has to offer. There are many barriers to be overcome, but if schools are going to use the curriculum as a tool to take children beyond their own experience, they must ensure that they find ways of ensuring all children can and do participate. This means tackling cost, but also tackling issues of representation (such as girls' participation in rugby and football) and wider cultural barriers to ensure every child is able to count themselves into every opportunity.

Case Study 2 Continued The PP Strategy statement is a statement of intent for schools to lay out their vision and plans to support some of the most vulnerable members of their school community. The compulsory strategy statement template, new for 2021 onwards, asks schools to identify the main challenges faced by their disadvantaged students, what the success criteria to overcome these barriers would be and what research informed approaches they plan to undertake to achieve this.

Nevertheless, our vulnerable students are not a homogenous group who all face the same range of problems. It is imperative that schools develop their PP strategy with a pupil led, not label led, approach. There is no one size fits all approach when working with disadvantaged pupils, in particular when looking at gender and the different barriers all genders can face. Once again, I stress the need for a systematic assessment of pupil need which encompasses the voice of the pastoral team, the teaching and learning team, the students and their families. By becoming experts in our students, we can ensure the right intervention is put in place for the right student.

The EEF Guide to Pupil Premium identifies three key areas for schools to focus their efforts on to best support disadvantaged students. These three areas then form the basis of the activities section of the PP Strategy template schools must complete and publish on an annual basis. They are discussed as follows.

High-Quality Teaching

High-quality teaching should be rooted in high expectation and high challenge. Classroom teaching should clearly address the needs of the individual pupil and all pupils should be given the opportunity to participate fully in the lesson. As Dylan Wiliam says, 'Raising the quality of teaching within existing schools is probably the single most effective thing we could do to promote both overall attainment and equity' (Wiliams, 2014, p. 2). This means dismantling unconscious bias within the classroom that some genders are better at different subjects and ensuring that high expectation and high participation of all genders takes place in every lesson and subject.

The EEF Teaching and Learning toolkit helps us to identify the 'best bets' when it comes to effective classroom teaching. Coupled with celebrated research led techniques such as Rosenshine's Principles of Instruction, classroom teachers and teaching and learning leads can develop a toolkit of strategies to employ in their lessons to ensure pupils are accessing the best-quality education on offer (Sherrington, 2019).

As previously mentioned in the Literacy as a Bedrock for Equity section, this particular aspect of teaching and learning is key in developing our more vulnerable students as the language gap is the attainment gap for our disadvantaged students and the aforementioned section outlines the best way to support students with their literacy. It is important teachers are aware of the 'Matthew effect'—ensuring pupils who are not language rich do not lose out on opportunities to present their ideas in lessons and to have their voice heard, to the detriment of their more language-rich classmates. With girls more likely to be selective mutes than boys, it's important that educators scaffold classroom talk and make it common. Woolley (2020) adds to this, stating:

> Speaking up and speaking out is the best way to claim equality. Women need the confidence to speak out in all aspects of their lives. There are two main reasons to develop female students' oracy. The first is to empower them to speak up for themselves and for others, to share their ideas openly and to be heard. The second is to shift the way that oracy is perceived, away from its classical origins rooted in patriarchal performance and show …. Studies show that women in business and politics are repeatedly silenced in different ways … It's too common for girls to be taught to change how they speak, right down to pitch and tone …. Disadvantaged children are subject to the same silencing … Everyone—girls and boys—benefits when whole-class discussion is academic, thoughtful and collaborative. (Woolley, 2020, pp. 45–48)

Common strategies such as no-hands-up approaches to questioning, oracy writing frames and thinking time can be useful ways to ensure that all students engage in purposeful classroom dialogue, regularly.

Targeted Academic Support

What is key to emphasise here is the idea of *targeted* academic support—that, once again, the intervention is put in place based on pupil need, not pupil label. It is also important that schools consider what intervention is right for each child; not just what subject, but what format (small group, 1:1 etc.), what time (before-school, after-school, during school) and what additional resources pupils may need to support themselves within accessing the intervention (such as a laptop or Wi-Fi dongle).

A targeted aspiration programme is another aspect which can be used to support some of our PP pupils, once again, under the caveat that not all PP pupils lack aspiration, but acknowledging that for some, exposure to the world of higher education may be more limited. University visits in which pupils can envision themselves accessing such establishments, myth-busting sessions on university support and finance and talks delivered by school-alumni can all be useful tools in helping pupils better understand their post-18 options. Moreover, a strong CEAIG (Careers Education, Advice, Information and Guidance) programme in school, which meets the Gatsby benchmarks, should ensure that all pupils have access to these opportunities, and that aspiration and attainment go hand in hand in motivating students in their future endeavours.

Wider Strategies

At the local secondary school where I work, we have worked with Children North East's Poverty Proofing the School Day audit, a fantastic programme which helps schools understand and mitigate the effects of poverty on pupils accessing the school day. The audit allowed us to identify what barriers some pupils faced and therefore what wider strategies we needed to put in place. The Canny Clean hygiene bank is one aspect of this, but the adaptation of our school uniform policy in line with the new school uniform Bill is another. During the pandemic and cost of living crisis, we have looked at supporting our families with food parcels and access to technology and we are acutely aware of the mental health strain these crises have put on our school community, particularly those who were already struggling. As mentioned earlier, girls were disproportionately affected by the pandemic due to the pressures of supporting within the home with care, further adding to their sense of isolation from peers and the wider world. Coupling the economic pressures that came with furlough and redundancy with the 'pink tax' costs of products such as tampons, the physical needs of young girls were adversely affected and so contributed to a decline in their wellbeing. Government studies highlight how 'girls had higher levels of emotional distress. Young women (16–24) were more likely to report psychological distress than young men' (Office for Health Improvement and Disparities, 2021). Consequently, we have increased the mental health support we have on offer in school via increased access to school counselling and a safe space in school designed for student wellbeing.

Inclusion should be at the heart of everything we do as a school. It is our moral imperative to get this right for our whole school community and whilst schools can't make *THE* difference in tackling poverty, they can make *A* difference and that is something we must challenge ourselves to do in order to ensure a just, equitable education system that works for all.

Strategically Identifying Children in Need of Support

Girl-Kind

Gender inequality is still an undeniable truth in modern Britain and something those young women, trans-women and trans-men and non-binary students experience regularly. A key target of the UN Sustainable Development Goals is 5.1, to 'End all forms of discrimination against all women and girls everywhere' (United Nations, 2016) and a range of various different projects and programmes have been set up in order to tackle discrimination and create opportunities for empowerment.

One such project is Girl-Kind, which is a project inNorth-East England. Within areas such as the North-East, young women and trans-women are subject to multiple barriers to achieving their aspirations, such as: gender, socio-economic status in a region that is less affluent than other (usually southern) regions, and negative cultural and societal stereotyping of 'Geordies' and 'Northerners'. In order to overcome these barriers, Girl-Kind was established to engage young women and trans-women 11–18 to take part in an annual event to explore their experiences through workshops and a showcase event. The first workshop starts with one open question: what are your experiences of growing up as a girl in the North-East of England? This is all it takes to open up a rich seam of ideas. Working together in groups, the girls decide what topic or theme they want to focus on, and how they want to express it to others. All this leads up to the celebration event in October for the UN's International Day of the Girl. At this Girl-Kind Celebration Day, the girls present the work they have created to family, friends and special guests, who have the power to influence change (Holland et al., 2018).

Typically, schools will also ensure that a diverse range of students are involved, including those who qualify for PP and FSM. By engaging the students in the opportunity to explore issues which affect them and channel this into a project, such as creating period hygiene bags or distributing feminist literature around Newcastle as 'Book Fairies', there has been a demonstrable positive impact upon their confidence and wellbeing. Participant reflections include comments such as stated that they had changed as 'my courage to challenge sexist beliefs' and 'speaking up about more what I believe in' (Holland et al., 2018, p. 6). By working with organisations such as Northumbria University, Newcastle University, the Tyneside Cinema and the Young Women's Film Academy, students were given opportunities to visit universities, to create a film to be presented at a local cinema focusing on an issue that affected them, as well as showcase their project within a university with invited guests such as local Members of Parliament. The data collated on confidence measures confirmed qualitative data such as:

> [U]sually … loads of thoughts will go through my head: … 'I can't do this' … 'You are not supposed to do that!' 'You can't talk.' 'You are not allowed to do this!' and stuff like that. But ever since I went to Girl-Kind I am able to open up more, and just tell people. And even talk to older people. (Holland et al., 2018, p. 8)

It is such project as this which can help students to become more knowledgeable about the world around them, share and discuss ideas in safe spaces, and collaboratively work to challenge the status quo.

This chapter has outlined a range of different strategies within education to tackle discrimination and to work towards ensuring an equitable and equal education system for all. The overriding theme recommendation should be to start conversations. Look at the demographic and the data, listen to voices of all your stakeholders, invest in training and access quality projects and programmes which can provide opportunities beyond the parameters of the four walls of a building. A caveat will also be to ensure that any strategy you adopt has the 'why' at the centre and that it is rooted in evidence and fit for your own context; what works in one educational setting may not work the same (or at all) in another. To achieve the UN Sustainable Development Goals set out for education, it must be that we adopt the approach of 'the mirror and the window'; the mirror to self-reflect and bring about institutional change and opportunities, and the window to maximise using opportunities and training locally, regionally, and nationally.

References

Cairns, S. (2019). What Is Cultural Capital? *Cultural Learning Alliance.* [Online] Retrieved August 2, 2022, from https://www.culturallearningalliance.org.uk/what-is-cultural-capital/#:~:text=Bourdieu%20believed%20that%20cultural%20capital,might%20call%20'high%20culture'

Child Poverty Action Group. (2022). Cost of the School Day: Breaking Down the Financial Barriers, *Children Poverty Action Group.* Retrieved July 24, 2022, from https://cpag.org.uk/cost-of-the-school-day

Clark, C., & Teravainen, A. (2017). Book Ownership and Reading Outcomes, *National Literacy Trust.* [Online] Retrieved June 22, 2022, from https://cdn.literacytrust.org.uk/media/documents/National_Literacy_Trust_-_Book_ownership_and_reading_-_December_2017.pdf

Coleman, R., & Quigley, A. (2021). Improving Literacy in Secondary Schools. Education Endowment Foundation. Accessed April 2023: https://educationendowmentfoundation.org.uk/education-evidence/guidance-reports/literacyks3-ks4

Criado-Perez, C. (2019). *Invisible Women: Exposing Data Bias in a World Designed for Men.* Random House.

Department for Education. (2021). *Cost of School Uniform Guidance.* Department for Education. Retrieved July 2, from https://www.gov.uk/government/publications/cost-of-school-uniforms/cost-of-school-uniforms

Department for Foreign Affairs. (2021). *Declaration on Girls' Education: Recovering from COVID-19 and Unlocking Agenda 2030.* Department for Foreign Affairs. [Online] Retrieved August 1, 2022, from https://www.gov.uk/government/publications/g7-foreign-and-development-ministers-meeting-may-2021-communique/declaration-on-girls-education-recovering-from-covid-19-and-unlocking-agenda-2030

Equality and Human Rights Commission. (2010). *Your Rights Under the Equality Act 2010.* Equality and Human Rights Commission. [Online] Retrieved June 29, 2022, from https://www.equalityhumanrights.com/en/advice-and-guidance/your-rights-under-equality-act-2010

Fairlamb, A. (2020). *Being Ambitious with the First World War – Blended Not Binary.* One Big History Department. [Online] Retrieved June 28, 2022, from https://onebighistorydepartment.com/2020/09/09/being-ambitious-with-the-first-world-war-blended-not-binary/

Farthing, R. (2014). The Costs of Going to School, from Young People's Perspective: Child Poverty Action Group. Retrieved July 24, 2022, from https://cpag.org.uk/sites/default/files/The%20Costs%20of%20Going%20to%20School%20FINAL.pdf

Government Office of Science. (2021). Gov.uk. [Online] Retrieved May 20, 2022, from https://www.gov.uk/government/publications/trend-deck-2021-demographics/trend-deck-2021-demographics#:~:text=In%20 2020%20there%20were%2019.4,over%20the%20last%2010%20 years

Hamer, J. (2016). *Gender Issues in Teaching History.* Council of Europe [Online] Retrieved June 2, 2022, from https://rm.coe.int/1680687d66

Hochman, J. et al. (2017). *The Writing Revolution.* [Online] Retrieved June 29, 2022, from https://www.thewritingrevolution.org/wp-content/uploads/2017/07/SPO.pdf

Holland, T. et al. (2018). Hearing Girls' Voices: Girl-Kind North East's Story So Far, *Girl Kind.* [Online] Retrieved June 29, 2022, from https://www.girlkind.co.uk/_files/ugd/0042dd_34db85ada2244d0c99ab3f23b5ef3ab3.pdf

Kwauk, et al. (2021). *What Do We Know About the Effects of COVID-19 on Girls' Return to School?* Brookings [Online] Retrieved August 1, 2022, from https://www.brookings.edu/blog/education-plus-development/2021/09/22/what-do-we-know-about-the-effects-of-covid-19-on-girls-return-to-school/

Office for Health Improvement and Disparities. (2021). *Research and Analysis. Children and Young People.* Office for Health Improvement and Disparities. [Online] Retrieved August 2, 2022, from https://www.gov.uk/government/publications/covid-19-mental-health-and-wellbeing-surveillance-report/7-children-and-young-people

Ofsted. (2022). *School Inspection Handbook.* [Online] Retrieved June 29, 2022, from https://www.gov.uk/government/publications/school-inspection-handbook-eif/school-inspection-handbook

Plan UK. (2021). *Nearly Two Million Girls in the UK Miss School Because of Their Period.* Retrieved July 2, 2022, from https://plan-uk.org/media-centre/nearly-two-million-girls-in-the-uk-miss-school-because-of-their-period

Reid, A. (2020). Cultural Capital, Critical Theory and Curriculum. In *The researchED Guide to the Curriculum.* John Catt Edu.

Rowland, M. (2017). *Learning Without Labels. Improving Outcomes for Vulnerable Students.* John Catt Edu.

Sherrington, T. (2019). *Rosenshine's Principles in Action.* John Catt Edu.

United Nations. (2016). *4 Ensure Inclusive and Equitable Quality Education and Promote Lifelong Learning Opportunities for All.* United Nations. [Online] Retrieved June 9, 2022, from https://sdgs.un.org/goals/goal4#targets_and_indicators

United Nations. (2021). *100 Million More Children Fail Basic Reading Skills Because of Covid-19.* United Nations [Online]. Retrieved August 1, 2022, from https://news.un.org/en/story/2021/03/1088392

Wiliams, D. (2014). *Teacher Quality: Why It Matters, and How to Get More of It*. Institute of Education, University of London. [Online] https://view.officeapps.live.com/op/view.aspx?src=https%3A%2F%2Fdylanwiliam.org%2FDylan_Wiliams_website%2FPapers_files%2FSpectator%2520talk.doc&wdOrigin=BROWSELINK

Woolley, C. (2020). *The Lost Girls: Why a Feminist Revolution in Education Benefits Everyone*. John Catt Edu.

CHAPTER 6

The Sustainable Development Paradox: The Economics of Child Marriage and Prevention Within India's Neoliberal Landscape

Jodie Weatherston

Introduction

Over the last two decades gender has been placed at the forefront of development through two of the largest global initiatives aimed at solving some of the world's biggest issues impacting humanity and the planet. The Millennium Development Goals (MDGs), which paved the way for gender-related issues between 2000 and 2015, however, fell short in their attempt to tackle gender inequality, leaving the most vulnerable and disadvantaged women and girls behind (OECD, 2010). The Sustainable Development Goals (SDGs) (2015–2030) developed a more directed and intersectional approach at achieving gender equality, informed by the failings of the MDGs, which mapped out specific targets and indicators to

J. Weatherston (✉)
University of Sunderland, Sunderland, UK
e-mail: jodie.weatherston@sunderland.ac.uk

D. Dalton, A. Smith (eds.), *Gender, Sexuality and the UN's SDGs*, Sustainable Development Goals Series,
https://doi.org/10.1007/978-3-031-31046-1_6

ensure that gender was interwoven throughout the new development agenda. This led to the development of SDG 5, which incorporates nine targets and 14 indicators aimed at achieving gender equality and empowering women and girls across the globe. In recent years, child marriage has been recognised as a hindrance to development and has been incorporated in the global agenda through target 5.3 which aims to 'eliminate all harmful practices, such as child, early and forced marriage and female genital mutilation' (UN DESA, 2022). This is due to the recognition that empowering women leads to more resilient, inclusive, and productive economies, more sustainable development and reduced global issues (UN Women, 2018).

In an era of SDGs and an emphasis on gender equality through global initiatives to end harmful practices, child marriage still occurs. Although rates are decreasing globally due to a more intense emphasis on child marriage than ever before, 12 million girls are still married each year before the age of 18, having immense impacts on their social development (UNICEF, 2018; Selby, 2018). Without significant progress on child marriage, eight SDGs will not be achieved, including those related to poverty, hunger, health, education, economy, peace, and inequality (GNB, 2023). This was demonstrated by the MDGs which undermined the extent of child marriage as a development issue through lack of consideration and implementation when designing the goals. This resulted in a shortage of achievement in gender- and equality-related goals as some widespread gender-based issues, like child marriage, were not included (GNB, 2023). Discouragingly, the United Nations (2022) claims that no country is on track to achieve gender equality by 2030 and progress has stalled, and even reversed due to the recent pandemic. Since addressing child marriage through the SDGs, global rates have decreased, with 25 million child marriages prevented during the last ten years; however, Covid-19 poses a threat to this progress, placing approximately another 10 million girls at risk of child marriage by 2030 (UN DESA, 2022; UNICEF, 2018).

Current prevention methods include female empowerment, family and community interventions, access to education, law enforcement and financial incentives (Bessa, 2019), however, doubts have emerged around the effectiveness of these methods and the intentions of the global actors who enforce them. This chapter will explore financial incentives focusing on the use of conditional cash transfers as a prevention technique for child marriage and as a solution to poverty. Evidence provided throughout this chapter attempts to unveil the neoliberal agenda rooted within the prevention of child marriage as well as providing insight into how young girls are being used as neoliberal entities to meet the economic needs of the world. It will aim to shine light onto the exploitation, dehumanisation, and control which young girls endure despite conditional cash transfers promising autonomy and empowerment as well as investigating how conditional cash transfers have perpetuated gender inequality through the commodification and marketisation of girls' bodies. Drawing upon child marriage and neoliberalism, this chapter attempts to evaluate the likelihood that no one will be left behind, exposing the SDG paradox that exists making it almost impossible to achieve SDG 5 alongside other goals. Although the focus of this chapter is global, India will be used as a case study to situate child marriage in a more specific context. It will do this through exploring India's marriage laws, levels of poverty, and the influence of culture and dowry on rates of child marriage. It will also analyse how successful the use of conditional cash transfers have been as a solution to child marriage in India.

Global Overview of Child Marriage

The term 'child' is a globally contested term; therefore, this section will begin by identifying the definition of a child to provide context for this chapter. Across the globe age is used as a marker of childhood in which most countries maintain that anyone under the age of 18 is a child. This is supported by the United Nation's Convention on the Rights of the Child (1989) (UNCRC), which has established a global definition of childhood, defining anyone under the age of 18 as a child. The UNCRC is the most widely ratified convention, with all countries apart from the United States ratifying, which has attempted to create a global consensus on the definition of childhood. The UNCRC is a legally binding document which outlines the rights of a child, including civil, political, economic, social, and cultural rights, and is governed by the Committee on the Rights of the Child (UNICEF, 2022). Despite this, some countries fail to comply with the standards set by the UNCRC and obligate conflicting messages which are written into their national laws. India is an example of a country which defines childhood differently within different national laws, providing conflicting messages to the public. For example, many of India's laws constitute a child as being under the age of 14 through acts such as the Child Labour (Protection and Regulation) Act (1986), the Constitution Act

(2002), but the Juvenile Justice Act (2015) states that a child is anyone under the age of 18. UNICEF (2020) assert that without a universal definition of the child, it is impossible to ensure children are protected and safeguarded against things like child marriage. For consistency and clarity, this chapter will follow the global definition of the child used by the UNCRC which states that a child is anyone under the age of 18.

Child marriage is a global issue which affects every country in the world, albeit at different rates (UNICEF, 2021). Sub-Saharan Africa has the highest rates of child marriage with 34% of girls married before the age of 18, closely followed by South Asia where approximately 24% of girls are married as children (ibid.). This practice is also common in Latin America, the Caribbean, the Middle East, and North Africa (ibid.). Eastern Europe and Central Asia are reported to have the lowest rates of child marriage with approximately 11% of the population married during their childhood (ibid.). Although child marriage disproportionally affects girls in every country, boys are subject to the practice, illustrated by UNICEF (2019) who state that more than 650 million women and 150 million boys across the world entered a child marriage before the age of 18 displaying astounding prevalence rates. Poverty, gender inequality, patriarchy, cultural traditions, and lack of education have regularly been outlined as drivers of child marriage globally, and although these drivers vary across regions and countries, they have been identified as key drivers in almost every context (Freccero & Whiting, 2018).

Over the last decade, child marriage has been placed at the forefront of several government and non-government organisations (NGOs) as well as being recognised as a development issue by the United Nation's Sustainable Development Goals (SDGs) for the first time in history, resulting in significant reductions in child marriage rates (UNICEF, 2021). Global rates of child marriage have decreased by 15% in the last decade with South Asia seeing the largest decline in rates, dropping by 30% between 1995 and 2020 (ibid.). Latin America and the Caribbean are the only areas where rates of child marriage have stayed the same over the last two decades (ibid.). Additionally, global momentum towards ending child has intensified with several international and national initiatives aimed at ending the harmful practice such as the 'Global Program to Accelerate Action to End Child Marriage', formed by UNICEF in partnership with UNFPA in (2016), which promotes female rights, strengthens local services, and works alongside governments and local organisations to help prevent child marriage. Individual governments have also introduced cash transfers which are initiatives aimed at preventing parents marrying off their children before the age of 18 (Girls Not Brides, 2021).

One of the biggest current global initiatives to end child marriage is through the SDGs which provide a framework for sustainable development in relation to gender through Goal 5 (UN DESA, 2022). A total of 193 countries have pledged to work towards ending child marriage by 2030 through the adoption of Goal 5.3, with 11 countries forming national initiatives (UN, 2019). This has been absorbed into the agenda of governments as child marriage has been identified as a significant barrier to female development, having wider impacts on the economy and country development (UN, 2019). The World Bank (2017) have alleged that child marriage could cost developing countries trillions of dollars by 2030 if rates do not decrease, due to the wider impacts of child marriage. Acknowledging child marriage from human rights perspective and an economic perspective has led to the collation of more than 500 organisations worldwide, most which implement programmes and advocacy initiatives to prevent child marriage (Freccero & Whiting, 2018).

Despite decreasing rates of child marriage, numbers remain high due to social, cultural, and political factors making elimination in certain areas of the world increasingly difficult (UNICEF, 2021). The pandemic has also slowed progress placing a further 2.5 million girls at risk of child marriage by 2025 which has the potential to undo 25 years of progress (Save the Children, 2022). To achieve the elimination of child marriage in line with the SDGs by 2030, progress must be accelerated significantly and wider social structures which underpin child marriage must be tackled in the process (UNICEF, 2020).

Development as an Economic Endeavour

Development, as we understand it today, emerged as a paradigm built upon Western concepts with the motive to economically rebuild states which were damaged after the Second World War (Rapley, 2007). To support this operation, the World Bank and the International Monetary Fund were formed as instruments to spread capitalism to postcolonial states with the incentive of exploitation for self-development (Hopper, 2018). Development as an economic endeavour manifested, as the Modernisation paradigm articulated by Rostow in his non-communist manifesto suggested five stages of economic development (Isbister, 2006). These five stages mirrored the process of economic development in the West presenting a single model of modernity which circulated the belief that economic progress is synonymous with development, further reinforcing economic enhancement as the ultimate goal of development (ibid.). Descending from modernisation theory the neoliberal development paradigm emerged in the 1980s which advocated for market involvement in development and government reforms to achieve development purely in economic terms (Hopper, 2018).

Neoliberalism is an economic ideology which encourages free markets, privatisation, and deregulation (Cahill & Konings, 2017). It supports that economic control should be transferred from public control to private control and has been implemented within global politics through the undertaking of global development (ibid.). This has created a free but unfair market which has led to global disconnect and has been labelled by Pramono (2003) as a genocidal, self-destructive 'suicidal, global social structure' (115). This is due to the nature of neoliberal policy which creates winners and losers, the latter being the majority group, which suffer from 'alarming [rates of] poverty, hunger, diseases and death [...] environmental degradations... and dehumanisation of human societies' (Pramono, 2003, p. 120). Understanding the global structure of neoliberalism which underpins development practice is paramount when exploring issues such as child marriage as neoliberalism often impedes the strategies used in prevention techniques. This leaves the question of whether potential child brides are being supported or whether they are being used as neoliberal entities in the development landscape. This chapter will argue the latter.

Neoliberalism has remained hegemonic across the development landscape, largely due to its ability to co-opt alternative visions of development which correlate with human rights issues such as child marriage. This is apparent when exploring the discourse ingrained within large development actors and global initiatives such as the SDGs which have been accused of being embedded in neoliberal policies (Weber, 2017). Weber states that 'the SDG project looks set to reinforce the conditions which sustain deprivation of fundamental entitlements to life sustaining needs for many' (ibid., p. 401) through the veiling of human rights discourse to justify its economic project. Furthermore, the World Bank, the United Nations and other mainstream development actors regularly focus on the economic gain of reducing rates of child marriage, viewing girls as untapped resources, a view reproduced in the neoliberal paradigm (WB, 2017). This focuses on macro economy losses rather than taking a human rights approach to child marriage. It is in this climate that child marriage has come to the forefront of development, sold as a solution to underdevelopment by transforming potential child brides into monetary value. This has led to the commodification of young girls whose status exists as monetary value for the benefit of others as can be seen with current schemes aimed at child marriage prevention, such as cash transfer schemes, which will be discussed further in this chapter.

Gender Blindness and Development

The history of global development is entwined in 'gender-blind and male-centred conceptualisations' (McIlwaine & Datta, 2010, p. 369) which have steered the development agenda and shaped many development projects since 1945. As a result of this, women have been largely excluded from the global development agenda whilst suffering from many of the harmful impacts imposed upon developing nations in an attempt to 'modernise' them (Escobar, 2011). This exclusion was largely caused by the discourse underpinning Rostow's Modernisation theory which constructs Southern women as passive and non-contributors to economic growth (Giles, 2008). Furthermore, patriarchal beliefs around women's roles led to the assumption that women added very little to society, and therefore, their inclusion within the development process was deemed unnecessary (Escobar, 2011). Viewing women as passive recipients meant that women's unpaid labour was ignored which largely sustained the work force allowing neoliberalism to progress (ibid.). This legacy has not only caused a gender division of labour where women's work has been undervalued but, but also marginalised women's needs in development planning and practice (ibid.). Such exclusion has led to direct consequences for women, as traditional gender norms which are reinforced through modernisation reproduce the conditions for child marriage by keeping women in domestic roles.

This led to the emergence of the 'Women in Development' (WID) approach in the 1970s which recognised women as important bodies within the development agenda for the first time and focused largely on incorporating women into the existing economic domains (Pearson, 2005). Although the WID approach recognised women as important factors within economic development bringing about positive change, it was largely criticised as an approach for simply adding women into patriarchally oppressive systems, without considering larger constraints which cause inequality, creating a process of 'add women and stir' (Giles, 2008, p. 501). Furthermore, the WID approach has been accused of using girls as 'untapped resources' (Moser, 1993, p. 2), focusing on the benefits for development rather than the benefits for women. For these reasons, the WID approach has been labelled a very uncritical approach to development having very little impact on the recognition of women's development issues, reinforcing neoliberalism and the modernisation project by co-opting feminist concerns (Aguinaga et al., 2013).

As a development of this, the 'Gender and Development' (GAD) approach emerged in the 1980s as a combination of third-wave feminism and socialist feminist thought, providing a critique of WID by recognising that the roles of women and men are socially constructed and reinforced by multiple social structures and categories, which have led to the subordination of women (Moser, 1993). GAD criticised WIDs assumption that economic change alone is the solution to women's empowerment arguing that modernisation and neoliberalism have often had adverse and harmful impacts on women's development through the perpetuation of gender inequality (Young, 2002). GAD criticises the assumption that women are a homogenous group as it recognises underlying social structures which impact women's roles such as the intersections between race, class, and gender (Young, 2002). The GAD approach and social feminists of the 1980s view women as 'agents of change, rather than recipients of development' (Aguinaga et al., 2013, p. 45), emphasising the importance of women within global development. However, when GAD approaches have been adopted by mainstream development organisations 'they have often been depoliticised, losing much of their feminist edge' (McIlwaine & Datta, 2010, p. 371), stripping the GAD approach of its initial intention to dismantle patriarchal definitions of gender whilst absorbing it into the neoliberal development paradigm (Wilkins, 1997). The adaptability of neoliberalism has allowed it to submerge itself into new development issues such as child marriage, embedding them in development discourse in the modern paradigm (Capraro & Rhodes, 2017). This has resulted in the manifestation of neoliberalism in child marriage, framing it as an economic issue, whilst undermining other social structures which underpin the practice (ibid.). Neoliberalism has shaped both the WID and GAD paradigms through the mainstreaming of development, depoliticising them and arguably causing them to be ineffective in the wider development agenda (ibid.).

Child Marriage as a Development Issue

Child marriage has been distinguished as a hindrance to social and economic global development as it 'perpetuates poverty, inequality and insecurity' (Girls Not Brides, 2023) as well as denying women and girls their basic human rights. It prevents women's self-development, can cause severe health issues, and prevents educational attainment, as well as impacting their wider development within the economy and within society (Jack, 2011). It is true that socioeconomic change is heavily reliant on the participation of women in society, therefore, 'countries that undervalue women limit their own possibilities for growth, stability and transformation' (GNB, 2023), but efforts to tackle child marriage need to place girls and their needs at the heart of the solution. Gender equality is vital for a sustainable and progressive world, however, the prevalence of harmful practices towards women limit the full potential of development and sustainability (ibid.). When attempts have been made to prevent child marriage this has been done with an economic motive, co-opting girls into neoliberal subjects where their value is determined through the money value which is placed upon them by governments and the wider development agenda. To tackle child marriage successfully, individual socioeconomic conditions must be considered and understood to develop culturally appropriate and specific strategies as banning child marriage risks intensifying underlying issues at the root of child marriage (WEF, 2013).

Poverty, Dowry, and the Commodification of Girls

This section will use India as a case study to situate child marriage in a global and cultural context, exploring dowry, poverty, laws, and gender inequality. India has signed and ratified various laws and policies against child marriage and child exploitation, including the Prohibition of Child Marriages Act (2006), the United Nations Convention on the Rights of the Child (UNCRC) (1989), and the Convention on the Elimination of All Forms of Discrimination against Women (CEDAW) (1979) (Action Aid, 2021). Each of these laws and conventions pledges to protect women and children from harmful practices such as child marriage, gender discrimination and sexual and physical exploitation and abuse, allowing women the freedom to enter a marriage through their own will (HRW, 2014).

The Prohibition of Child Marriages Act (2006) sets the minimum age of marriage for women at 18 and for men at 21, however, there have been recent discussions about moving the minimum age of marriage for women from 18 to 21 to curb gender inequality, delay motherhood and maternal mortality, and to equivalate the minimum age between men and women. Many issues have been identified with this, with fears emerging around further inequalities developing, and instead requests have been made to bring the minimum age of marriage for men down to 18 (OXFAM India, 2020). Differences in minimum marriage ages between men and women in India are rooted in harmful patriarchal ideologies which provoke sexism and perpetuate harmful stereotypes (Jurist, 2020). There is very little evidence to suggest that raising the age from 18 to 21 for women in India to marry would prevent child marriage, instead this would lead to the criminalisation of the poorest and most vulnerable women and girls, void marriages from the ages of 18–21, force more women and girls into economic instability, increase the price of dowry and prevent social protection (ibid.). It would also take away autonomy from women to choose when to marry having adverse effects on empowerment.

Despite government efforts, India has the highest absolute numbers of child marriage in the world with around 15,648,000 children married before the age of 18 (Girls Not Brides, 2022). The perpetuation of child marriage is caused several intersectional factors, including poverty, social norms, lack of education, insecurity, patriarchy, and gender inequality (ibid.). Poverty in India is widespread with approximately 176 million people living in extreme poverty and has been identified as the leading cause for child marriage (World Bank, 2020). Where deprivation and poverty exist within family systems, alongside patriarchy, females are often denied equal access to resources and are treated as an economic burden on the family (Lal, 2015). Girls are forced into child marriages to keep dowry demand low, prevent parents from investing in education and to avoid caring costs for their daughters (Paul, 2019; Singh & Vennam, 2016). Although education has been a successful tool in tackling child marriage, where the practice is customary families are less likely to educate their daughters due to a lack of return in investment when that girl moves to another household (Lal, 2015). In many Indian households, there is a preference for sons and an aversion for daughters which continues to be a huge issue due to patriarchal and religious beliefs which have constructed harmful gender ideologies which devalue female children (Pande, 2021). Patriarchy, poverty, and religion have created a toxic combination which has led to the continuation of child marriage. It is a process submerged in constructed gendered roles which emphasise a women's status of inferiority in comparison to the belief that men are superior (Godha et al., 2013). Child marriage is 'a direct outcome and consequence of patriarchal power over women's bodies and lives' (Wadhwa, 2017). It is rooted in the idea that women are possessions which belong to men and can be gifted from one man to another which has led to the objectification of women (Wadhwa, 2017).

In India and wider South Asia, dowry is part of the cultural and social marriage contract whereby the bride's family are required to pay cash or market goods to the groom's family (Khanal & Sen, 2020). The practice of dowry is ancient and tracing its origins is complex, however links have been made to Hindu mythology and the ancient text Manusmriti from 1500 BC which states that a father's social and religious position can be firmly established through gifting a bejewelled and expensively clothed daughter (Banerjee, 2014). Dowry is also known to be rooted in Hindu practices such as Kanyadan which means giving away the bride, and Varadakshina which are voluntary gifts given by the father of the bride to the groom (Khanal & Sen, 2020). Misinterpretations of these practices have led to dowry becoming a 'widespread evil' (Umar, 1998, p. 67) through modernisation which has employed the growth of dowry into the current capitalist climate. Dowry in modern society has now taken on a different meaning which has surpassed the original practices of Kanyadan and Varadakshina, perpetuating violence against women and upholding gender inequality (ibid.). Demands for dowry usually include property, land, jewels, gold, or money and in contemporary society, requests are becoming more unrealistic and difficult to uphold placing a burden on the poorest of families (Banerjee, 2014). Expensive dowry requests have become an incentive for child marriage as marrying girls at a younger age reduces the cost of dowry (UNICEF, 2022). Therefore, girls from poorer families are much more likely to be married before the age of 18 to decrease the cost of dowry and to adhere to ancient cultural standards which are closely guarded by the wider society. Despite child marriage being used as a solution to poverty for many families, this only delivers a short-term solution and leads to an intergenerational cycle of poverty which impacts the individual, the economy and the wider society (UNICEF, 2022).

The contemporary dowry system in South Asia can be applied to the concept of commodification where in the current capitalist climate, the child bride has become a neoliberal entity in which she can be sold by her own family to another. This perpetuates the objectification of girls and their bodies and supports harmful gender ideologies which allow control over women's bodies. Placing monetary value on girls has led to them becoming commodities in the capitalist market of marriage, a mistake made through previous attempts to include women and girls in the development agenda. This has also been made easier through the secondary social positioning of women and girls where boys are favoured. In a patriarchal cultural setting where marriage is regarded a significant milestone, and dowry exists, child marriage is difficult to overcome and poses a number of obstructions in prevention. It is apparent from the evidence above that in order to tackle SDG 5.3 that bigger efforts must be made at tackling the root causes of poverty and gender discrimination which would mean a whole uprooting of religious and culture-based practices, as well as the capitalist market.

Development Efforts Through Cash Transfers

Numerous strategies have been employed by development organisations to tackle global poverty for some of the most vulnerable populations worldwide (Dake et al., 2018). Governments have often turned to cash incentives in the hope that this will provide a solution to child marriage. Of these, there has been an increase in the use of cash transfers which have become one of the most widely implemented strategies aimed at alleviating poverty and supplementing the incomes of the poorest (ICAI, 2017). Cash transfers provide a small and regular amount of money to individuals and households and in recent years have been used as an initiative to prevent child marriage, protecting girls and their well-being (Haider, 2020; Sekher & Ram, 2015). Alongside cash transfers, conditional cash transfers also exist which are given to families when certain conditions of the cash transfer are met, for example, not marrying a female child before the age of 18 (Amin et al., 2017). Conditional cash transfers were introduced with the aim to strengthen female agency, reduce gender inequality, and increase the value of female children which should in theory lead to reduced rates of child marriage (Nanda et al., 2016). This strategy has been adopted by the Indian government who have implemented multiple conditional cash transfers schemes to help the prevention of child marriage. One of these is the Dhanalakshmi scheme, which was introduced in 2008 and provides staggered financial incentives in seven stages, which encourages birth registration, immunisation, school enrolment and retention, and delaying marriage before the age of 18 (Haider, 2020; Jejeebhoy et al., 2015; Sekher & Ram, 2015). These schemes have been aimed the poorest households in an attempt to change the economic value attributed to girls to even out the sex ratio in India (Rahm, 2020). Evidence provided by the Foreign, Commonwealth and Development Office (FCDO) suggests that these conditional cash transfers have been successful in reducing rates of forced child marriage, particularly in South Asia, which has also led to educational attainment up until the age of 14 (Haider, 2020; Sekher & Ram, 2015).

Despite some positive progress, thorough evaluation of the schemes has revealed a wealth of negative impacts. Nanda et al. (2016) found that conditional cash transfers had very little impact on changing parental social attitudes towards their female children and marriage was still urged at the age of 18 when the conditional cash transfer scheme had ended. Currently, India accounts for 46 million missing women as a result of sex selective abortions, neglect, discrimination, and infanticide, which has continued to increase since the 1970s (State of World Population, 2020). India also has the highest rate of postnatal sex selective deaths, with one in every nine girls below the age of five being murdered for being female (ibid.). This evidences the patriarchal nature of Indian society in the treatment of women and girls. Additionally, money gained from the conditional cash transfers was used to fund dowries and wedding costs which has aided the commodification of girls' bodies, having an adverse effect on preventing child marriage (Nanda et al., 2016). This has enabled dowry to become more affordable with the government essentially paying money towards dowry systems unconsciously. Although rates of child marriage have decreased in South Asia, attitudes towards gender equality have in many instances remained unchanged and unchallenged through conditional cash transfers. Essentially, development organisations and governments, in their efforts to tackle child marriage have reinforced harmful ideologies surrounding the value of girls in which they have become a cash transfer in the capitalist market. By introducing conditional cash transfers in the current climate, this has reinforced the belief that girls are financial burdens on the family and that their value equates to money (ICRW, 2015). This has solidified the marketisation of female children and encourages harmful ideologies which suggest that girls can be sold, owned, and controlled through cash transfers in line with patriarchal ideologies. This is what Sen (1997) refers to as the 'subordination of sexuality' whereby young women's sexuality is guarded and owned by older men and women who reinforce patriarchal hierarchies for the purpose of men. This leads to the subordination and oppression of young women as owners of their own sexuality, driving the continuation of forced child marriage. Alongside sexual subordination, Hinduism is increasingly being used as a political tool in India, to control women and prevent their empowerment (Haldar, 2020). Ancient Hindu texts are used to justify the subordination of women, such as the Manusmriti which outlines human purpose and duty. These misogynistic texts teach that 'women are never fit for independence' (1886 cited in Oldenburg & Talwar, 2010, p. 2) and should be guarded throughout their life by their father, husband, and son. Providing conditional cash transfers to parents who are known to be the gate keepers of their daughter's sexuality takes away autonomy and reinforces subordination and disempowerment for young girls and women. Rather than transforming views on child marriage, conditional cash transfers have played into the patriarchal status quo which dehumanises and devalues girls through monetising them to meet the neoliberal development agenda.

Furthermore, conditional cash transfers have been accused of co-opting strategies which blend in with neoliberalism to suit western development, as human capital is at the core of neoliberalism (Goeury, 2016; Holborow, 2012). The concept of making a cash transfer conditional is a key aspect of neoliberal discourse as it promotes neoliberal ideologies which teach that poverty is the fault of the individual, thus, making the individual responsible for their own actions (Goeury, 2016). Using this discourse undermines the structural causes which underpin poverty and child marriage shifting blame from the wider social structures to the individual. Doing this results in the continuation of both poverty and child marriage through a structured power dynamic which essentially aids patriarchy. The nature of conditional cash transfers require individuals to earn cash through adhering to socially desirable behaviours in line with western development standards who mask themselves behind the narrative of 'empowering the poor' (ibid.). This contributes the current power imbalance which has dominated the development agenda since the 1940s through the 'development myth' which has persuaded its global viewers that poverty occurs due to laziness and individual fault (Hickel, 2017). In reality, poverty is actively created through global power dynamics in which countries and individuals are deliberately prevented from progressing which has created a development delusion and lies at the very heart of neoliberal policy (ibid.). Child marriage has become a product of poverty, among other factors, and is a hindrance to the neoliberal agenda which has led development actors and governments viewing girls as 'untapped resources', presenting their involvement in the economic market as necessary for their personal development whilst lubricating the underlying motive of an increased facilitation of neoliberal agendas (Banet-Weiser, 2015; Boyd, 2016). The global development agenda recognises that the contribution of women and girls is vital for the progression of neoliberalism and so conditional cash transfers ascribe a price to young girls to excel the neoliberal mission whilst masking behind development discourse (Nafstad et al., 2007).

By increasing the use of conditional cash transfers, many families do not avoid child marriage, but use this as an incentive for child marriage. In this regard, potential child brides are being turned into neoliberal entities. ICRW (2015) stated that 'uprooting deep-seated discriminatory norms around girls and marriage requires more than just a simple cash transaction ... it requires sustained, multi-sectoral interventions that change attitudes and aspirations for girls'. There is a clear intersection between capitalism, patriarchy, and culture which breeds harmful gender ideologies, impacting the most vulnerable girls in society. It can be concluded that conditional cash transfers cannot sufficiently tackle the complexity of socially constructed gender roles and the importance placed on marriage in Indian society. This poses questions around how achievable the SDGs are in ensuring that 'no one is left behind' in the current neoliberal climate which has created a paradox of impossibility, a concept which will be discussed further in the next section.

The SDG Paradox

The interlinking nature of the SDGs makes it difficult to achieve single goals alone which is apparent when investigating the progress of child marriage as part of SDG 5. According to Girls Not Brides (2023) without the prevention of child marriage, eight SDGs will not be achieved, including goals related to poverty, food security, health, education, gender equality, economic growth, and peace and justice. This is due to the cross-cutting nature of child marriage which perpetuates aspects of key global issues (ibid.). However, the SDGs pose a major paradox. The success of some SDGs will inevitably cause the failure of others due to the neoliberal policies which underpin economic development at the expense of human development (Scharff, 2014). Where neoliberalism is involved, economic development is being achieved but at the risk of gendered implications (ibid.). It is this paradox that Weber (2017) argues that the SDGs are built upon. She claims that, despite the SDGs being framed as universal, this has been adopted strategically, 'to promote and consolidate a highly contested neo-liberal variant of capitalist development' (Weber, 2017, p. 1). Evidentially, social policies which underpin the SDGs create unsustainable development through the current neoliberal agenda. This challenges the initial aim of sustainability rooted within the SDG agenda and promoted through the very title of the goals. Considering conditional cash transfers within this agenda brings to light the neoliberal intensions where governments have attempted to deal with child marriage. Rather than truly tackling the root causes of poverty, girls are turned into monetary value which devalues and undermines girls, defeating the purpose of SDG 5. Additionally, where neoliberalism is enacted, poverty increases creating mass inequality and poorer living conditions (Feldman, 2019). Where poverty rises so do rates of child marriage and gender inequality. Neoliberalism breeds inequality whilst framing the poor as free agents in charge of their own choices (ibid.). However, this is strictly untrue. Neoliberalism creates a poverty trap which impacts the most vulnerable people and can be extremely difficult to escape (ibid.). This creates a concern when the development landscape is governed by neoliberal policies which has generated a suicidal, self-destructive social structure yet claims to be 'sustainable'. As long as neoliberal policies underpin international development, we will not see the majority of SDGs met, particularly those aimed at gender, equality, peace and poverty. To change the current landscape would mean to dismantle global systems embedded in power dynamics, backed by the international policy agenda, which is unlikely given that neoliberalism benefits those who currently hold global power. Within this argument the SDG paradox is unveiled.

Conclusion

It is evident that global efforts from policymakers, governments, and global initiatives have rallied child marriage into the development limelight in the last few decades which has triggered a decrease in global rates. This has been led largely by the SDGs which have brought child marriage into the development agenda through SDG 5.3, providing a time constrained target in which the world has pledged to achieve by 2030. Efforts have been successful to some extent; however, the world is not on target to eradicate child marriage by 2030 in line with the SDGs, despite several efforts. Numbers remain particularly high in India and across South Asia due to contradictory laws, patriarchal cultural ideologies which devalue girls, poverty and dowry fees, and family pressures.

The global development agenda is underpinned by neoliberal policies and ideologies which has created a destructive landscape, especially in addressing gender-based issues. Consequently, this has resulted in child marriage being treated in purely economic terms, stalling wide-scale prevention. A closer investigation into current development efforts and the use of conditional cash transfers has revealed that these are mainly ineffective in tackling child marriage and have often had adverse effects, sometimes aiding early marriage to occur. Evidence has also revealed that conditional cash transfers are ineffective in changing cultural attitudes on child marriage and gender norms, and they only provide a short-term solution to poverty. One of the key reasons identified for the failure of conditional cash transfers is the neoliberal nature of them, and where they have been used, they have turned girls into neoliberal commodities placing economic value upon them, which in contrast, has led to girls being further devalued. Conditional cash transfers as a solution to child marriage echo some of the downfalls of both the WID and GAD approaches which were criticised for adding women into the development agenda and stirring. This has often led to women and girls being exploited by neoliberal systems which underpin development, where they have been removed from one exploitative system and dropped into another to serve the neoliberal agenda. Conditional cash transfers in their current form are unlikely to offer anything more than a temporary prevention at best and will continue to be unsuccessful, especially when the value of women and girls is transferred into monetary value and underpinned by harmful gender stereotypes.

This chapter has unveiled an SDG paradox outlining the influence of neoliberal policy in which the SDGs are built upon. The complexity of achieving gender-related goals within the current neoliberal climate is questionable when neoliberalism is responsible for creating conditions for poverty and child marriage to prevail. To make any significant progress in global child marriage prevention, a multidimensional approach is required which tackles each of the social structures which underpin child marriage in each individual context. Neoliberalism has managed to mask behind human rights but is set to sustain more deprivation and inequality than ever before if not prevented in the global development agenda.

References

Action Aid. (2021). *Child Protection Laws in India*. Retrieved October 2, 2022, from https://www.actionaidindia.org/blog/child-protection-laws-in-india/

Aguinaga, M., Lang, M., Mokrani, D., & Santillana, A. (2013). Development Critiques and Alternatives: A Feminist Perspective. In M. Lang & D. Mokrani (Eds.), *Beyond Development: Alternative Visions from Latin America* (pp. 41–59). Rosa Luxemburg Foundation.

Amin, S., Asadullah, M. N., Hossain, S., & Wahhaj, Z. (2017). *Can Conditional Transfers Eradicate Child Marriage*. Germany, Institute for the Study of Labor. IZA Policy Paper No. 118.

Banerjee, P. R. (2014). Dowry in 21st-Century India: The Sociocultural Face of Exploitation. *Trauma Violence Abuse, 15*(1), 34–40.

Banet-Weiser, S. (2015). Confidence You Can Carry! Girls in Crisis and the Market for Girls' Empowerment Organizations. *Continuum: Journal of Media & Cultural Studies, 29*(2), 182–193.

Bessa, T. (2019). Informed Powerlessness: Child Marriage Interventions and Third World Girlhood Discourses. *Third World Quarterly, 40*(11), 1941–1956.

Boyd, G. G. D. (2016). The Girl Effect: A Neoliberal Instrumentalization of Gender Equality. *Consilience: The Journal of Sustainable Development, 15*(1), 146–180.

Cahill, D., & Konings, M. (2017). *Neoliberalism*. Polity Press.

Capraro, C., & Rhodes, F. (2017). *Advancing Feminist Alternatives Group in the Context of Neoliberalism*. Retrieved October 3, 2022, from https://static1.squarespace.com/static/536c4ee8e4b0b60bc6ca7c74/t/59e8cb18fe54ef8e23644372/1508428571304/Rhodes+Capraro+-+Advancing+feminist+alternatives+in+the+context+of+neoliberalism+.pdf

Dake, F., Natali, L., Angeles, G., De Hoop, J., Handa, S., & Peterman, A. (2018). Cash Transfers, Early Marriage and Fertility in Malawi and Zambia. *Studies in Family Planning, 49*(4), 295–317.

Escobar, A. (2011). *Encountering Development: The Making and Unmaking of the Third World*. Princeton University Press.

Feldman, G. (2019). Neoliberalism and Poverty: An Unbreakable Relationship. In B. Greve (Ed.), *Routledge International Handbook of Poverty* (pp. 340–350). Routledge.

Freccero, J., & Whiting, A. (2018). *Toward an End to Child Marriage: Lessons from Research and Practice in Development and Humanitarian Sectors*. Human Right Centre.

Giles, A. R. (2008). Beyond 'Add Women and Stir': Politics, Feminist Development, and Dene Games. *Leisure/Loisir, 32*(2), 489–512.

Girls Not Brides. (2021). *Cash Transfers and Child Marriage*. Retrieved September 4, 2022 from https://www.girlsnotbrides.org/learning-resources/resource-centre/cash-transfers-and-child-marriage/,1

Girls Not Brides. (2022). *Where It Happens.* Available at: https://www.girlsnotbrides.org/learning-resources/child-marriage-atlas/atlas/. Accessed 28/04/2023.

Girls Not Brides. (2023). *What Is the Impact of Child Marriage: Sustainable Development Goals (SDGs).* Retrieved September 12, 2022, from https://www.girlsnotbrides.org/themes/sustainable-development-goals-sdgs/

Godha, D., Hotchkiss, D. R., & Gage, A. J. (2013). Association Between Child Marriage and Reproductive Health Outcomes and Service Utilization: A Multi-Country Study from South Asia. *Journal of Adolescent Health, 52*, 552–558.

Goeury, H. (2016, April 28–29). *Conditional Cash Transfers (CCTs) and Neoliberalism in Latin America.* Paper Presented at the Ideas and Transformations in the Americas conference, London, UK.

Haider, H. (2020). *Financial Incentives to Reduce Female Infanticide, Child Marriage and to Promote Girls' Education.* Institute of Development Studies. K4D Helpdesk Report no. 943.

Halder, A. (2020). Hinduism as a Political Weapon: gender socialization and dis-empowerment of women in India. Univeristy of San Farancisco. Available at: https://repository.usfca.edu/thes/1295/. Accessed 28/04/2023.

Hickel, J. (2017). *The Divide.* Windmill Books.

Holborow, M. (2012). What Is Neoliberalism? Discourse Ideology and the Real World. In D. Block, J. John Gray, & M. Holborow (Eds.), *Neoliberalism and Applied Linguistics* (pp. 14–32). Routledge.

Hopper, P. (2018). *Understanding Development* (2nd ed.). Polity Press.

Human Rights Watch. (2014). *25th Anniversary of the Convention on the Rights of the Child.* Retrieved September 10, 2022, from https://www.hrw.org/news/2014/11/17/25th-anniversary-convention-rights-child

ICAI. (2017). *The Effects of DFID's Cash Transfer Programmes on Poverty and Vulnerability.* Retrieved October 4, 2022, from https://icai.independent.gov.uk/html-version/effects-dfids-cash-transfer-programmes-poverty-vulnerability/

ICRW. (2015). *New Study Shows That Cash Incentives Ate Not Enough to Tackle Child Marriage.* Retrieved October 4, 2022, from https://www.icrw.org/press-releases/new-study-shows-that-cash-incentives-are-not-enough-to-tackle-child-marriage/

Isbister, J. (2006). *Promises Not Kept.* Kumarian Press.

Jack, D. C. (2011). Reflections on the Silencing the Self Scale and Its Origins. *Psychology of Women Quarterly, 35*(3), 523–529.

Jejeebhoy, S. J., Acharya, R., Basu, S., & Zavier, A. J. F. (2015). *Addressing Gender-Biased Sex Selection in Haryana, India: Promising Approaches.* Retrieved October 3, 2022, from https://knowledgecommons.popcouncil.org/cgi/viewcontent.cgi?article=1646&context=departments_sbsr-pgy

Jurist. (2020). *Right to Vote But Not to Marry? Analyzing the Proposed Increase in the Minimum Marriage Age for Women in India*. Retrieved October 3, 2022, from https://www.jurist.org/commentary/2020/12/srinivasa-swar-marriage-age/

Khanal, K., & Sen, R. (2020). The Dowry Gift in South Asia: An Institution on the Intersection of Market and Patriarchy. *Journal of Economic Issues, 52*(2), 356–362.

Lal, S. B. (2015). Child Marriage in India: Factors and Problems. *International Journal of Science and Research (IJSR), 4*(4), 2993–2998.

McIlwaine, C., & Datta, K. (2010). From Feminising to Engendering Development. *A Journal of Feminist Geography, 10*(4), 369–382.

Moser, C. (1993). *Gender Planning and Development: Theory, Practice and Training*. Routledge.

Nafstad, H. E., Blakar, R. M., Carlquist, E., Phelps, J. M., & RandHendriksen, K. (2007). Ideology and Power: The Influence of Current Neo-liberalism in Society. *Journal of Community & Applied Social Psychology, 17*, 313–327.

Nanda, P., Das, P., Datta, N., & Lamba, S. (2016). *Making Change with Cash? Impact of a Conditional Cash Transfer Program on Girls' Education and Age of Marriage in India*. International Centre for Research on Women.

OECD. (2010). *Gender Inequality and the MDGs: What Are the Missing Dimensions?* Retrieved October 2, 2022, from https://www.oecd.org/dev/development-gender/45987065.pdf

Oldenburg, V. T., & Talwar, V. (2010). *Dowry Murder: Reinvestigating a Cultural Whodunnit*. Penguin Books.

Oxfam India. (2020). *5 Reasons Changing the Minimum Age of Marriage Is a Bad Move*. Retrieved October 3, 2022, from https://www.oxfamindia.org/blog/5-reasons-changing-minimum-age-marriage-bad-move

Pande, R. (2021). Time to End Daughter Aversion in India. *The Lancet Global Health, 9*(6), E732–E733.

Paul, P. (2019). Effects of education and poverty on the prevalence of girl child marriage in India: A district–level analysis. *Children and Youth Services Review, 100*, 16–21.

Pearson, R. (2005). The Rise and Rise of Gender and Development. In U. Kothari (Ed.), *A Radical History of Development Studies: Individuals, Institutions and Ideologies* (pp. 157–179). Zed Books.

Pramono, S. (2003). The Genocidal Global Politics and Neoliberalism. *Journal of Economic and Social Research, 4*(2), 115–138.

Prohibition of Child Marriage Act. (2006). India. Retrieved October 4, 2022, from https://legislative.gov.in/sites/default/files/A2007-06.pdf

Rahm, L. (2020). *Gender-Biased Sex Selection in South Korea, India and Vietnam: Assessing the Influence of Public Policy*. Springer International Publishing.

Rapley, J. (2007). *Understanding Development: Theory and Practice in the Third World* (3rd ed.). Lynne Reinner Publishers.

Save the Children. (2022). *Covid-19 Places Half a Million More Girls at Risk of Child Marriage This Year, Warns Save the Children.* Retrieved October 4, 2022, from https://www.savethechildren.org.uk/news/media-centre/press-releases/covid-19-places-half-a-million-more-girls-at-risk-of-child-marri0#:~:text=%E2%80%9CA%20growing%20risk%20of%20violence,who%20are%20often%20much%20older

Scharff, C. (2014). *Gender and Neoliberalism: Exploring the Exclusions and Contours of Neoliberal Subjectivities.* Retrieved October 3, 2022, from https://www.theoryculturesociety.org/blog/christina-scharff-on-gender-and-neoliberalism

Sekher, T. V., & Ram, F. (2015). *Conditional Cash Transfers for Girls in India: Assessment of a Girl Child Promotion Scheme from Beneficiary Perspective.* International Institute for Population Sciences (IIPS).

Selby, D. (2018). *Child Marriage Numbers are Falling Worldwide.* Retrieved August 12, 2022, from https://www.globalcitizen.org/en/content/child-marriage-decrease-unicef-report-india/

Sen, G. (1997). Subordination and Sexual Control: A Comparative View of the Control of Women. In N. Visvanathan, L. Duggan, L. Nisonoff, & N. Wiegersma (Eds.), *The Women, Gender and Development Reader* (pp. 142–149). Zed Books.

Singh, R., & Vennam, U. (2016). *Factors Shaping Trajectories to Child and Early Marriage: Evidence from Young Lives in India.* Retrieved October 5, 2022, from https://www.younglives.org.uk/sites/default/files/migrated/YL-WP149-Trajectories%20to%20early%20Marriage.pdf

State of World Population. (2020). *Against My Will: Defying the Practices That Harm Women And Girls and Undermine Equality.* Retrieved September 14, 2022, from https://www.unfpa.org/publications/state-world-population-2020

The Child Labour (Prohibition and Regulation) Act. (1986). India. Retrieved October 4, 2022, from https://clc.gov.in/clc/acts-rules/child-labour-prohibition-and-regulation-act-1986#:~:text=It%20came%20on%20the%20Statute,1986%20(61%20of%201986).&text=An%20Act%20to%20prohibit%20the,children%20in%20certain%20other%20employments

The Constitution (Eighty-sixth Amendment) Act. (2002). India. Retrieved October 4, 2022, from https://www.india.gov.in/my-government/constitution-india/amendments/constitution-india-eighty-sixth-amendment-act-2002#:~:text=Right%20to%20education.%2D&text=The%20State%20shall%20provide%20free,new%20article%20for%20article%2045

The Juvenile Justice (Care and Protection of Children) Act. (2015). India. Retrieved October 4, 2022, from https://www.indiacode.nic.in/handle/123456789/2148?sam_handle=123456789/1362

The World Bank. (2017). *Child Marriage Will Cost Developing Countries Trillions of Dollars by 2030.* Retrieved September 20, 2022, from https://www.worldbank.org/en/news/press-release/2017/06/26/child-marriage-will-cost-developing-countries-trillions-of-dollars-by-2030-says-world-bankicrw-report

Umar, M. (1998). *Bride Burning in India: A Socio Legal Study.* A.P.H. Publishing Corporation.

UN. (2022). *Without Investment, Gender Equality Will Take Nearly 300 Years: UN Report.* Retrieved October 4, 2022, from https://news.un.org/en/story/2022/09/1126171

UN DESA. (2022). *Do You Know All 17 SDGs?* Retrieved September 20, 2022, from https://sdgs.un.org/goals

UN Women. (2018). *Facts and Figures: Economic Empowerment.* Retrieved October 2, 2022, from https://www.unwomen.org/en/what-we-do/economic-empowerment/facts-and-figures

UNFPA & UNICEF. (2016). *UNFPA-UNICEF Global Programme to End Child Marriage.* Retrieved October 4, 2022, from https://www.unicef.org/protection/unfpa-unicef-global-programme-end-child-marriage#:~:text=The%20UNFPA%2DUNICEF%20Global%20Programme,through%20education%20and%20alternative%20pathways

UNICEF. (2018). *Child Marriage: Latest Trends and Future Prospects.* Retrieved September 9, 2022, from https://data.unicef.org/resources/child-marriage-latest-trends-and-future-prospects/

UNICEF. (2019). *115 Million Boys and Men Around the World Married as Children.* Retrieved June 20, 2022, from https://www.unicef.org/press-releases/115-million-boys-and-men-around-world-married-children-unicef

UNICEF. (2020). *A Universal Definition of What It Means to be a 'Child'.* Retrieved September 10, 2022, from https://www.unicef.org/sudan/stories/universal-definition-what-it-means-be-child

UNICEF. (2021). *Towards Ending Child Marriage: Global Trends and Profiles of Progress.* Retrieved June 20, 2022, from https://data.unicef.org/resources/towards-ending-child-marriage/

UNICEF. (2022). *How We Protect Children's Rights with the UN Convention on the Rights of the Child.* Retrieved October 4, 2022, from https://www.unicef.org.uk/what-we-do/un-convention-child-rights/

United Nations. (1979). Convention on the Elimination of All Forms of Discrimination Against Women. Treaty Series, Vol. 1429, p. 13. Retrieved October 4, 2022, from https://www.ohchr.org/en/treaty-bodies/cedaw

United Nations. (1989). United Nations Convention on the Rights of the Child. Treaty Series, vol. 1577, p. 3. Retrieved October 4, 2022, from https://www.unicef.org.uk/what-we-do/un-convention-child-rights/

United Nations. (2019). *Sustainable Development Goal 5*. Retrieved June 14, 2022 from https://sustainabledevelopment.un.org/sdg5

Wadhwa, M. (2017). *Acknowledging Sexual Violence in Forced Marriage*. Retrieved June 7, 2022, from http://www.safelives.org.uk/practice_blog/acknowledging-sexual-violence-forced-marriage

Weber, H. (2017). Politics of 'Leaving No One Behind': Contesting the 2030 Sustainable Development Goal Agenda. *Globalizations, 14*(3), 399–414.

Wilkins, K. (1997). Gender, Power and Development. *Journal of International Communication, 4*(2), 102–120.

World Bank. (2020). *Poverty and Equity Brief*. Retrieved October 5, 2022, from https://databankfiles.worldbank.org/data/download/poverty/33EF03BB-9722-4AE2-ABC7-AA2972D68AFE/Global_POVEQ_IND.pdf

World Economic Forum. (2013). *Five Challenges, One Solution: Women*. Retrieved June 24, 2022, from http://www3.weforum.org/docs/WEF_GAC_WomensEmpowerment_FiveChallangesOneSolution_Compendium_2013.pdf

Young, K. (2002). WID, GAD and WAD. In V. Desai & R. B. Potter (Eds.), *The Companion to Development Studies* (pp. 321–325). Arnold.

CHAPTER 7

(In)decent Work for All? How the Decriminalisation of Sex Work Is Crucial to Achieving the SDGs

Helen Williams

Goal 8 of the UN's Sustainable Development Goals (SDGs) aims to 'promote sustained, inclusive and sustainable economic growth, full and productive employment and decent work for all'. In many places, the sex industry is constructed as the very opposite of 'decent'—criminalised, stigmatised and attracting intervention, regulation and punishment. Yet, in this chapter, I argue that despite its reputation as 'indecent', the sex industry is one of the more inclusive forms of employment, particularly amongst migrant, transgender or disabled workers, who are often excluded from other forms of work. This chapter takes a broad approach in understanding the construction of sex work beyond dominant narratives of exploitation and abuse. Using a sex-positive perspective, sex work is represented as the viable strategy of income generation, economic participation

H. Williams (✉)
University of Sunderland, Sunderland, UK
e-mail: helen.williams@sunderland.ac.uk

D. Dalton, A. Smith (eds.), *Gender, Sexuality and the UN's SDGs*, Sustainable Development Goals Series,
https://doi.org/10.1007/978-3-031-31046-1_7

and productive employment that it represents for many workers and argues that the decriminalisation of sex work is a necessary step in the achievement of Goal 8.

Acknowledging the Work in Sex Work

Sex work is a broad term which incorporates a multitude of sexual activities in exchange for money or other resources. These can include webcamming (performing intimate or explicit acts online); stripping, pornography and sugaring (dating or relationships in exchange for money or gifts); as well as the embodied sexual services traditionally understood and described in legal terminology as prostitution. Digital technology has transformed the ways in which individuals can earn a living using their sexual labour and there are advantages in terms of safety, legality and control for those working online, but technology is not universally available, especially for the most economically deprived. This chapter is principally concerned with in-person sex work as the most legally restricted and stigmatised of these activities and also the mode of work most accessible to workers in different cultural and economic contexts. Prostitution is a problematic term with gendered connotations of criminality, shame and victimhood (Empower Foundation, 2016), which are not helpful or appropriate for the arguments presented here. To counter these assumptions, sex worker activist Carol Leigh coined the term sex work in 1978 to highlight the work done by those in the sex industry and to reject stigma (Mac & Smith, 2018; Sanders et al., 2018). Sex work is necessarily consensual and between adults—non-consensual acts do not constitute sex work, but rather sexual exploitation, which is both a crime and a distinct subject. Thus, 'sex work' is used intentionally here to foreground the author's consideration of sex work as work and the legitimacy of labour which is sexual in nature.

The sex industry represents a considerable, mainly female, workforce (Ross et al., 2012) although accurate numbers of workers are impossible to gauge. Workers may leave and return to sex work continually (Balfour & Allen, 2014) and the illicit nature of the work means that many are unable to be open about their professional life. What is known is that, globally, selling sex is a multibillion-dollar industry and underpins tourism to such a degree that in some countries, the national economy depends on it, even when sex work is illegal or stigmatised (Kempadoo, 2003). The assumption that sex workers are female and clients are male underpins most policy interventions and theoretical understandings of sex work.

Although numbers of male and trans sex workers are significant, this chapter focuses mainly on the targets of such policy—women.

Motivations for working in the sex industry can be multiple and various yet, as with other work, money is the overwhelming factor. For female workers, this is often underpinned by the increased feminisation of poverty worldwide (O'Neill & Jobe, 2016), barriers to employment for women (Swendeman et al., 2015) and disproportionate familial responsibilities (Bowen, 2021). Sex work provides income for those whose access to other forms of employment may be limited (Swendeman et al., 2015), making sex work one of the more inclusive and accessible industries. For example, migrant workers may not have the right to work in their new country, may be exempt from claiming benefits, may not speak the language sufficiently or their qualifications may not be recognised (Mai, 2009). Members of the transgender community are often precluded from other forms of employment due to discrimination in the workplace (Balfour & Allen, 2014; Orchard et al., 2021) and in many places, they may face substantial medical bills. For workers with disabilities, chronic illness, mental health issues or substance misuse, sex work can provide flexible employment, offering the ability to work when well (Bowen, 2021; Mac & Smith, 2018). Access to some forms of employment can be limited if a prospective employee has previous convictions (Balfour & Allen, 2014), limited educational qualifications, or if their caring responsibilities impact their attendance at work. Some jobs require cash outlay which may not be feasible for some—for travel, training, criminal record checks or new attire. However, motivations for engagement in sex work are not limited to subsistence (Orchard et al., 2021). Particularly in the West, the proliferation of unpaid internships in some industries, the debts incurred during university study, the effects of the Covid-19 pandemic and increasing prices mean that sex work can sometimes provide a lucrative side-line (Bowen, 2021; Orchard et al., 2021). The rise of female-headed households worldwide and reduced state welfare programmes means that sex work can often bridge the gap between formal earnings and the cost of living (Kempadoo, 2003). Sex work provided a quick and convenient source of income for research participants (Bowen, 2021; Comte, 2014; Orchard et al., 2021) and workers described sex work as less exploitative or demeaning than other, low-paid employment (Mac & Smith, 2018). Yet, sex work is, by some definitions, 'indecent'—that is, outside the bounds of accepted standards of (sexual) behaviour. Historical constructions of women as naturally chaste and sexually passive underpin the criminalisation and stigmatisation of sex work while the sexual double standard and slut-shaming persist in the modern age (Comte, 2014; Williams, 2021).

Theoretical Perspectives and Legal Regulation

The sex industry is subject to challenging and complex debates underpinned by dichotomous theoretical positionings. Given that these debates have been covered extensively and in detail previously (e.g. see Sanders et al., 2018; Comte, 2014), what follows here constitutes an overview of the dominant positions. On one side, abolitionist feminists argue that sex work is indicative of patriarchy, gendered inequality and women's exploitation at the hands of men. The term sex work is opposed as it is argued that prostitution is abuse and can never be work, it perpetuates the oppression of women and the entitlement of men to access women's bodies (Dworkin, 1993). Similarly, abolitionist feminists argue that it can never be undertaken by choice when social and structural inequalities impinge on the availability of alternative options (Comte, 2014; Farley, 2018) and, from this perspective, female sex workers are always victims (Jackson, 2016). By constructing sex work as a choice, it is argued that the underlying gendered, racialised and classed power imbalances that provide the context for this choice are ignored and that the exchange of money constitutes coercion, even when there is consent (Farley, 2018). From this standpoint, the sex industry represents male-perpetrated violence against women and should be eradicated in its entirety in order to wipe out exploitation and abuse (Comte, 2014). This results in the conflation of sex work and sex trafficking (Sanders et al., 2018), that is, forced or coerced involvement in selling sex for the benefit of a third party, usually involving transportation and/or debt bondage. From this perspective, organised crime supplies women to feed the demands of the sex industry via trafficking (Jackson, 2016)—thus, trafficking exists because sex is available for sale and the availability of sex is underpinned by forced, coerced or trafficked labour. The resulting policies and legislation to eliminate the sex industry are then ideologically and politically driven rather than founded on evidence from research (Lerum & Brents, 2016). It should be emphasised that trafficked labour is present in many other industries. For example, in the UK, nail bars have been highlighted as particular destinations for trafficked individuals (Gentleman, 2020). While efforts are made to raise awareness and eradicate exploitative conditions and modern slavery in the beauty industry, in contrast to sex work, there is no parallel campaign to outlaw nail bars altogether.

Human trafficking, for sexual or other purposes, is a crime and victims/survivors should be protected. However, there are important differences between sex trafficking and sex work which should not be ignored—consent being the most important. A preoccupation with constructing the industry as universally dangerous and exploitative and, therefore, in need of abolition has meant that legal regulation, in one form or another, has become justified. Policy is, thus, driven towards punitive measures in a bid to end sex work even though this fails to account for 'the complex and multifaceted organisation of labour within the sex industry as well as sex workers' diverse experiences working in it' (van der Meulen, 2012, p. 152). The criminalisation of transactional sex has never eradicated sex work in any time or place (Empower Foundation, 2016; Mac & Smith, 2018) and the legal system remains an ineffective tool for regulating the industry. The insistence of framing sex work solely in terms of gendered inequality and male violence towards women, obscures the perspectives of male, trans or non-binary workers (Chu & Glass, 2013; Pitcher & Wijers, 2014) and the perpetuation of narratives that see the profession as inherently dangerous, normalise violence perpetrated against sex workers (Kenny et al., 2021). Similarly, it denies female sex workers the ability to consent to the types of work they wish to undertake and furthers paternalistic viewpoints of women in need of protection. When criminalisation of the whole industry is seen as a necessary, protective measure designed to root out traffickers and rescue their victims (Jackson, 2016; Lerum & Brents, 2016), consensual sex workers are further marginalised and impeded from claiming worker's rights (Mac & Smith, 2018)—rights which can and do make them safer (Armstrong, 2019; Kempadoo, 2003; Plumridge & Abel, 2001; Ross et al., 2012). As argued by Empower Foundation in Thailand:

> The overriding conditions of exploitation in the sex industry cannot be addressed if these situations of abuse are automatically considered to be outside the context of work. Such divisions create a hierarchy of merit in which sex workers must be criminally exploited, e.g., trafficked, in order to be seen as deserving of support, opportunities or protection under the law and in society. (Empower Foundation, 2016, unpaginated)

To bridge the gap between viewing sex workers as victims and the need for legal regulation, attention turned to the criminalisation of those paying for sexual services. The Nordic model, first implemented in Sweden in 1999 and increasingly popular in other countries, aims to disrupt the demand for transactional sex and is underpinned by abolitionist assumptions that the sex industry is inherently exploitative and dangerous (Kingston & Thomas, 2019). Despite the theoretical aim to hold buyers (which this model assumes are always male) to account, few have been charged under this model (Kingston & Thomas, 2019) and most consequences are felt by workers (Chu & Glass, 2013; Jackson, 2016). In the same vein, little social attention is paid to how these laws are implemented in practice (Mac & Smith, 2018) and the policing of the purchase of sex.

Levy and Jakobsson (2014) found that the Nordic model failed to demonstrably reduce sex work in Sweden and has, conversely, made some forms of sex work more dangerous. Studies show that workers are forced to operate more covertly, often with less time to screen clients (Kingston & Thomas, 2019; Levy & Jakobsson, 2014) and less power to negotiate condom use (Chu & Glass, 2013). Workers are also less trusting of the police and more likely to be subjected to police harassment (Chu & Glass, 2013; Lerum & Brents, 2016). Other research emphasises that in places where buying or selling sex is legally regulated, workers are more likely to suffer violence but less likely to report it, have poor health outcomes, including increased likelihood of HIV infection and mental ill health, and diminished access to health services, criminal justice and alternative sources of income (Balfour & Allen, 2014; Elmes et al., 2021; McBride et al., 2022; O'Neill & Jobe, 2016; Platt et al., 2018). Ross and colleagues conclude that the significant barriers to health and safety among sex workers are rooted in legal regulation (Ross et al., 2012) and this context affects the (re)production or rejection of social stigma (Sanders, 2016; cited in Armstrong, 2019).

The opposite position is taken by those who understand sex work as work and therefore, as valid and socially valuable as other intimate service work typically undertaken by women such as care work or nursing (Califia, 1994). This standpoint challenges the stigma associated with sex work (Armstrong, 2019), demands an end to moral debates and the legal recognition of workers (Mac & Smith, 2018; Sanders et al., 2018). While it is acknowledged that sex work can be dangerous, it is argued that it is made so by criminalisation and punitive measures which place sex workers underground and at risk (Armstrong, 2019). It is considered the right of individuals to exercise agency and to capitalise on their sexuality and the viewpoint that all sex work is demeaning or exploitative constitutes a denial of individual agency (Califia, 1994; Comte, 2014; Jackson, 2016). It has been argued that sex work can be empowering (Califia, 1994) and allow women to resist their construction as a conduit for male pleasure (Comte, 2014). While this may be true at times, wholehearted subscription to empowerment narratives should be avoided as they can obscure the intersectional nuances involved in choice and both personal and collective experience (Mac & Smith, 2018). What is clear is that sex work provides a route to financial independence (Swendeman et al., 2015), particularly for disenfranchised individuals and this can be empowering (Lawless, 2021). It is worth noting that few other professions necessitate individual feelings of empowerment to be seen as legitimate (Lawless, 2021). Sex work can be arduous, boring, demanding and exploitative in the same way that any work can (Empower Foundation, 2016; Mac & Smith, 2018) although this is often a discomforting observation given the perceived blending of selling sex and selling oneself (Pitcher & Wijers, 2014). Sex workers are often adversely affected by legislation designed to deter traffickers which threatens their ability to advertise, work openly and, crucially, report crimes committed against them (Jackson, 2016).

While both sides of the debate are oppositional in how they view sex workers and how they believe the sex industry should be (de)regulated, they often have shared goals. Both advocate for gender equality, the ability for individuals to achieve financial independence and an end to violence against women, however the means to these ends and what the completion of these goals would look like are highly contested. Abolitionist feminists would argue that sex work represents the very opposite of 'decent work' while those in support of sex workers rights would consider them as entitled as other workers to access 'decent work' benefits, such as improved health and safety and the abolition of discrimination. Sex work and 'decent work' itself are contentious concepts as the following sections will highlight.

'Everyone Works, But Not Everyone Is Employed'

'Decent work' is terminology associated with an aspirational agenda from the International Labour Organisation (hereafter ILO[1]), a specialised subsection of the UN which deals with labour policy and practice and which strives to promote working conditions which uphold dignity, equality, stability and safety around the world (1999). The aim is to address compulsory or forced work, child labour and abuse or discrimination at work (Ghai, 2003) and to promote worker's rights and gender equality (Burchell et al., 2014). While the economic growth in Goal 8 is a quantifiable target, the measurement of 'decent' work is much more troublesome (Ghai, 2003). A lack of clear definition and universally understood parameters which denote 'decent work' renders comparison between diverse cultures and international labour markets difficult if not impossible (Burchell et al., 2014). It may seem pertinent to examine the 'terms and conditions' of work (Deranty & MacMillan, 2012) to denote decency—for example, is the worker willing, fairly paid and adequately recognised, respected and safeguarded? While this may seem to simplify measurements of 'decent work', the authors go on to trouble this, arguing that the content of the work itself may preclude it from 'decency', even if the worker chooses to undertake it. This may be the case if the tasks involved are overly dangerous, dirty or stressful (Deranty & MacMillan, 2012). While Goal 8 aims to eradicate poor working conditions, these are, in some cases, integral to particular industries—mining, for example, will always be dirty and dangerous work even when the 'terms and conditions' are favourable. Thus, it has been argued that 'decent work' is not synonymous with desirable work, and only an individual worker can decide if their work is 'decent' (Deranty & MacMillan, 2012). If understanding what constitutes 'decent work' is subjective and understanding how it can be measured is complex, then its inclusion as an aim in Goal 8 is rendered almost meaningless.

Similarly, access to 'decent work' is not equal and vulnerable or marginalised populations are often excluded from making choices about the kinds of work they undertake (Blustein et al., 2016). Kempadoo (2003) argues that global trends indicate women are increasingly required to support household income with paid employment, yet the opportunities for waged work for women are often in sectors which are poorly paid, unregulated and precarious such as manufacturing or agriculture. Furthermore, the use

[1] ILO (1999, p. 3).

of 'decent' comes with connotations of morality and respectability which set it apart from comparable terms such as 'good' or 'acceptable' work. What is considered decent, both in terms of an acceptable standard and in terms of morality, is culturally and contextually bound, changing across time and place, making this questionable as a measure of development. Despite the problems associated with multiple and changing definitions of 'decent' and 'decent work', the imposition of single understandings on an international level has connotations of colonialism and the promotion of cultural hegemony which make it difficult to support.

The SDGs pledge that 'no one will be left behind' as part of their Agenda 2030 (Elias & Holliday, 2019) yet the World Employment and Social Outlook report from the International Labour Organisation (ILO) recognised that of the employed population worldwide, almost half continue to work in conditions which are not representative of 'decent work' (2015, p. 27). It is significant that the majority of these workers are women. The International Labour Organisation asserts:

> All workers have the right to decent work, not only those working in the formal economy, but also the self-employed, casual and informal economy workers, as well as those, predominantly women, working in the care economy and private households. (ILO, 2012, p. v)

Goal 8 aims specifically to eradicate poor working conditions and forced labour, yet it frames this by focusing explicitly on economic growth as measured by GDP. Deranty and Macmillan (2012) argue that this focuses attention on formal, waged employment, which is carried out disproportionately by men. Despite the rise of women in waged work, there has been no simultaneous sharing of domestic duties which are predominantly performed by women (Rai et al., 2019). While the recognition of unpaid and/or informal reproductive, social and caring work is stated in Goal 5 in the context of the achievement of gender equality, it has been argued that its lack of specific inclusion in Goal 8 causes unresolved tension between competing goals (Elias & Holliday, 2019; Rai et al., 2019)—if women's informal work is to be valued as per Goal 5, it should surely be explicitly included in the work of Goal 8? Thus, gendered inequality is engrained by the patriarchal organisation of formal employment (Deranty & MacMillan, 2012) in which the work of women is underpaid and undervalued (Rai et al., 2019) and domestic/reproductive work underpins the economy but is not counted towards GDP growth and development. It is argued that this leaves an unworkable policy in which neither goal can be truly met.

There are similar tensions when we consider sex work as 'decent work'. Goal 5:2 of the SDGs aims to eliminate all forms of violence against women. If the sex industry is conceptualised as inherently violent and exploitative towards women, then Goal 5 must include the sex industry as a target to be eradicated. Yet, this is highly contested by sex workers themselves and their supporters. The ability to advocate for decent work for all is predicated on the acceptance of sex work as legitimate work, however the ongoing criminalisation of the industry and entrenched stigmatisation make this almost impossible. The illegality of sex work is the foremost barrier to the recognition of sexual labour and the claim for workers rights. Ultimately, this means that, worldwide, a substantial demographic of people are excluded from pertinent debates on working conditions, discrimination and exploitation and ultimately, sex workers are left behind. If decent work is the goal for everyone, then specific and explicit consideration of sex workers should be included. For this to happen, the first step must be the decriminalisation of sex work. In the next section, I outline the impact decriminalisation could have on the accessibility of decent work.

The Case for Decriminalisation

Decriminalisation refers to the removal of criminal laws which restrict the sale of sex. This differs from legalisation, which refers to the state control of the sex industry and the implementation of new laws which sometimes include compulsory STI testing, zoning or official registration (O'Neill & Jobe, 2016). Where a legalised, state-controlled approach has been implemented, such as the Netherlands and some states in the US, there is greater surveillance of workers and more legal rights but the improvement in working conditions is inconsistent and often dependent on migration status, leaving some workers on the wrong side of the law (Pitcher & Wijers, 2014).

Decriminalisation does not mean that there are no rules or regulations to follow, and it does not mean that there are no crimes associated with exploitative or abusive practice. In 2003, sex work in New Zealand was decriminalised using the Prostitution Reform Act, affording sex workers occupational rights in line with workers in other industries. This increased the autonomy of workers to control when, where and whether they worked and the ability to use the legal system to resist coercive, exploitative or abusive working conditions (Abel, 2018). Subsequent research associates a decriminalised context with greater health and well-being outcomes (Platt et al., 2018; Seib et al., 2009), although deeply entrenched stigma still exists (Armstrong, 2019). Decriminalisation can reduce the covertness of the industry and work to decrease exploitation, violence and abuse, creating safer workspaces for sex workers (Plumridge & Abel, 2001). Prior to the decriminalisation of sex work in New Zealand, Plumridge and Abel describe the vast differences between workers working semi-legally in brothels operating under the guise of massage parlours, and illegal workers soliciting on the street. Illegal workers tended to have started sex work at a younger age, were more likely to be dependent on drugs and more at risk of violence and abuse (Plumridge & Abel, 2001). A similar Australian study found that sex workers operating illegally reported poorer mental health and more negative experiences than those employed in licensed brothels (Seib et al., 2009). Immigration status impinges on individuals' ability to claim employment rights, yet sex industry work enables this population to maintain good living standards and avoid other exploitative industries (Mai, 2009). Exploitation and abuse are exacerbated when workers and clients are criminalised and forced to operate out of sight. When sex workers fear the police and the consequences of receiving criminal charges are potentially dire, there is little incentive to report crimes perpetrated against them.

British legal regulation of sex work prohibits brothel-keeping meaning that workers preferring to share working space with each other for safety are unable to do so within the law. It is argued that this makes those working together a target for violence, robbery or abuse as it is known that they cannot engage with police without highlighting their own criminality (Pitcher & Wijers, 2014). Similar legislation in Canada was judged unconstitutional and to infringe the rights of sex workers because the law prevented workers from 'taking steps that could reduce the risk of violence' (Chu & Glass, 2013, p. 102). It has been noted that participation in formal employment has an emancipatory effect on women (in particular), increasing female agency and power (Kabeer et al., 2011 cited in Swendeman et al., 2015). Thus, it follows that the decriminalisation and therefore, the incorporation of sex work into formal employment could support efforts towards gender equality and female financial and social independence. There is a certain epistemic injustice in the production of policy and legislation which fails to consult the very people it will impact most (Siegmann, 2019). Advocacy for the decriminalisation of sex work has taken place by sex workers around the world for many years (Kempadoo, 2003; Mac & Smith, 2018; Sanders et al., 2018) and it continues to gain traction on an international level. Currently, the World Health Organisation, Amnesty International and UNAIDS, among other organisations, support calls for the decriminalisation of the sex industry (Empower Foundation, 2016). Thus, decriminalisation and sex work's subsequent inclusion under Goal 8 of the SDGs is not an unrealistic appeal. There is, of course, exploitation in sex work and this chapter does not seek to deny that some sex workers, particularly those with less social power such as those with impairments, transgender people and migrants, work in objectionable conditions. However, workers in many other industries also work in poor or exploitative conditions—in factories, mines or agriculture, for example—and they are not denied worker status nor is their labour considered unproductive or invalid. Opponents of decriminalisation suggest that sex work is inherently dangerous, yet there is little similar outcry over workers in the military or in prison where violence is commonplace. The difference is that those workers are afforded the protection of legal and occupational rights, upheld by the state:

> As with any other industry, the existence of exploitation, forced labour or substandard working conditions experienced by workers does not negate the State's responsibility to protect workers' rights, nor should it negate the individual's right to seek recognition or redress as a worker. (Empower Foundation, 2016, unpaginated)

Rights for All?

When debates on sex work are reduced to the dichotomy of choice and empowerment vs exploitation and oppression—that the sex industry is wholly one or the other—there is limited scope for moving forward. Elias and Holiday argue for the '*simultaneous* existence of perspectives on sex work framed in terms of anti-trafficking *as well as* a labour rights perspective' (Elias & Holliday, 2019, p. 24; emphasis in original). Furthermore, we need to consider rights that are beyond traditional labour legislation when discussing the decriminalisation of sex work and how this might impact other goals in the SDGs. For example, the right to family life is enshrined in The Human Rights Act (1998) yet criminalisation and the concomitant stigma mean sex workers are framed as inherently dangerous to their children and often have their children removed by the state which can have severe and long-lasting consequences (Kenny et al., 2021). The right to healthcare is listed as a goal in the SDGs (3.7 and 5.6) yet criminalisation hinders access to healthcare services (McBride et al., 2022; Platt et al., 2018). Similarly, achievement of the goal to end the HIV epidemic (3.3) is impeded if sex workers are afraid to carry condoms because they may be used as evidence of criminal activity—something reported by workers in countries such as Russia, the US, South Africa and Kenya (Chu & Glass, 2013; Shields, 2011). Aiming to eliminate corruption (16.5) is not helped if police routinely profit from raids on brothels, are offered money or sex to turn a blind eye and can perpetrate violence against sex workers in the name of upholding the law (Mac & Smith, 2018).

Sex work can represent a valuable and legitimate source of income, because of the constrained choices and the barriers to employment that some groups of people face. Criminalisation does not prevent sex work from taking place nor does it do anything to address the social and economic inequalities faced by women, migrants, people who are transgender and those with disabilities which make sex work a logical and attractive choice.

Decriminalisation is not a panacea, rather it represents the first step in recognising the validity of sexual labour, to promoting the health and safety of sex workers and to challenging deeply entrenched stigma (Armstrong, 2019). It represents a move towards 'decent work', free from discrimination, poor working conditions and exploitation, and the recognition that workers, and particularly women workers, can make informed decisions about the type of work they engage in. Viewed through this lens, it becomes imperative that sex workers are included in the goal to promote safe and secure working environments for all workers. Much has been written about the vulnerability of sex workers, yet this is fuelled by their status as operating outside the bounds of 'decent' employment, as criminal, deviant or disreputable—in short, as workers who do not matter. Goal 8 must really apply to all workers, as stated, or risk perpetuating inequality and exclusion for the very groups it aims to support. Therefore, to ensure safe workplaces, labour rights and to advance the ability of marginalised groups to participate in employment, the UN must advocate for the full decriminalisation of sex work around the world as part of the SDGs.

References

Abel, G. (2018). Commentary: Sex Work Is Here to Stay and Decriminalisation Improves Safety and Social Justice. *British Medical Journal, 361*, k2687.

Armstrong, L. (2019). Stigma, Decriminalisation and Violence Against Street-Based Sex Workers: Changing the Narrative. *Sexualities, 22*(7–8), 1288–1308.

Balfour, R., & Allen, J. (2014, April). *A Review of the Literature on Sex Workers and Social Exclusion*. UCL Institute of Health Equity. Retrieved June 19, 2022, from https://assets.publishing.service.gov.uk/government/uploads/system/uploads/attachment_data/file/303927/A_Review_of_the_Literature_on_sex_workers_and_social_exclusion.pdf

Blustein, D. L., Olle, C., Connors-Kellgren, A., & Diamonti, A. J. (2016). Decent Work: A Psychological Perspective. *Frontiers in Psychology, 7*, 407. https://doi.org/10.3389/fpsyg.2016.00407

Bowen, R. (2021). *Work, Money and Duality: Trading Sex as a Side Hustle*. Policy Press.

Burchell, B., Sehnbruch, K., Piasna, A., & Agloni, N. (2014). The Quality of Employment and Decent Work: Definitions, Methodologies and Ongoing Debates. *Cambridge Journal of Economics, 38*(2), 459–477.

Califia, P. (1994). *Public Sex: The Culture of Radical Sex*. Cleis Press Inc.

Chu, S., & Glass, R. (2013). Sex Work Law Reform in Canada: Considering Problems with the Nordic Model. *Alberta Law Review, 51*(1), 101–124.

Comte, J. (2014). Decriminalisation of Sex Work: Feminist Discourses in Light of Research. *Sexuality and Culture, 18*, 196–217.

Deranty, J.-P., & MacMillan, C. (2012). The ILO's Decent Work Initiative: Suggestions for an Extension of the Notion of "Decent Work". *Journal of Social Philosophy, 43*(4), 386–405.

Dworkin, A. (1993). Prostitution and Male Supremacy. *Michigan Journal of Gender and Law, 1*(1), 1–12.

Elias, J., & Holliday, J. (2019). Who Gets 'Left Behind'? Promises and Pitfalls in Making the Global Development Agenda Work for Sex Workers – Reflections From Southeast Asia. *Journal of Ethnic and Migration Studies, 45*(14), 2566–2582.

Elmes, J., Stuart, R., Grenfell, P., Walker, J., Hill, K., Hernandez, P., ... Platt, L. (2021, October 26). Effect of Police Enforcement and Extreme Social Inequalities on Violence and Mental Health Among Women Who Sell Sex: Findings from a Cohort Study in London, UK, Sexually Transmitted Infections. [Advance Online Publication]. https://doi.org/10.1136/sextrans-2021-055088.

Empower Foundation. (2016). Moving Towards Decent Sex Work. Sex Worker Community Research Decent Work and Exploitation in Thailand. : Empower Foundation. Retrieved June 19, 2022, from https://nswp.org/sites/default/

files/Moving%20Toward%20Decent%20Sex%20Work%20Summary%2C%20EMPOWER%20-%20April%202016.pdf

Farley, M. (2018). Risks of Prostitution: When the Person is the Product. *Journal for the Association of Consumer Research, 3*(1), 97–108.

Gentleman, A. (2020, January 21). What Does Your £10 Manicure Really Cost? The Unvarnished Truth About Nail Bars. *The Guardian*.

Ghai, D. (2003). Decent Work: Concept and Indicators. *International Labour Review, 142*(2), 113–146.

International Labour Organisation. (1999). Decent Work. Report of the Director-General. *International Labour Conference*, 87th Session. ILO.

International Labour Organisation. (2015). *World Employment and Social Outlook Report: Trends 2015*. Retrieved July 7, 2022, from https://www.ilo.org/wcmsp5/groups/public/%2D%2D-dgreports/%2D%2D-dcomm/%2D%2D-publ/documents/publication/wcms_337069.pdf

Jackson, C. A. (2016). Framing Sex Worker Rights: How U.S. Sex Worker Rights Activists Perceive and Respond to Mainstream Anti-Sex Trafficking Advocacy. *Sociological Perspectives, 59*(1), 27–45.

Kempadoo, K. (2003). Globalising Sex Workers' Rights. *Canadian Woman Studies, 22*(3–4), 143–150.

Kenny, K. S., Krüsi, A., Barrington, C., Ranville, F., Green, S. L., Bingham, B., Abrahams, R., & Shannon, K. (2021). Health Consequences of Child Removal Among Indigenous and Non-Indigenous Sex Workers: Examining Trajectories, Mechanisms and Resiliencies. *Sociology of Health and Illness, 43*, 1903–1920.

Kingston, S., & Thomas, T. (2019). No model in practice: A 'Nordic model' to respond to prostitution? *Crime, Law and Social Change, 71*, 423–439.

Lawless, T. (2021). *Beyond 'Exploitation' and 'Empowerment' in Sex Work*. Retrieved June 23, 2022, from https://www.sydneyoperahouse.com/festivals/all-about-women/digital/articles/beyond-exploitation-empowerment-sex-work-tilly-lawless.html

Lerum, K., & Brents, B. G. (2016). Sociological Perspectives on Sex Work and Human Trafficking. *Sociological Perspectives, 59*(1), 17–26.

Levy, J., & Jakobsson, P. (2014). Sweden's Abolitionist Discourse and Law: Effects on the Dynamics of Swedish Sex Work and on the Lives of Sweden's Sex Workers. *Criminology & Criminal Justice, 14*(5), 593–607.

Mac, J., & Smith, M. (2018). *Revolting Prostitutes: The Fight for Sex Workers' Rights*. Verso.

Mai, N. (2009). *Migrant Workers in the UK Sex Industry: Final Policy-Relevant Report*. Institute for the Study of European Transformations: London Metropolitan University.

McBride, B., Goldenberg, S. M., Murphy, A., Wu, S., Mo, M., Shannon, K., & Krüsi, A. (2022). Protection or Police Harassment? Impacts of Punitive Policing, Discrimination, and Racial Profiling Under End-Demand Laws

Among Im/Migrant Sex Workers in Metro Vancouver. *SSM: Qualitative Research in Health, 2*, 100048.
O'Neill, M., & Jobe, A. (2016). Policy Briefing: Adult Sex Work, Law and Policy. *Discover Society, 39*.
Orchard, T., Salter, K., Bunch, M., & Benoit, C. (2021). Money, Agency and Self-Care Among Cis-Gender and Trans People in Sex Work. *Social Sciences, 10*(1), 6.
Pitcher, J., & Wijers, M. (2014). The Impact of Different Regulatory Models on the Labour Conditions, Safety and Welfare of Indoor-Based Sex Workers. *Criminology and Criminal Justice, 14*(5), 549–564.
Platt, L., Grenfell, P., Meiksin, R., Elmes, J., Sherman, S. G., Sanders, T., Mwangi, P., & Crago, A. (2018). Associations Between Sex Work Laws and Sex Workers' Health: A Systematic Review and Meta-Analysis of Quantitative and Qualitative Studies. *PLoS Medicine, 15*(12), e1002680. https://doi.org/10.1371/journal.pmed.1002680
Plumridge, L., & Abel, G. (2001). A 'Segmented' Sex Industry in New Zealand: Sexual and Personal Safety of Female Sex Workers. *Australian and New Zealand Journal of Public Health, 25*(1), 78–83.
Rai, S. M., Brown, B. D., & Ruwanpura, K. N. (2019). SDG 8: Decent Work and Economic Growth – A Gendered Analysis. *World Development, 113*, 368–380.
Ross, M. W., Crisp, B., Månsson, S., & Hawkes, S. (2012). Occupational Health and Safety Among Commercial Sex Workers. *Scandinavian Journal of Work, Environment and Health, 38*(2), 105–119.
Sanders, T., O'Neill, M., & Pitcher, J. (2018). *Prostitution: Sex Work, Policy and Politics* (2nd ed.). Sage Publications.
Seib, C., Fischer, J., & Najman, J. M. (2009). The Health of Female Sex Workers from Three Industry Sectors in Queensland, Australia. *Social Science and Medicine, 68*(3), 473–478.
Shields, A. (2011). *Criminalising Condoms*. Open Society Foundations. Retrieved July 7, 2022, from https://www.opensocietyfoundations.org/publications/criminalizing-condoms
Siegmann, K. A. (2019). Decent Work for Sex Workers' as ILO's Centenary Treat. *Global Labour Column, 317*.
Swendeman, D., Fehrenacher, A., Ali, S., George, S., Mindry, D., Collins, M., Ghose, T., & Dey, B. (2015). "Whatever I Have, I Have Made by Coming into this Profession": The Intersection of Resources, Agency, and Achievements in Pathways to Sex Work in Kolkata, India. *Archives of Sexual Behaviour, 44*(4), 1011–1023.
Van der Meulen, E. (2012). When Sex is Work: Organising for Labour Rights and Protection. *Labour/Le Travail, 69*, 147–141.
Williams, H. (2021). 'You Can Spot Them a Mile Off' – Young Women's Negotiations of Class and the Sexual Culture of Shame. Sexuality and Culture, 25, 1273–1289.

CHAPTER 8

Sharing Stories of an Experience Shared: From 'Me Too' as Narrative to #MeToo as Political Movement

Joanna Thornborrow and Pierre Chartier

Introduction

This chapter addresses the problem of gender inequality (Sustainable Development Goal—SDG 5), specifically the empowerment of all women and girls to speak up against the sexual abuse and violence they experience, and hold the (often institutionally powerful) men accountable for their actions (SDG 16). To this end we focus on Twitter, the affordances of social media, and the creation of the hashtag movement #MeToo in 2017–18. As this emerged from the context of sexual exploitation, harassment, and assault in the film industry, we can also align this chapter with SDG 9, which, amongst other things, seeks to promote full and

An earlier version of this chapter was published in French in Patron (ed) 2020.

J. Thornborrow (✉) • P. Chartier
University of Western Brittany, Brest, France

D. Dalton, A. Smith (eds.), *Gender, Sexuality and the UN's SDGs*, Sustainable Development Goals Series,
https://doi.org/10.1007/978-3-031-31046-1_8

productive employment and decent work for all. In this introductory section we briefly give the context for Milano's first tweet, before setting out our theoretical approach to the data in Sect. 2. In Sect. 3, we move to a presentation and comparative description of the corpora, and Sect. 4 develops this description into a more in-depth analysis and discussion of the discursive activity on each day.

Small Stories, Big Stories, and Social Networks

On 5 October 2017, *The New York Times* published allegations by Rose McGowan and Ashley Judd against Hollywood producer Harvey Weinstein of sexual harassment spanning several decades. In the following days, further allegations appeared from a long list of prominent female actors, including Meryl Streep and Judi Dench. More recently, in January 2019 British actor Emma Thompson resigned from her role on a film for Skydance Animations in protest against John Lassiter's appointment as head of that company. Lassiter had been sacked from Pixar in March 2018 after claims of sexual harassment were made against him. In her letter of resignation, Thompson says: 'I can only do what feels right during these difficult times of transition and collective consciousness raising.'[1]

On 15 October 2017, Alyssa Milano had 3,220,500 followers on her Twitter account. One year later, this number had risen to 3,457,758.[2] #MeToo had thus boosted her audience on the social network by well over 200,000. In the intervening months between these two events, women all over the world, and some men too, were telling their stories of sexual harassment on social media, and particularly prominently on Twitter. The hashtag *#MeToo* celebrated 12 months of existence in October 2018, and has now become a global movement, with similar sites being created both within and across national and cultural boundaries (e.g. *#BalanceTonPorc*, *#Cuéntalo*, *#YoTambien*, *#quellavoltache*, *#TimesUp*, and many others).[3]

[1] https://womenintheworld.com/2019/02/27/i-can-only-do-what-feels-right-emma-thompsons-rallying-cry-against-abuse-of-power/.

[2] Sourced from Trackalytics, https://www.trackalytics.com/.

[3] The Me Too movement was first started in 2006 by Tarana Burke, currently Senior Director of Girls for Gender Equity.

Twitter, Public Spaces, and Mediated Narratives

Among other affordances, social media platforms, including Twitter, offer 'a space where fragmented individual experiences and personal narratives aggregate to act collectively' (Saki, 2017, p. 168). A virtual space like *#MeToo* can be considered as an ideal site for 'small' storytelling (Georgakopoulou, 2017), that is, a short, fleeting, undeveloped narrative that is structurally minimal, with a single narrator. However, for the gathering force of a movement like *#MeToo* to be transformed into the collective action of a political campaign, the publication of such small stories has to move beyond the multiple production online of individual accounts of a common experience, into a form of large-scale collective social protest. What evidence is there of corresponding transformations in the discursive actions on the *#MeToo* site, one year after its launch?

Extensive research in sociolinguistics, discourse, and conversation analysis clearly shows that narrative discourse is pervasive in all contexts for social interaction (Blum Kulka, 1993; Goodwin, 1990; Johnstone & De Fina, 2015; Thornborrow, 2015). Narratives are built in different ways according to locally situated contexts and activities, but all stories are designed for recipients, and those told on social media are no exception. However, investigating socially mediated storytelling poses various challenges for discourse analysts, and, as in all domains of socially mediated interaction, various researchers have warned against the dangers of generalising and over-simplifying socially mediated activity (Androutsopoulos, 2006). As De Fina notes in an analysis of audience reactions to storytelling in social media, narrative practices 'differ in terms of the media used, the platform in which narratives are embedded, and the communities that access and use such media' (De Fina, 2016, p. 477).

Research on storytelling that focuses specifically on Twitter narratives (Dayter, 2015; Page, 2012) suggests that the format of a tweet and limited number of characters available for each post results (predictably) not just in smaller stories than those found on media platforms with fewer constraints, but also in changes to the classic Labovian narrative in terms of structure and form (Labov, 1972). Dayter notes that 'the episodic quality of storylines is a feature of the eyewitness microgenre' and also that 'life events are reported as they are unfolding and the teller does not have an opportunity to process them according to a narrative template and present a packaged story' (Dayter, 2015, p. 24). This suggests that *Twitter* stories may in fact share a number of features with other forms of mediated breaking news, be it in the press, where there are constraints on space which means that typically the resolution comes first (Bell, 1994), or in broadcast TV news, which often has much more in common with the discourse of commentary than with narrative (Montgomery, 2007). Life-logging in the *Twittersphere* might be equally appropriately considered as a form of commentary rather than narrative, firstly because micro-blogging is primarily concerned with the current and unfolding events of an emergent now, and secondly because it is predominantly deictic, assuming shared contextual frames and background knowledge with recipients.[4]

These reservations notwithstanding, we consider the initial posts to Milano's *#MeToo* site as narrative actions that are elicited, situated, and take shape within the specific social context described above. They thus represent a particular form of storying past events in relation to that context. In the second stage of the analysis we compare this narrative activity to the posts one year later, in order to see what may have changed and whether the context and impact of the *#MeToo* movement has had an effect on narrative activity in tweets.

Theoretical Framework

In order to examine the development of narrative and other discursive activity on the Twitter site *#MeToo*, we focus first of all on how personal accounts of harassment and abuse initially emerged within a socially mediated framework and in relation to a particular temporal and socio-political context, that is, the international headline news of accusations of sexual harassment against Harvey Weinstein in early October 2017. We then consider how and to what extent discursive activity on the same site one year later has moved beyond narrative, as the contextual/temporal environment changes and the tweeted stories transition into other forms of social and political action. Using a lexico-metrical and functional analysis of the data,[5] we compare both corpora and identify any significant lexico-grammatical differences between them. We follow this with a more in-depth comparison of the pragmatic and discursive framing of the tweets,

[4] These features can be observed in the frequent use of non-finite verb forms, present and present perfect tenses and deictic terms, an orientation to immediacy in relating the now and the just now, an orientation to the future (what is going to happen next) as well as to what has just happened, and the presence of prediction, speculation, and evaluation (Marriott, 2007).

[5] In this analysis we draw on functional grammatical categories from Halliday (1994).

drawing on conversational analysis and research on mediated discourse analysis to examine the interactional aspects of the activity on the site for each corpus.

The application of conversational analytic (CA) methods—the analysis of situated talk-in-interaction—to digital data is comparatively new, and sometimes contested, but nevertheless slowly expanding in research on socially mediated interaction (Giles et al., 2015). Several points raised by Giles et al. are particularly relevant in respect of the *#MeToo* data. Firstly, that 'to ignore the interactional dynamics [on Twitter] at the local level would be losing sight of the trees in order to understand the wood' (ibid., p. 46). In other words, we can usefully use 'small data' to understand a bigger picture. Secondly, that online interaction is conditionally framed by the norms and conventions of its particular technological context and therefore cannot be treated as locally managed conversation, or talk, in general. Again, Giles et al. point out that 'a tweet would not necessarily accomplish the same discursive actions in any context other than Twitter' (Giles et al., 2015, p. 48). Thirdly, like other media contexts for talk-in-interaction, socially mediated activity is 'doubly articulated' (Scannell, 1991) in that it is designed for a non-co-present, potentially unlimited number of recipients, who may at any point join the interaction as current participants. While this can raise complex ethical considerations in collecting data from some social media platforms where divisions between public and private interactions can be very blurred (Thornborrow, 2017), on Twitter, self-promotion, seeing and being seen, is recognised as one of its primary functions (Marwick & boyd, 2011), this is much less likely to be the case. Participants are aware that to tweet is to communicate in the public domain. Finally, since CA is primarily the study of the organisation of interaction, and individual identity is not treated as relevant unless made so by participants, we propose to deal with identity as it may emerge as a membership category created through postings to the site *#MeToo*. In the next section we provide a brief overview of the formal structure and lexico-semantic content of the two data sets, then move to an analysis of the tweets as discursive actions.[6]

[6] We reproduce all tweets exactly as they were posted, without corrections or alterations.

Data Description

Some Numbers

We divided the corpus into two parts, each corresponding to the same date in 2017 and 2018, and used a lexico-metric analysis to identify any significant lexical and semantic similarities/differences between them. The 2017 corpus consists of 254 tweets, and contains 2939 words, an average of 11.57 words per tweet. 83 tweets begin with #MeToo and 73 end with it. The distinguishing feature of this corpus is that over one third (88) of the total number of tweets contain simply the hashtag #MeToo, or the hashtag accompanied with 'me too', combined in six different formats as illustrated here:

> 85. Me too #metoo
> 87. me too #MeToo
> 117. Me too. #metoo
> 139. #Metoo 'me too'
> 183. #MeToo Me Too
> 187. Me too. #MeToo

The 2018 corpus is shorter, containing 131 tweets, but denser in terms of the number of words: a total of 3475, giving an average of 25.74 words per tweet. This represents an increase of about 50% in the average length of a tweet compared to the 2017 corpus. The construction of these 131 tweets is also different since only seven begin with the #MeToo, whereas 61 end with it. Lastly, in 2018 no tweet is composed simply of #MeToo, nor of the repeated forms '#MeToo me too' found in 2017.

Narratives of Personal Experience

Of the remaining response tweets in the 2017 corpus, only five were not narrative: two were hostile responses to Milano, the other three contained comments comment on the medium and use of #. In the narrative tweets, 62 had first-person 'I' narrators:

> 27. Me too. When I was three years old. When I was 13. When I was 30. It has taken years to be able to say it. #MeToo
> 46. #metoo I found him on an online dating app so I 'was asking for it'. 'women don't use the net unless they want it.' His words to me.

We also found occasional use of a third-person, generic 'you' in accounts of the experience of sexual harassment, producing a strong semantic link between the subject 'me' of 'me too', and a collective 'you' in the accounts of those experiences, as, for example:

> 18. " #MeToo Early in life, and often still. Where, when, who … you never can anticipate. Cld be ANYWHERE, ANY TIME, ANY ONE. Every day.
> 44. Me too … And each time, the perpetrator makes you feel like you 'asked for it'. #MeToo

The generic 'you' functions here as a narrative device that both distances the teller from the violence or trauma of the recounted events, while extending the frame of reference to others sharing the same kind of experience.

Representing Acts of Sexual Aggression

In the 2017 corpus, representations of sexual violence are frequent, but vary little. These include nominal forms, for example, 'the assault' (seven instances) or 'the rape' (four instances), but occur most frequently as past tense passivised verb phrases 'was assaulted' (11 instances) 'have been harassed' (15 instances) and 'was raped' (4 instances). The two actions 'harassed' and 'assaulted' are often combined in the same tweet. In terms of agency, the subject position is either third-person pronoun 'he' (11 occurrences), represented as male (uncle, boy, male cousins, mother's boyfriend, uni guy,) or otherwise made explicit through pronominal co-reference 'he/his/him' (referring to neighbour, teacher, boss, preacher). Only one tweet specifically refers to a woman as agent. First-person 'I', on the other hand, occurs 47 times as the affected entity in passive forms: 'I was assaulted', while in addition to the 217 instances of 'me' in the phrase 'me too', 'me' occurs 24 times as affected entity of a violent act, as in the following two examples:

> 38. #MeToo\nThe teenage neighbor when I was barely a teen. Pinned me in his garage. Told my brother to stay out, but he came when I yelled for him.
> 192. My sec hubby and I were good friends with another couple. My guy and the other woman had an affair. Her hubby raped me to get even #metoo

The #MeToo tweets on this first day, for the vast majority, took the form of personal accounts of subjective experience, centred around a first-person 'I', or third-person 'me', in a series of individual tellings that bear witness to a world in which sexual and sexist aggression is systematically carried out by men.

A Lack of Familiarity with the Medium

One of the most noteworthy differences observed between the two corpora was the level of familiarity with the communicative medium. We found this most obviously in the a priori unnecessary repetition, as in the following tweet:

> 92. Me too. (#MeToo)

where the bracketed form appears as an afterthought, and possible uncertainty about hashtags and their function. This also suggests that, as well as being the first time they have spoken up publicly about experiencing sexual aggression, for some it may be also their first experience of using the 'techno-discursive' forms of Twitter (Paveau, 2015). The following examples further illustrate a certain lack of familiarity with the medium:

> 95. It works! Thank Your friend. I thank you! #MeToo = me too.
> 230. Not to mess up this thread but should we have put #MeToo to get it to trend?
> 239. You need to add the hashtag #MeToo
> 254. #metoo (forgot the # in my response)

In tweet 95, the poster indicates their realisation that #MeToo means 'me too', while tweet 239 is a clear instruction from one poster to another. Tweet 230 asks for an explanation of how to the thread 'trending', and 254 is a repair of a prior tweet, signalling the importance of the hashtag as a techno-discursive marker in Twitter. This discursive amateurism is completely absent from the 2018 corpus; it seems that the intervening year provided a kind of initiation into the techno-discourse of Twitter, as indeed the proliferation of other hashtags in the 2018 corpus (from 13 in 2017 to 76 in 2018) suggests.

A New Discursive Arena

In the 2018 corpus, the discursive framework and participant roles have shifted and become more explicitly defined. We found 134 instances of 'you' compared to 22 in 2017 (most of which were generic) and 31 instances of 'your' compared to four in 2017. The majority are used in direct address to Alyssa Milano, thanking her, encouraging her and occasionally criticising her. The name 'Alyssa Milano' appears 37 times in all, with or without the prefix '@'. However, there are far fewer references to men (pronominal or role defined) as the discursive subject shifts from individual I/me narrators of an act of aggression, into a more generalised and systematic framing of sexual violence.

This transformation of the discursive arena can also be observed in the predominant orientation towards the future in many tweets where the actors are constructed as forming a collective, and the subjective self of 'me' of 2017 becomes 'you' and 'us' (22 instances compared to three in 2017):

> 12. I hope your daughter will never have to say #MeToo!
> 14. Can we start the conversation about #MeTooInMyChurch.
> 45. #MeToo I was 13y.o. Blamed and bullied out of Middle School due to it. Never told anyone again until I was in my 20's. I want to ♡ every one of these posts! Sadly they are too numerous to be able to, and the list keeps growing. We will be heard!

Tweet 45 combines these two discursive arenas—the first part comprising the personal narrative and the second part addressing the online collective: 'every one of these posts' with a rallying call for future action 'we will be heard'. Also noteworthy is the occurrence of 'for' (70 instances): 'for her', 'for us' 'for my little girl': here we see the subjective 'me' of the 2017 tweets again giving way to the collective 'us', the participatory framework broadens to include 'daughters' (23 instances compared to four in 2017). However, the gendered dimension of the problem remains, as there is no reference to sons. Finally, we note the 17 occurrences of 'movement' (of which 12 are classified by 'the MeToo movement'), indicating that the semantics of the phrase 'me too' is broadening in scope. In the 2018 corpus the phrase is now being used to refer to a phenomenon that has grown on a global scale, transcending the individual narration of 'Me Too' accounts of sexual violence in 2017.

In our comparison of the two corpora above we have found significant differences between the lexico-grammatical content of tweets in 2017 and those of 2017, suggesting that this difference indicates a shift in scope from the individual to the collective, and from an orientation towards past events to an orientation towards the future. We now move to a more detailed investigation of this shift, and of what is going on in the tweets in terms of discursive action and interaction in 2017 and 2018.

The Me Too Narrative

In this section we offer a qualitative analysis of the tweeting activity on the two selected dates, focusing on the tale, on how #MeToo develops as a 'second story', on aspects of teller identity as an emergent category, and on different forms of telling this story. We then compare this initial narrative activity to the discursive actions found in the second corpus from 2018, where narrative is much less prevalent, and where posters engage in other forms of discursive activity. We will show how at this point, #MeToo has shifted in its scope and is no longer functioning simply as a second story; rather, its use in the 2018 tweets tends either to be a marker of collective identity, or to denote a social movement, one that is either affiliated with, or explicitly critiqued and in some cases attacked.

#MeToo as 'Second Story'

Sacks (1995) observed that often 'stories come in clumps, and clumped stories have an apparent similarity between them' (Sacks, 1995, p. 249). A 'second story' is sequentially placed by a story recipient straight after the telling of the first one and made relevant by that placement. Tweets to *#MeToo* are actions that produce the smallest kind of second story, one which can situate the next teller in the same kind of tale as the first, that is to say, this happened to 'me too' or as Sacks describes it, 'the search for a story in which you are the character the other one was in their story' (ibid., p. 5). However, unlike conversational second stories, these are mediated narratives. They are told at a spatial and temporal distance from the first story, by multiple tellers, and to a potentially vast audience of story recipients. The 'Me Too' Twitter stream thus constitutes a public environment for the sequential emergence of a series of second stories.

Milano's opening post on 15 October 2017 is a directive: 'If you've been sexually harassed or assaulted write "me too" as a reply to this tweet.' It functions as a request for a very specific next action, directly addressed to multiple recipients: it is in effect a second story elicitation, where the first story is invoked, rather than told, by her tweet. The backdrop to the request is a 'big' story, the headline news of the moment involving Harvey Weinstein and his sexually abusive behaviour towards women he worked with, which is treated as contextually and relevantly available to the recipients, that is, her followers in the first instance. In the analysis below we focus on aspects of the tale, on how 'me too' develops as a second story, on features of teller identities and on different forms of telling this story (Blum Kulka, 1993).

The 'Tale'

As noted above, Milano's tweet invites the most minimal of second stories, 'me too'. The first reply is brief: 'Me too. #MeToo'. This opening exchange forms an adjacency pair, a directive request and a response which not only complies with the request, but also contains the most relevant further action, the addition of a hashtag, thereby making it visible, searchable, and retweetable as a topic on Twitter. At this point we can differentiate between two components of the response which accomplish two separate actions: the first 'me too' tells the second story, and the '#MeToo' creates a meta-discursive space in relation to that story. #MeToo has thus an additional pragmatic force which de-individualises/depersonalises the narrative and shifts it into a techno-discursive domain, one based neither on social identity, nor on community, but on the collective construction of a shared experience.

The opening adjacency pair is rapidly followed by a stream of second story posts, as shown here:

3. #MeToo for the majority of my life. Happens far too often. Glad to see its finally being talked about
4. Me too\n#MeToo
5. The first time I was sexually assaulted I was 3. My aunt's LT boyfriend, whom I called uncle. I remember it. #MeToo
6. Me too #MeToo
7. Me too #MeToo
8. #Metoo I have been sexually harassed many times, several times as a nurse trying to care for a male patient.

9. He was a Baptist minister. Once found out, he got 'spiritual help' we didn't go to church ever again. Me too #MeToo
10. I was first raped when I was 8 years old by my mother's boyfriend & have been harassed & assaulted several times since then #MeToo
11. #metoo Me too. It runs rampant in all industries.

These posts can be read both individually, as serial, unrelated follow-up second stories in response to the initial call in the opening post, but also sequentially, as they emerge consecutively in their real-time production. Specific elements in the posts begin to develop the Twitter feed, and each tweet provides a slightly different version of the same story in relation to the prior post and sets the context for the following one. For instance, in tweet 3 there is reference to frequency and two evaluations, first of the act itself and then of its public revelation. The next post 'me too/#MeToo' in 4 can be read as both a response to the initial tweet and an agreement with the evaluations. In 5 there is a situated narrative action in the past tense, with (in Labov's terms) orientation details and a coda 'I remember it'. In 7 there is a mention of 'many times', building on the prior mention of 'the first time', and in 9, the use of pronominal 'he' refers anaphorically to the prior given identity of the abuser as a man. In 10 there is an explicit statement which amplifies the severity of the action; 'I was raped', as well as the frequency, 'the first time' and 'several times', and orientation details, by whom, and when (I was eight years old). Tweet 11 also contains an evaluative statement with anaphoric reference to the main act in the story 'it runs rampant'.

Other features which invite a sequential reading of the tweets are that, for these first few posts, there are no replies (though some are retweeted or liked). Also, in some cases a post disrupts the seriality of second stories by doing something different, as in the following sequence which looks like a request for clarification:

15. The number of times I can fit #metoo into 140 charas, or even 280, won't come even close to the # of times I've been groped by strange men.
16. You mean like this? #MeToo

Tweet 16 is one of the rare direct questions in the 2017 corpus, and has a male username. 'You' could potentially address multiple recipients, including Milano and the poster of tweet 15, or just the prior post, depending on a serial or sequential reading. The deictic 'this' refers to eight photographs of famous women actresses also posted with the caption 'Clinton's lifelong war on women'. The pragmatic force of this tweet as criticism is only contextually recoverable in relation to another aspect of the big story, which becomes prominent as a topical focus of further critical actions the 2018 corpus which we will return to later.

As noted above, over one third of the posts in the 2017 corpus tell simply the minimal second story, the double 'me too', #MeToo. The same 'tale' is told, over and over, as well as through the more extended narrative discourse of posts which develop variations of the same story. We are thus dealing with narrative situated in two domains, the individual serial second story tellings and their collective status as shared experience via the hashtag.

Me Too #MeToo 2017 Tellers

The social identity of posters is rarely present in the tweet text, although it can accessible in the *Twitter* username handle, when a full name is used. But by and large social identity is not made relevant by posters except in certain specific cases. Only one refers to her professional status, a nurse (tweet 9), although some infer other social roles through the mention of a context: at school, at college; or at work. Also, we should bear in mind that sexual assault and harassment is not only experienced by women, and three posters do self-identify as male, thus extending #MeToo explicitly to men as well as women, as can be seen in the following extracts:

106. I'm not a woman, but me too. A widespread issue #MeToo
210. @Alyssa_Milano I'm not a woman, however, Me Too. #MeToo
215. Tain't just you girls ... #MeToo

The following tweet breaks the pattern by just using #MeToo, remaining in the techno-discursive domain rather than the narrative 'me too', and with no accessible identity:

248. #metoo. Hell, let's just see how it trends

But the majority teller identity appears to be female, particularly as we saw above, in the overwhelming use of masculine pronouns ('he', 'his', and 'him'), and male perpetrators (uncle, boyfriend, stepfather, husband) in the accounts of assaults.

Forms of Telling

As we have seen in the extracts above, while many contain the minimal second story and hashtag, 'Me too #MeToo', many others contain more developed second stories that are very close to Labovian narrative syntax in form. The following tweet begins with extensive orientation details that is continued as a complete narrative on the author's blog:

> 155. Matt and I went in to London last weekend to see a show in the West End. When the play let out we walked through Leicester Square toward the underground station to get the train home, stopping …

However, this use of a written narrative style, with standard spelling and sentence structure, is unusual as a form of telling on the site. Most response tweets are short, more conversational in their telling, and fall within the 280-character limit. However, within that limit not all take the same form. In the next two extracts, the tweet-initial '#MeToo' serves as an abstract to the tale:

> 38. #MeToo\nThe teenage neighbor when I was barely a teen. Pinned me in his garage. Told my brother to stay out, but he came when I yelled for him.
>
> 46. #metoo I found him on an online dating app so I 'was asking for it'. 'women don't use the net unless they want it.' His words to me.

Here we find details of orientation (where when who), as well as some past tense narrative clauses. The first tweet contains a resolution and the second some reported speech. In contrast, the posters in the next four extracts all refer to how difficult it is to tell the tale at all, and all place #MeToo in tweet-final position. In this position, #MeToo functions as the act of telling, it is the minimal second story and is placed at the end of the tweet:

> 19. don't know if i'll ever be ready to talk about my experiences, but #MeToo
>
> 21. Never thought I'd admit this, but … #metoo

27. Me too. When I was three years old. When I was 13. When I was 30. It has taken years to be able to say it. #MeToo
86. I sat here for almost 20 mins looking at this tweet before I typed. Amazing how 2 small words could be so hard.\n#MeToo

In tweets 19 and 21, both posters provide a meta-discursive preface to the act of telling, as 'talking about', and 'admitting'. The upcoming tale is generalised as 'my experiences' in 19, and in 21 and 27, 'this' and 'it' refer deictically to the upcoming minimal story '#MeToo'. Both 19 and 21 syntactically embed #MeToo as the tale after 'but'. Posts 27 and 86 also refer to the difficulty of telling. In 27, 'me too' and '#MeToo' frame the 'when' of the orientation, and in 86 the poster develops a meta-level story of how difficult this tale is to tell, using past tense narrative clauses 'I sat here' and 'I typed', followed by an evaluation and finally, like 27, starts a new sentence for the second story: \n#MeToo.

One final observation to make about the shape of these '#MeToo' stories concerns what is *not* there. Most narratives contain some form of evaluation which positions the teller 'I' in relation to the content of the tale, often in the form of expression of feelings/emotions. But not in these tweets. There is no emotional evaluation, no expression of feelings, or of any negative emotion (e.g. fear, shock, pain) relating to events recounted in the tales. Expressions of sadness are found, but in relation to the situation in general, not the teller in particular, as in the following:

28. Me too (countless times), and sadly, it's true for almost every woman I know. #MeToo.
221. #MeToo It's sad that ppl don't already recognize the magnitude of the problem but powerful that women are speaking up #StrongerTogether

Posters can be ironically self-deprecating, as in the following:

33. #MeToo\nWas told that the multiple assaults I've survived make me hard to date because I'm inherently untrusting now. Guess that's my bad

But mostly, the more extended second story tweets contain simple narrative clauses with no explicit negative evaluation of the perpetrator or the feelings of the victim. It is the frequency of the event that is commented on, as in 3 above: 'happens far too often', or the lack of consequences, of being ignored, or worse, as in the next two extracts:

23. Junior year of HS would ask me sex questions and try to cheat off me. Teacher refused to acknowledge cause he was on Basketball team. #MeToo
198. at 18 coming home from uni guy passed by on a bike and grabs my breasts I told my dad he said I should feel flattered I was pretty #MeToo

These response stories are dispassionate, objectivising accounts which differ greatly from the mediated narratives of shared experiences of assault and rape analysed by researchers in other media platforms, such as, for instance, those told in women's magazines like *Cosmopolitan*.[7]

Non-narrative Actions

About halfway through the 2017 corpus, posters engage in other forms of action which are not narrative. Rather than telling a second story, posters start to express thanks, or appreciation, as in the following tweets:

82. So much respect for YOU #MeToo
95. It works! Thank Your friend. I thank you! #MeToo = me too.
129. #MeToo Too many times. I stopped talking about it Bc I was told I was 'bragging' or to 'take it as a compliment'. Thank you for hearing us.
219. Me too. And it's my first time speaking out online about this. Thanks to all of you that gave strength to say #MeToo

In tweet 82, 'YOU' could potentially have multiple recipients, as in 16 above, or just one, Milano. Tweet 95 starts with a declarative 'it works!', referring to the creation of the hashtag that is now functioning as a techno-discursive domain. The poster directly addresses Milano, with the directive 'thank your friend', then 'I thank you' before finishing with #MeToo = me too. In 129 the poster thanks 'you' (Milano) for hearing 'us', at which point 'us' is starting to exist as a collective membership category, and towards the end of the corpus, in tweet 219, the poster addresses thanks to 'all of you', the collective identity is now established.

[7] Rodi-Risberg and Höglund (2018).

Posts which also break the series of me too stories are the following—rare on the first day—hostile tweets:

16. You mean like this? #MeToo
20. @Alyssa_Milano raped her contractors! #MeToo
107. @Alyssa_Milano you have known about Corey Haim for years but decided to keep quiet. Don't play the hero, it's too late. #MeToo

As noted, tweet 16 is critical of Milano's political stance. Although 20 and 107 contain past tense clauses relating to past events, their pragmatic force is not narrative. Both are accusations directly addressing Milano '@ Alyssa_Milano'. Tweet 20 addresses her followers, talking about her, as well as to her, and here the final placement of #MeToo is part of a hostile accusation, not an alignment with the other second stories. The same applies to 107 where the form '@Alyssa_Milano' is also used, but with direct address to her: 'you' and a pragmatic force that is also hostile and accusatory, with the warning 'don't play the hero' and tweet-final #MeToo. Towards the end of the day posters start to introduce the idea of a political objective and possible social change, as in the next examples:

206. Me too. And I want to change this sickness in the world so my daughter won't have to say #MeToo when she's my age.
221. #MeToo It's sad that ppl don't already recognize the magnitude of the problem but powerful that women are speaking up #StrongerTogether

To summarise, in this analysis of the 2017 corpus, two significant points emerge. Firstly, that the narrative actions, in their form and in their content, are overwhelmingly similar 'second stories'. While each tells an individual story, the serial construction of shared experience is laying the foundations for building the collective #MeToo as an emergent movement. The disruptions to this seriality are rare, but nevertheless present, and as we will see in the 2018 corpus the nature of the activity changes, as narrative gives way to other forms of discursive action.

#MeToo as a Collective

One year later the development of #MeToo as a social movement around the globe is in full swing, with its adherents and its critics. Writing in *The Guardian*, 2 October 2018, Eva Wiseman says: 'The past 12 months have seen a sea change in our approach to the way sexual abuse is covered, but in some ways it feels like the real work is only starting now.' In a similar vein, on 5 October 2018, *The Washington Post* comments: 'In the year since, the global conversation about sexual harassment – and worse – has shifted, but the lasting impact of the moment remains unclear.'

An analysis of the 2018 corpus shows clearly that the form and content of the tweets on Milano's page have changed in various ways. As noted in Sect. 3, the tweets are on average much longer, and the discursive actions are more complex. Narrative discourse has decreased and minimal #metoo stories have disappeared altogether, while other types of actions emerge within the new, contextually relevant frames of adherence to the movement or protest against it. The tweets are no longer a sequence/series of second stories; rather, posters take up positions in relation to Milano herself, many tweets contain multiple techno-discursive forms, that is, @ Alyssa_Milano, and the use of multiple hashtag sites to connote either support for, or criticism of the #MeToo movement.

To mark the one-year anniversary of #MeToo on Twitter Milano published a video entitled 'message to my daughter' that she had recorded a year earlier. Most posts to her page that day reference this video and construct a position in relation to it. Several actions can be observed in this second corpus of tweets that clearly differentiate them from those in the first corpus and we describe these below.

Firstly, use of 'you' to directly address 'Alyssa' is much more frequent. Posters thank her, congratulate her, compliment her and produce other acts of encouragement and support as illustrated in the following extracts:

1. Your daughter will grow up knowing that her Mama loves her, stands up for her, and fights for her. Hopefully her world will be a better place. #Metoo
8. Thank u for that platform u share with us. Thank you for ur bravery, resilience, & the hope u give us! We appreciate you! We care!/ #Metoo
13. You are an amazing mama! Keep up the good fight #MeToo
40. Thank you for your video. #metoo
102. I love you Alyssa! Thank you for sharing this story with us. You have one lucky daughter to have such an amazing mommy like you! #MeTooOneYearLater #MeToo

Contrasting with the generic 'you' found in 2017, here 'you' refers to Milano, and the use of inclusive 'us' refers to the collective membership of #MeToo. Secondly, the placement and discursive function of the hashtag #MeToo have both shifted. In 2018, there are only seven tweets that start with #MeToo compared to 97 in 2017. In the 2018 corpus it frequently occurs at the end of the tweet, and as such, functions predominantly as an affiliative sign off, rather than a second story. This affiliative action can be observed in all the extracts above.

Thirdly, in 2018 #MeToo becomes nominalised. It is often placed in the grammatical subject position of agency, as well as in the complement position of affected entity, and in these positions it refers to a concept, the #MeToo movement. It is therefore no longer telling a second story. Examples of this change of functional status can be seen in the following tweets, where Milano's political affiliation is attacked:

26. you need to tell her the truth that #metoo stands for liberal women, not all women ... just ask #MonicaLewinsky #metoo hates men, hates our @POTUS #metoo are haters, and i'm sure it didn't start out that way, but you made it that way ... that is what her mother, you Alyssia did!
62. Sorry this happened to you, or anyone else. But you people, by using Ford, have damaged the #metoo movement. It will now be harder for real victims to be believed.
97. The main issue @Alyssa_Milano has being recognized as a #Metoo champion is that she refuses to denounce Bill Clinton or acknowledge accusations against Ellison. #metoo should be larger than political affiliation and her hypocrisy harms the movement more than she helps it.
132. Congratulations on how you turned #metoo into a brand to further advance your acting career and relevance

In tweets 26 and 97 the hashtag occurs in subject position, while in 62 and 97 it functions as a nominal classifier in the phrases, 'the #metoo movement', 'a #Metoo champion'. In 132 it is the affected entity 'you turned #metoo into a brand'. These tweets contain directives: 'you need to tell her the truth', and accusations: 'you make it that way', 'congratulations on how you turned #metoo into a brand'. Milano is addressed directly by 'you', or as talked about, 'she/her' and in 97, '@Alyssa_Milano'. Nominalisation is also found in the next examples where 'a #metoo' is used to indicate affiliative membership identity:

174. @Alyssa_Milano I am a #MeToo over 30 years ago. I feel it is SO important to have proof, evidence before anyone is accused. I want to protect the men I love from false accusations. Christine had no memory, no proof, no witnesses. Who, what, where & when is very important.

212. My 5 year old daughter became a #metoo member on the school bus last week. No words for how it feels to be parents going through this right now.

The transformation of #MeToo from personal narrative to social movement is clearly observable in all these examples, in the context of a very different set of discursive actions. Posters take up positions as either critical of Milano, or supportive of her. The movement is topicalised, polemicised, blamed and praised, and other stories are made contextually relevant (particularly the Blasey Ford testimony in September 2018, where Alyssa Milano and Tarana Burke appeared together in the Kavanaugh hearing before his appointment as Supreme Court judge). Posters regularly and competently use the full range of Twitter's techno-discursive forms, as in these two final examples:

91. And yet still you do NOTHING to protest Bill Clinton Keith Ellison or others because they are democrats! is that what you want to teach your daughter? its ok to assault women only if they agree with your political beliefs? #MeTooLiars #Hypocrites #metoo

119. While you are taking credit, are you going to take responsibility for all the lives that have been wrecked with #FalseAllegations? #MeToo is yelling 'Fire!' in a crowded theater, inviting disturbed people to belong to something. #IWasFalselyAccused #DontCryWolf

The pragmatic force of #MeToo has changed, and alongside that change other hashtags develop which express support for, or make polemical points against, the #MeToo movement, rather than contributing to its construction *as* a movement.

Concluding Remarks

In this micro-analysis of a tiny corpus of tweets, given the global context of a social network like Twitter, we have attempted to provide an in-depth account of posting activity at two very specific moments for the hashtag

#MeToo. In applying theoretical concepts from CA and from narrative analysis to our data, we examined the emergence of 'me too' accounts in 2017 as 'second stories', a posting activity that consisted of sharing a shared experience online. In the 2018 corpus, we observed significant changes in posters' discursive activity, and a transformation of individual narratives into a collective story, the movement 'Me Too', which enables posters to take up a position in relation to that movement. Narration thus gives way to other discursive actions which not only respond to a changing social context, but also construct and shape that context.

We also want to draw attention to the specific characteristics of Twitter as a communicative network compared to other media sites where women talk about their experiences of sexual violence. In their study of the online version of *Cosmopolitan UK*, Rodi-Risberg and Höglund (2018) note the preference of women's magazine editors for emotional stories where individuals overcome their problems to those that focus on underlying complex social and political dynamics, because happy endings sell more. They argue that 'polarizing perpetrator and victim and isolating trauma from its sociopolitical context through a Manichean discourse may be emotionally appealing but does not allow for needed cultural and structural changes' (2018, p. 118). As we showed in Sect. 3, 'me too' narratives on the #MeToo site do exactly the opposite. Twitter thus provides up a public space which offers the possibility of changing social structures through the creation of a dynamic political movement.

References

Androutsopoulos, J. (2006). Introduction: Sociolinguistics and Computer-Mediated Communication. *Journal of Sociolinguistics, 10*(4), 419–438.

Bell, A. (1994). Telling Stories. In *Media Texts: Authors and Readers* (pp. 100–118). Graddol, Boyd-Barrett. Multilingual Matters.

Blum Kulka, S. (1993). You Gotta Know How to Tell a Story: Tellings, Tales and Tellers in American and Israeli Narrative Events at Dinner. *Language in Society, 22*, 361–402.

Dayter, D. (2015). Small Stories and Extended Narratives on Twitter. *Discourse, Context & Media, 10*, 19–26.

De Fina, A. (2016). Storytelling and Audience Reactions in Social Media. *Language in Society, 45*, 473–498.

Georgakopoulou, A. (2017). Small Stories Research: A Narrative Paradigm for the Analysis of Social Media. In A. Quan Haase & L. Sloan (Eds.), *The Sage Handbook of Social Media Research Methods* (pp. 266–281). Sage.

Giles, D., Stommel, W., Paulus, T., Lester, J., & Reed, D. (2015). Microanalysis of Online Data: The Methodological Development of "Digital CA". *Discourse, Context & Media, 7*, 45–51.

Goodwin, M. H. (1990). *He-Said-She-Said: Talk as Social Organization Among Black Children*. Indiana University Press.

Halliday, M. A. K. (1994). *An Introduction to Functional Grammar* (2nd ed.). Edward Arnold.

Johnstone, B., & De Fina, A. (2015). Discourse analysis and narrative. In D. Tannen, H. Hamilton, & D. Scheffrin (Eds.), *The Handbook of Discourse Analysis* (Vol. 1, pp. 152–167). Wiley Online Library.

Labov, W. (1972). The Transformation of Experience in Narrative Syntax. In *Language in the Inner City: Studies in the Black English Vernacular* (pp. 354–396). University of Pennsylvania Press.

Marwick, A., & boyd, d. (2011). To See and Be Seen: Celebrity Practice on Twitter. *Convergence, 17*(2), 139–158.

Marriott, S. (2007). *Live Television: Time, Space and the Broadcast Event*. Sage.

Montgomery, M. (2007). *The Discourse of Broadcast News*. Routledge.

Page, R. (2012). *Stories and Social Media: Identities and Interaction*. Routledge.

Patron, S. (Ed.). (2020). *Small Stories: Un nouveau paradigme pour les recherches sur le récit*. Paris: Hermann Editeurs.

Paveau, M. (2015). *Dictionnaire d'analyse du discours numérique, Technologies discursives*. http://technodiscours.hypothèses.org/?p=431

Rodi-Risberg, M., & Höglund, M. (2018). From Victims to Survivors: The Discourse of Trauma in Self-Narratives of Sexual Violence in *Cosmopolitan* UK Online. *Discourse, Context & Media, 25*, 114–121.

Sacks, H. (1995). In G. Jefferson (Ed.), *Lectures on Conversation* (Vol. 2). Blackwell.

Saki, M. (2017). #Notinmyname, Twitter, Aambient Affiliation and Heteropic Public Space of Appearance. In M. Burger, J. Thornborrow, & F. Fitzgerald (Eds.), *Discours des réseaux sociaux: enjeux publics, politiques et médiatiques* (pp. 163–178). Deboeck.

Scannell, P. (Ed.). (1991). *Broadcast Talk*. Sage.

Thornborrow, J. (2015). *The Discourse of Public Participation Media: From Talk Show to Twitter*. Routledge.

Thornborrow, J. (2017). The Interactional Spaces of Social Media: Ethics, Methods and Research Practice. In M. Burger, J. Thornborrow, & F. Fitzgerald (Eds.), *Discours des réseaux sociaux: enjeux publics, politiques et médiatiques* (pp. 43–62). Louvain-la-Neuve, BE.

CHAPTER 9

Gender-Based Violence in Higher Education: A Case Study of an Institution in England

Donna Chambers and Angela Smith

It is evident that there are strong interconnections between all 17 United Nations Sustainable Development Goals (SDGs). However, what is also apparent is that gender equality, expressed in UN SDG5, lies at the heart of all the SDGs. In this chapter, we will specifically explore SDG16, which seeks to promote peaceful and inclusive societies for sustainable development; provide access to justice for all; and build effective, accountable, and inclusive institutions at all levels. We will address its overlap with SDG8 which seeks, amongst other things, to promote full and productive employment and decent work for all. The employment of women and their fair and equitable treatment within the workplace are important to the achievement of these two interlocking SDGs. However, organisations are gendered (Acker, 1992) in so far as they have a substructure that

D. Chambers (✉)
Northumbria University, Newcastle, UK
e-mail: donna.chambers@northumbria.ac.uk

A. Smith
Faculty of Arts and Creative Industries, University of Sunderland, Sunderland, UK
e-mail: angela.smith@sunderland.ac.uk

D. Dalton, A. Smith (eds.), *Gender, Sexuality and the UN's SDGs*, Sustainable Development Goals Series,
https://doi.org/10.1007/978-3-031-31046-1_9

promotes inequality for women. Kelly (1987) further suggested that most women have experienced gender-based violence (GBV) in their lifetimes, including in the workplace. That said, victims of GBV can have different gender identifications, although Watts and Zimmerman (2002) found that most victim-survivors of GBV are women and girls, with most perpetrators being men. Mahlori et al. (2018) describe GBV as a 'silent scourge' that affects mostly women 'who are frequently marginalized and made invisible through their inability to speak out about their experiences' (Mahlori et al., 2018, p. 12). Consequently, it would be true to say that GBV is an issue that is of serious concern in our societies and in our institutions. We seek in this chapter to explore GBV within a specific institutional context: higher education (HE).

According to Humphreys and Towl (2023) the first study on sexual violence towards women by men at universities was published in 1957. Since then, there has been a well-established body of literature on GBV in HE (Anitha & Lewis, 2018; Dziech & Hawkins, 2012; Forbes-Mewett & McCulloch, 2016; Marine & Lewis, 2020). However, many of the studies on GBV in higher education have focused on students and have elided university staff as victims-survivors of GBV. There are a few exceptions: for example, Kirkner et al. (2022) conducted a study on the reporting and disclosure of sexual harassment amongst a sample of academic staff in US universities, Mahlori et al. (2018) examined GBV amongst a tiny sample of staff in a university in South Africa, while Finniear et al. (2020), in a conceptual paper, examined GBV specifically in tourism academia. In the UK context, Anitha and Lewis (2018) claim that GBV in student communities has only been the focus of academic research since the mid-2000s. In 2010 the National Union of Students (NUS) published what was then seen as a ground-breaking study on the experiences of GBV of women students in HE institutions in the UK (NUS, 2010) and in 2014–2016 the first Bystander Programmes[1] were piloted in the UK (Anitha & Lewis, 2018). For the first time in 2016 Universities UK (UUK) focused on violence against women, specifically sexual harassment and misconduct. In 2018, UUK's focus shifted to GBV in universities (see Humphreys & Towl, 2023). It was clear from these studies that GBV was taking place in UK universities and involved both students *and* staff. Yet,

[1] Bystander Programmes refer to training delivered on how to safely intervene in instances where sexual violence, relationship violence or stalking may be occurring or where there may be risk that it will occur—Bringing in the Bystander® | Culture of Respect.

in the UK there has been a dearth of studies that explore GBV amongst staff in HE and this has been described by Anitha and Lewis (2018) as a 'missed opportunity'. This chapter is an attempt to address this lacuna. Specifically, we present empirical research conducted to investigate GBV amongst staff (academic and professional services) in HE using a case study of a university in England.

Our study is twofold: first, the barriers to promotion and career advancement will be viewed through a gendered lens. The consequent paucity of positive role models for women in Higher Education can be partly explained by these barriers, thus perpetuating the notion that HE is a male-appropriate career, not 'decent work' for females. The second element of our argument is that there has been an under-reporting of cases of GBV in HE, and some of the reasons for this will be discussed, such as the lack of confidence in a reporting mechanism within institutions which are perceived as 'silencing'.

In our discussion, we draw on Gelfand et al.'s (1995) categorisation of GBV, where they define three overlapping but distinct parts:

a. Sexual coercion, where sexual favours are demanded to ensure promotion or employment;
b. Unwanted sexual attention, such as sexual objectification, touching, and comments;
c. Gender harassment, which involves degrading someone because of their gender.

The latter two subcategories include electronic communication and social media. We will begin with a discussion of Fourth Wave Feminism which was, arguably, motivated by GBV in education.

Fourth Wave Feminism in the UK

Any discussion of gender-based violence will involve reference to the MeToo movement, which places rape and sexual assault at the centre of discussions about GBV. However, the MeToo movement did not emerge out of nowhere in 2017. To understand where it came from, as a culmination of what became Fourth Wave feminism, we need to look briefly at the post-feminist context.

The multi-faceted term 'post-feminism' emerged in the mid-1990s and, in the UK, became associated with girl power and the Spice Girls in particular. Coinciding with the rise of 'new lad' culture, the prototypical post-feminist ladette drove an agenda that saw the 'freedom, choice, empowerment' mantra that unites post-feminism embrace the sexualisation of women and girls as being 'empowering'. Unlike the empowered Second Wave feminists, post-feminist culture espoused female equality and rights but with a feminine slant. The equality that the ladettes embraced was lager-drinking, loud, football-loving, and pink. The freedoms that had been so hard won by a previous generation were taken for granted by the young women of the 1990s, but post-feminist culture associated with girl power mirrored the darker side of Second Wave feminism that led to some young women who had been given control over their fertility (through the prescription of the contraceptive pill in the late 1960s) being made to feel they must engage in casual sexual activity. This is something the first editors of pioneering Second Wave feminist magazine *Spare Rib*, Rosie Boycott and Marsha Rowe, both write about in their autobiographies: the feeling of being obliged to engage in sexual activity that was 'risk free' (Smith, 2017). Twenty years later, young women were again being made to feel that they were empowered through casual sexual activity, whether this be the rise in popularity of pole dancing as a fitness routine or the normalisation of pornography through the incredible popularity of lads' mags of this decade.

Feminist academics sought to problematise such 'empowerment'. For example, Imelda Whelehan's *Overloaded: Popular Culture and the Future of Feminism* (Whelehan, 2000) argued that far from empowering young women, the ladette culture that was such a dominant thread of post-feminism was actually a form of retrosexism where media images of men in crisis and neurotic, sexually liberated single women abound. Any attempt to criticise such behaviour or representations, she argued, was greeted with a rebuttal that would likely include taunts of being 'politically correct' and a 'frigid old feminist'. This is also lamented by Natasha Walter in *Living Dolls* (Walter, 2010), where her interviews with young women in the UK reinforce her argument that, whilst the opportunities available for women have expanded as a result of Second Wave feminism, the ambitions of many young post-feminist women are actually limited by a culture that sees women's sexual allure as their only entry to success.

Whilst feminism is never static, the different strands of post-feminism eventually brought to the fore the strand that rejected ladette culture and prioritised a re-traditionalisation of gender where women would 'choose' to be highly educated and work in any occupation of their choosing, but then leave all this to be domesticated and housewiferly, supported not by their own employment but by a wage-earning partner. The rediscovery of the cult of the perfect housewife that emerged in the 1950s returned in the early part of the twenty-first century in a slew of TV programmes about cooking, home-making, and expert childcare. That is not to say that the ladette vanished: she just moved into the subcultural arena where all the cool girls lurked. The 'cool girls' who were sexually free and chose to be that way. All are caught up in what McRobbie (2009) refers to as the 'new sexual contract' which she glosses as allowing the young, post-feminist woman:

> To work, to gain qualifications, to control fertility and to earn enough money to participate in the consumer culture which [is] a defining feature of contemporary modes of feminine citizenship. (McRobbie, 2009, p. 54)

It is often argued, by McRobbie, Whelehan, Gill, and Walter (amongst many), that post-feminism saw gender equality as being achieved; it was common sense to believe that there were no more battles. As Lewis (2006) argues, this perceived progressiveness came to resemble a form of 'gender blindness', by which she refers to how women no longer see themselves as gendered actors and gender inequality is relocated as a problem of the past. As terms such as 'feminism' and 'sexism' were consigned to the domain of 'political correctness', this post-feminist gender blindness lacked a feminist vocabulary to enable the articulation of continuing inequalities as being structural rather than individual. This led to the perception of gender inequality across professions and hierarchies as being 'natural'. Banet-Weiser (2018) points to the belief that this is because of women's innate lack of ambition or confidence, whilst Lewis and Simpson (2017) suggest it also is used to explain women's supposed preferences for domesticity. Thus, there is an inequality born of innate biological difference rather than social factors.

The myths of equality, empowerment, and choice could be seen to unravel post-2008's financial crash, where the myth of equal employment was destroyed as women were the most affected by the downturn in the economy. This feel-bad post-feminism (see McDermott, 2022) came to dominate discourses about feminism, for example, in dramas such as *Hunger Games* (Suzanne Collins, 2008–10), as well as TV comedies such as *Fleabag* (BBC, 2016, 2019) and *Motherland* (BBC, 2016–2021). But at the same time, we started to see a rise in anger amongst women who were not satisfied with being discriminated against, no matter how compliant they had appeared in the preceding two decades.

The Rise of Feminist Activism and the Links with MeToo

The activism that we now know as 'Fourth Wave Feminism' can be traced back to the start of the second decade of the twenty-first century. As post-feminism's critics largely comprised the feminist academics, the activism started with young women who were largely outside of this theoretical abstraction. In her discussion of advertising, Judith Williamson (2003) observed that 'the problem is that sexism didn't go away; we just stopped talking about it'. In feminist academia, this was largely accepted as being true, but there is little evidence of anything being done about it. Whilst 'feminism' had become an unfashionable word, associated with the perceived kill-joys of disapproving feminists such as Whelehan and Waters, as Williamson comments, the term 'sexism' had also been rejected. No-one wanted to use this term for fear of being mocked as being 'frigid', or even worse, 'humourless'. One of the main triggers for the rise in Fourth Wave activism seems to be the arrival of social media around 2009. Social media gave women the public platform to present their arguments and, more importantly, to start to be heard.

The concept of 'rape culture' emerged in the early 1970s as part of the Second Wave Feminists' activism. In the UK, this manifested itself in women's marches in response to the media reporting of, and police investigating of, the so-called Yorkshire Ripper. This was a serial killer who stalked and murdered women in and around Leeds in Yorkshire from 1975, before finally being caught in 1981 and revealed to be lorry driver Peter Sutcliffe. Throughout his reign of terror, women were repeatedly told not to go out alone in the dark, and not to venture into certain areas of town. In other words, there was a policing of women that did not apply to men. The concept 'rape culture', in Second Wave feminist terms, is one that places the onus on society to change and thus challenges the idea that it is the victim's fault (she was walking on her own at night; she was drunk), and slut-shaming (she was wearing revealing clothing). The latter can be linked to the normalisation of pornography, partly as a result of post-feminism's acquiescence to sexualisation as a form of female empowerment.

Rape culture promotes social attitudes that normalise, trivialise, or joke about rape and sexual violence. It often shifts the responsibility of preventing rape onto women, rather than those most likely to perpetrate it: men. That shift in responsibility is structured in a myriad of ways. For example,

Attenborough (2014) has observed that it is found in telling women not to dress a certain way because they are 'asking for it', or that they are enticing men. More messages that are embedded in our cultural narratives include other female-centred directives: Do not drink too much. Do not wear revealing clothing. Do not walk the streets alone in the dark, or just don't walk alone, at any time. By ignoring these directives, the inference is that women are giving consent, if not encouraging, the assault. The result is that rather than protecting women, the predator is empowered. In such a way, gender-based violence becomes normalised, or at least is in some part the fault of the victim.

Early manifestations of Fourth Wave activism focused on gender-based violence. These include the 'SlutWalks' that began in 2011 in Toronto, Canada (although this strategy itself had emerged in the course of Second and Third Wave feminist activism previously). This was triggered by a 'safety on campus' talk given by Toronto Police in which Constable Michael Sanguinetti made the off-script remark that 'women should avoid dressing like sluts in order not to be victimized' (Pilkington, 2011). There were just ten women present at this talk, but they mobilised social media—Facebook, initially—and within three months had generated thousands of people across Canada and the US who were willing to take to the streets and march in protest at violence against women and women being blamed as victims because of their clothing. The SlutWalks became global, with major cities around the world holding their own versions. This form of grass-roots activism is primarily driven by young females but welcomes the participation of males.

Other forms of grass-roots activism started around the same time. In the UK, a young female office worker, Laura Bates, set up the Everyday Sexism Project as a blog in 2011. She had experienced 'casual sexism' on a day-to-day basis working in London, and when mentioning this to her co-workers, she found that they too had experienced the same things but hadn't thought to speak up. Bates's blog set out to challenge this normalisation of sexism by collecting stories of day-to-day sexism. The blog quickly spread to a dedicated Twitter account, which in turn became known for its hashtag activism. One Everyday Sexism Twitter campaign, for example, centred around the realisation that Facebook's rules at the time didn't ban pro-violence against women groups. The lack of engagement by Facebook in the calls to change their policy to include groups that promoted gender-based violence led to a hashtag campaign to 'call out' advertisers whose products appeared on the same pages as these groups using #FBrape. These advertisers included major international brands, who quickly threatened to withdraw their account from Facebook. Within a few weeks, Facebook had changed its policies to include prohibiting GBV sites, and Everyday Sexism won *Marketing Week's* Campaign of the Year award in 2013 (Vizard, 2013).

With great wit and humour, these grass-roots campaigns were demonstrating a form of feminism that was a version of feminism that Gill (2016, p. 618) claims is 'implicitly positioned against the figure of the "feminist killjoy"'. By this time, the very term 'feminist' was being reclaimed. For example, Beyoncé's MTV 2014 Awards appearance saw her silhouetted against the illuminated stage set that featured the word 'Feminist'. Mainstream fashion outlets were selling t-shirts emblazoned with slogans such as 'This is what a feminist looks like', t-shirts that were spotted on male politicians and high profile male actors. This rediscovery of the word is part of what Sarah Banet-Weiser calls 'commodity feminism' (2018), and links with McRobbie's (2009) concept of the new sexual contract.

This 'perfect storm' of activism brings us to the MeToo movement, and its drawing together of means of activism (social media) and a new-found readiness to listen to voices raised about GBV. The silencing of female voices in relation to sexual assault in the film industry cannot be underestimated. In fact, it could be said that the expectation of sexual assault by powerful men in the film industry was part of becoming a female actor: after all, the term 'casting couch' fell into common usage in Anglophone countries to mean just that, neatly glossing over the unwanted sexual advances of men in the film industry. As late as July 2017, Hollywood actor Rose McGowan was being silenced in her attempts to expose sexism in the film industry (Smith, 2018). She had used her own social media account to reveal details of a casting note that had required her to dress in a sexually provocative way. The mainstream media's response to this was to report her complaint as being invalid as she had worn 'attention-grabbing' red-carpet outfits. As is typical of mainstream print media, her appearance was being commented on and used as a form of victim-blaming that is not too far from the warning issued by Sanguinetti to the Toronto students in 2011. We can also see similar examples of women being silenced or at least muted when speaking about feminist issues across the media (see Smith, 2018).

The MeToo movement has its origins in 2006 when Tarana Burke wrote a blog posting to describe the sexism and racism she had experienced, intending this for the benefit of her daughter who was experiencing similar problems. She signed off this blog with 'me too' as a statement of solidarity. To see MeToo take off as a movement, we must go to 2017.

On 15 October 2017, Hollywood actor Alyssa Milano documented her experiences of sexual assault in the film industry, and expressed solidarity with other women who had previously made such reports, including Rose McGowan. At the end of her Facebook post, she used the hashtag, #MeToo. Within 24 hours, the hashtag had appeared on Twitter more than half a million times and was used in more than 12 million Facebook posts. There has been much criticism of the MeToo movement, with academics such as Alison Phipps (2020) pointing to the inherent whiteness and heterosexuality of the movement as it appears in social media. However, what it has done is facilitate a conversation where the voices of those affected by gender-based violence are being heard. Importantly, the phrase 'me too' has also been documented in the UK in campaign materials produced by feminist groups protesting against gender-based violence.

The UK Context

Inspired by the uses of social media seen in global activism against gender-based violence, another grass-roots campaign in the UK was started by Soma Sara in 2020. Soma had watched Michaela Coel's comedy-drama *I May Destroy You* (BBC/HBO 2020), which was written by Coel to document her own experience of rape and situated in the context of 'rape culture'. At the time, Soma was Instagramming of her own experiences of rape culture in education (she was 22 at the time, but documented the misogyny and sexual assaults that had been part of her life at school from the age of 10 or 11). As with #MeToo, she invited others to contribute their stories. Within a week, she had more than 300 anonymous responses detailing serious sexual abuse and sexual assault. This led to her setting up a web site to allow anonymous contributions from a wider area: this was called Everyone's Invited. Contributions were encouraged from victims of rape culture, sexual harassment, slut-shaming, of coercion into sharing nude photos on social media (Topping, 2021). Within a year, more than 16,000 stories had been collected, and by July 2022 this had risen to 50,045. Whilst the voices of #MeToo were most clearly from people who were no longer in the education system, or at least older than school-age, what came as a huge shock to many people in the UK was the extent of gender-based violence reported from primary school upwards. The web site carried anonymous stories from victims, but did record the names of the schools. The schools included the most prestigious in the UK: Wellington College; Latymer Upper School; it also included single-sex schools: Harrow, Eton, St Paul's. In 2021, the Everyone's Invited site opened to include universities and it was the same pattern: no institution was exempt, no matter what its reputation or fee-paying rate.

Given the age and legal status of most of the victims, the issue of rape culture in schools became a topic of political concern. The UK's government overseer of schools, OfSted, carried out an investigation into gender-based violence in schools, and in June 2021 published a report (Gov.uk, 2021) that revealed sexual harassment had been normalised in school-aged children, with children as young as nine or ten being sent explicit photos or videos via social media. Nearly 90% of girls and nearly 50% of boys had been sent unsolicited or unwanted sexually explicit images. About 80% of girls reported having been pressured into sharing sexualised images of themselves, and 60% said they had endured unwanted touching 'sometimes' or 'a lot'. The teachers, on the other hand, had little idea what to do in such cases, and had little or no guidance from the government.

Sexual misconduct cases are particularly found in Higher Education, as mentioned earlier. The rape culture that was exposed at school level by the Everyone's Invited site feeds into the long-standing reputation for sexual freedom that 18-year-olds are stereotypically expected to feel on leaving home and arriving at university, most of them living away from their parents for the first time. It was only in 2021 that this became an issue of public concern when university students started posting their stories on Everyone's Invited. This brought to wider attention research by the 1752 Group[2] which had been set up in 2015 as a national organisation to address sexual misconduct of academic and professional staff in UK universities (see, e.g., Bull & Page, 2021). However, gender-based violence is not only staff/student based: it is also found between staff but as mentioned in the introduction to this chapter this has scarcely been investigated. Our study therefore explores GBV in the context of a case study of a higher education institution in England.

[2] The name of this group comes from the derisory amount of money (£1752) offered to academics by their institution to set up a network event to research sexual misconduct in HE.

Methods

The University of Sunderland provides the case study context for this empirical investigation. The university is a long-standing holder of the national gender equality mark, the Athena Swan charter which it signed up to in 2006 making it one of the first universities to do so. At the time of the university's last renewal of this charter in 2019, academic staffing showed an above-sector average proportion of females (48% compared with the benchmark of 41%). At the highest academic level, that of professor, the institution again boasted of a higher number than the sector average at that point: 54% compared with 26%. In terms of professional and support staff, this again showed an above-average proportion of females: 65.2% compared with sector average of 62.6%. While the university has a higher-than-average number of female professors, this masks the lower proportion of senior managers who are female (e.g. in 2019 when our survey was conducted, 73% of Heads of Department were male).

Data was collected from all staff (academic and professional services) employed at the two campuses of the university (in Sunderland and in London) using an online survey. The survey was designed in Qualtrics (an online survey tool) and a link to access the survey was circulated to all staff through internal university communication channels. The survey had a total of 38 questions divided into four sections: about you as a professional (including faculty affiliation, job role, years employed); about work experiences of GBV; experiences of GBV at conferences; about you as an individual (demographic questions). The questions were close ended with four of the questions providing several statements with participants asked to indicate their level of agreement or disagreement with each statement using a six-point Likert scale (strongly agree, agree, neither agree nor disagree, disagree, strongly disagree, don't know). For example, Question 21 asked: 'Thinking about your academic/professional career so far, please indicate whether you agree or disagree with the following statements.' Here ten statements were provided, including 'senior managers take sexual harassment seriously' and 'sexual harassment is a large-scale problem in the academic workplace'. Other questions provided participants with several statements for them to choose from, allowing multiple options to be selected but with freedom to write in their own responses. For example, Question 13 asked participants: 'Have you personally experienced any of these behaviours in the workplace? (tick all that apply)?' Options here included 'persistent and unwanted invitations of a sexual nature' and 'talking about or spreading rumours about your sex life or attractiveness to others'. For this question an 'other' category was provided for participants to write in any other experiences not listed.

Prior to distribution the survey was piloted with five members of academic staff and post-graduate research students at the institution and based on feedback some of the questions were clarified in terms of the language used. Information on the purpose of the survey, and confidentiality and anonymity assurances were provided at the beginning of the survey. In addition, a definition of GBV was provided for participants to ensure they were familiar with how this concept was being interpreted in the survey. Participants needed to consent to completing the survey before accessing the questions and were free to end the survey at any point during completion without penalty. The survey received approval from the university's ethics committee and was distributed to all staff during the summer period of 2021.

We opted to use an online survey method for data gathering as its advantages include convenience, wider reach (the total number of staff at both campuses of the university at the time of the research was approximately 1922 according to the data from the university's Equality, Diversity, Inclusion and Social Responsibility (EDISR) 2020–21 Annual Report), cost effectiveness and the ability to collaborate in data analysis. Like other surveys, online surveys also have disadvantages (see Nayak & Narayan, 2019). One of the disadvantages is response rate which can be extremely low: this study was no exception with only 156 responses received which is approximately 8% of the total staff population. Another disadvantage is that sometimes participants choose not to answer some questions which happened with our survey, and this explains the varying totals in the analysis in the next section.

The data was exported to SPSS for analysis. Descriptive statistics and correlational analyses were performed, the latter to ascertain whether there were any associations between demographic variables (specifically gender), staff roles (professional or academic staff) and participants' experiences of GBV.

Data and Analysis

The participants were largely female (77%), heterosexual (82%), between 35 and 54 years old (65%), white (89%), not disabled (84%), and married (53%). In terms of organisational role more academic staff responded

(56%) compared to those in professional services roles (44%)—see Table 9.1.

In the survey we asked participants what the barriers were to their career progression and here 17 statements were provided with participants responding to each on a five-point Likert scale ranging from 'not at all' to 'a great deal' with a fifth option for 'Don't know/not applicable'. A total of 133 responses were received for this question and Table 9.2 illustrates the answers only for those who responded 'a fair amount' or a 'great deal' to each of the 17 statements.

Table 9.1 Profile of participants

Gender	Female—77%
	Male—21%
	Prefer not to say—2%
Organisational role	Academic staff—56%
	Professional services staff—44%
Sexual orientation	Heterosexual—82%
	Homosexual—6%
	Bisexual—5%
	Self-describe—3%
	Prefer not to say—4%
Age	18–24—2%
	25–34—18%
	35–44—28%
	45–54—37%
	55–64—14%
	65 and over—1%
Ethnicity	White—89%
	Black/Mixed—6%
	Asian—2%
	Prefer not to say—3%
Disability	Disabled—13%
	Not disabled—84%
	Prefer not to say—3%
Relationship Status	Married—53%
	Never married or in civil partnership—24%
	Civil partnership—3%
	Divorced—11%
	Separated—3%
	Widowed—1%
	Prefer not to say—5%

Table 9.2 Barriers to career progression

Barrier	*Fair amount/A great deal*
Perceptions and attitudes of senior academic colleagues	41%
Bullying	21%
Sexual harassment	3%
Sexual discrimination	14%
LGBTQI+ discrimination	3%
Race and/or ethnic discrimination	9%
Religious discrimination	3%
Disability discrimination	5%
Lack of role models or mentors	41%
Long hours working culture	42%
Lack of opportunities for professional development	48%
Lack of quality affordable childcare	15%
Partner's career	14%
Periods of less than full-time working	22%
Taking a career break	8%
Inability to easily relocate	20%
Change in academic specialism	17%

GBV can be physical, psychological, emotional, or a mixture of all three. What we found in our survey was that the main barriers to career progression were not obviously linked to GBV but to organisational culture namely, the perceptions and attitudes of senior academic colleagues, lack of role models or mentors, the long working hours, and the lack of opportunities for professional development. Qualitative responses to this question also supported this finding. However, it is important to note that some participants felt that bullying (21%) and sexual discrimination (14%) were barriers to career progression and while these percentages are not high in a relative sense, they are nevertheless very worrying. When cross-tabulations were done between these experiences and gender, and also in terms of academic versus professional services staff, the results were not significant.

Four participants mentioned the gendered nature of the institution (Acker, 1992), alluding to discrimination and sexism which they felt acted as barriers to their career progression (Table 9.3):

As we will see later in this chapter, such behaviour is rarely called out, challenged, or rectified and is thus another hidden barrier to progression.

Table 9.3 Gendered nature of the institution: selected comments

C.1	Difference in male/female CV characteristics
C.2	Also, as a female I am often tasked with pastoral support in ways which male colleagues are not (personal tutoring and other kinds of 'care' for both students and colleagues) which takes up a lot of time and does not further my career in ways that writing/research would. I don't see male colleagues being allocated PAT roles or being expected to offer an informal, listening ear to students/staff as much as female staff …
C.3	What is still a male-dominated culture
C.4	Sexism and invisibility

As indicated by one participant, this is sometimes manifest in the 'invisible' work that women do both inside and out with the institution, such as caring responsibilities and the expectation that female staff can 'mother' students as another participant indicated in the quotation in Table 9.3. This is cited as being a reason for lack of progress through an associated inability to devote time to research (and thus implicitly highlights the expectation that academics carry out research outside of work time). This has a more wide-reaching consequence in that fewer women rise to senior positions, and thus being seen as role models. This difficulty of achieving a work/life/study balance was reinforced by some participants (Table 9.4).

Our chapter focuses on GBV, so we will explore this in more detail to see how it finally links to the perception of there being no place for women in senior management.

To begin with, our survey showed a picture of perceptions of sexual harassment in HE in both the academic field and that of the professional services. Sexual harassment in higher education was a specific question in the survey. The question 'Do you think sexual harassment is a problem in higher education?' resulted in 130 responses, of which 35% (46) answered 'yes', and 49% (64) 'not sure'. This shows a wider culture of sexual harassment being acknowledged by a sizeable number of our respondents. So, what is this culture? Participants were asked to state whether they had personally experienced/witnessed/or knew of someone who had experienced unwanted sexual attention, harassment, and coercion in the workplace. Out of the 147 responses to this question just under 50% (49%) said they had not. However, 25% said they had personally experienced this in the last five years or more than five years ago, while 24% said they had witnessed/knew someone who had experienced it. Taken together this means that almost 50% had some personal experience/witnessing of

Table 9.4 Work/life/study balance: selected comments

C.5	Managing work/life/study balance being single parent
C.6	Maximum workload in face-to-face teaching and administration doesn't leave enough time for research
C.7	No time for self-study, RSA hours only allocated for cover (when you are working, not studying!)
C.8	lack of flexibility/ accommodating for being a full-time working parent—almost impossible to juggle both with a lengthy commute
C.9	Not enough time for research, I am struggling to complete my PhD at the moment due to my excessive teaching workload

sexual harassment in the workplace. Cross-tabulations between academic and professional services staff revealed no significant differences.

The question relating to personal experience of sexual harassment in the workplace was answered by 35 academic staff members and 20 professional services staff members. The most common experiences for academic staff were:

Non-verbal sexual harassment—26% (9)
Verbal remarks of a sexual nature—23% (8)
Unwanted touching—20% (7)

For professional services staff, this was:

Unwanted touching—35% (7)
Verbal remarks—25% (5)

These findings show a clear and present problem within HE and this is something we explore in more depth in the following question, which listed ten forms of sexual harassment. The sexual harassment can be linked to women being seen as intruders into a traditionally male working environment (both the academic and professional sides to HE), and thus their visibility leaves them open to comments that seek to re-domesticate or sexualise them.

By far the most common form of sexual harassment was 'verbal remarks of a sexual nature', with 36 (30%) of the 122 responses highlighting this. This was similarly the case for 'non-verbal sexual harassment, staring, or looking you up and down', which was reported in 21% (26) of the responses. Table 9.5 lists the responses to this question.

Table 9.5 Sexual harassment—behaviours

Behaviours	*Percentage (count) (excludes counts of 1)*
Persistent and unwanted invitations of a sexual nature	7% (8)
Unwanted touching, hugging, stroking, patting, or kissing	16% (19)
Stalking—online or physically	5% (6)
Non-verbal sexual harassment, staring, or looking you up and down	21% (26)
Verbal remarks of a sexual nature, jokes, and innuendo directed at you in your presence	30% (36)
Talking about or spreading rumours about your sex life or attractiveness to others	7% (9)
Sexual assault or rape	2% (2)
Message of a sexual nature sent to you via email, direct messaging, or social media	2% (3)
Other (open question)	9% (11)

The discursive comments relating to this reflect a male-dominated culture of women being intruders, with comments reported about female academics' clothing (sexualising her), breasts, and sex life (7%). In this regard one participant mentioned:

> One of the senior staff used to ask male lecturers how their research was going but made (complimentary) comments on my appearance instead. A different member of senior staff watched the admin staff and commented on their breasts, said another female lecturer dressed like a prostitute.

Another response is worth looking at in a bit more detail:

> I was only touched twice, and got asked out through a memo in internal mail and once kind of jokingly over lunch – all a very long time ago (when I was a new young lecturer and culture was different – and I was one of a relatively small number of women in a predominantly male Faculty)

The hedging around this harassment is clear: the respondent was 'only' touched twice: she was sexually assaulted twice. Then being pursued for a 'date' is framed as a 'joke'. The fact that this respondent refers to this happening a long time ago when there were a limited number of women in a male-dominated faculty does not lessen the seriousness of her underlying experience of unwanted sexual attention. Other comments in the discursive text relating to this series of questions also refer to experiences being at other institutions, indicating a more wide-spread problem. If we can link back to the earlier question about invisibility, then another comment in this section can be added to our growing picture: a problem in HE and an associated perception of lack of care for staff by the HR system.

Several respondents describe sexual harassment coming not from fellow employees but from students. One respondent writes in some detail of being 'chased by a student' but feeling that the student's mental health issues were taken more seriously than the safety of the academic concerned as the student returned to class and the behaviour did not go away entirely. The respondent refers to 'a rolled-eye culture', where the institution prioritises the students over the staff. That the gender-based harassment comes from students, who are typically younger than the staff, reflects the findings of Off et al. (2022), who found that sexism was increasing amongst those men in the 18- to 29-year age group who were most likely to see the advancement of women as a threat to men's opportunities.

There was one respondent who reported they had been made to feel their career would be progressed in return for sexual favours. Two reported serious sexual assault/rape. No discursive comments were made in connection to these two categories, but there is a very disturbing and serious point to be made here: the invisibility of gender-based violence is masking a very serious problem. The silence that is surrounding these issues is worryingly clear, not just in the HE sector in general, but in the supposedly safe confines of our survey.

The more insidious, less physical side of gender-based violence was teased out in a series of options. These are shown in Table 9.6.

Table 9.6 Have you personally experienced any of these instances of gender-based harassment in the workplace (tick all that apply)?

Experiences of gender-based harassment	*%*	*Count*
Bullying	14%	28
Mobbing	5%	9
Ghosting	8%	15
Insulting, undermining, or derisory remarks	16%	31
Coercive or controlling behaviour	8%	15
Gaslighting	8%	16
None of the above	36%	71
Other	6%	11
Total	100%	196

As we can see, there are multiple ways in which this can be manifest. The discursive comments reported experiencing this behaviour both within HE and in its associated partnerships. Other comments related to the closing down of discussions about gender and sex, with a silencing of views which do not conform to the dominant views about gender and sex which are glossed as 'gender critical'. In this regard one participant stated: 'Women are being silenced while women's spaces are at risk and safeguarding principles destroyed.'

Thus gender-based violence itself becomes a site for contention, something we see happening more widely in society in the often-poisonous debates about single-sex spaces.

In response to the question about just who is doing the harassment as reported in the previous questions, a sizeable percentage (36%) reported it was from someone more senior in the institution, with a slightly lower number reporting it coming from peers (33%). Again, students are cited as being responsible for such behaviour, with 15% of responses citing this group. The final group identified comes from outside of the institution, with 14% of cases originating in this area and seems more frequent in the case of professional than academic staff.

Our survey then posed the question, 'If you were harassed at work, what did you do about it?' See Table 9.7.

What is clear from Table 9.7 is that most victims of sexual harassment did not report their experience to the institution's HR department (only 12% did). Nine participants reported they had left the organisation (8%), and one reported they had taken this further by reporting to external

Table 9.7 Responses to workplace harassment

Responses	*%*	*Count*
I kept quiet	19%	23
I told the harasser it was wrong	11%	13
I told a friend/family member outside the organisation	22%	26
I told a colleague	20%	24
I reported it to HR	12%	14
I left the organisation	8%	9
I reported it to the authorities/police	1%	1
Other	8%	10
Total	100%	120

authorities. The discursive comments report that those who didn't refer their complaint to internal or external authorities 'felt there was no point'. One comment identifies a potential problem with HR, in that the participant felt there was no point in reporting their experience of gender-based violence to HR as there is a 'barrage of equality and diversity information' from HR. This indicates that the participant felt unable to report gender-based violence as the institution would not take it seriously owing to a smoke-screen of EDI news. The idea of not being taken seriously is one that is repeated in the comments and is not without foundation as several other comments report 'gaslighting' experiences where they were told 'it wasn't actually an issue' by senior managers.

It would seem that there is a lack of confidence in some staff. In our survey, 115 participants responded to this question and of these 16 (14%) 'disagreed' or 'strongly disagreed' that senior managers would take sexual harassment seriously. Of those who did take this to HR, the participants of our survey had mixed experiences. Of these, 42% (11) 'strong disagreed' that they felt supported by senior management, and 40% (10) strongly disagreed that they felt supported by HR. The lack of faith in those in power to act on accusations of gender-based violence is something we find elsewhere in our survey. As can be seen from our discussion, there is a long-standing culture of gender-based violence in HE, and if we turn to HE outside of the 'home institution', in conference spaces, then we can see the same pattern of toleration of sexual misconduct and lack of confidence in the complaints system repeated. Indeed, there have been few studies which have examined GBV at academic conferences despite these being an extension of the academic space with inherent unequal power relationships. Exceptions include Flores (2020) who interrogated the role of conference organisers and governing bodies in addressing GBV at these events; and Mair and Frew (2018) who used a duo-ethnographic approach to explore gendered behaviours of delegates at academic conferences.

Of the 119 responses to our question about the nature of sexual behaviour at conferences, 21 (18%) said that they believed sexual harassment was a problem, whilst 63% (75) responded 'don't know'. Eleven (9%) had experienced sexual harassment at conferences, with another 18 (15%) either witnessing it or knowing another person who had experienced it. In the case of residential conferences, 4% (5) people reported they had been asked for their hotel room number, and two people had been asked for sex (associating this with a promise of enhanced career prospects). One respondent reported she had been the victim of unwanted sexual attention at a conference, and this continued with unwelcome sexualised messaging for several weeks after the conference. Another academic commented that she had stopped going to conferences several years earlier because of the sexual harassment she had experienced. This is a point that needs to be seen in the broader context of academic reputations being enhanced by conference attendance, and so more junior academics would risk their careers stalling if they ceased attending conferences to avoid unwanted sexual attention.

The survey also shows that the people who experienced gender-based violence at conferences largely felt unable to report this. Of the 26 respondents who answered the question as to what they did in response to the sexual harassment, none reported it to the conference organisers or an external authority. The most common response (46%) was to keep quiet, with just two people saying they confronted the harasser. The reasons for not reporting this varied from 'I was told that it happens, and I should accept it' (three responses), to a lack of confidence that anything would happen in terms of consequences for the harasser (five responses). The discursive comments reflect this with statements such as 'not worth the effort' and the more dismal 'I stopped claiming over the years because no-one ever believes you and you are blamed'. From this, we can see a culture of silencing being enacted more widely when it comes to gender-based violence in HE.

Conclusion and Recommendations

This study is limited in its ability to offer more than tentative conclusions due to the small sample size, which as indicated previously is a limitation of online surveys. In addition, as a single case study, its generalisability to other higher education institutions is limited. Further research in this area should seek to widen the spatial parameters to include other higher education institutions not only in England but in the other UK nations (Scotland, Wales, and Northern Ireland) where there are some differences in higher education governance. In addition, researchers seeking to advance this topic might wish to use more qualitative and creative methods such as in-depth interviews, audio diaries or visual techniques that can help to further unpack the issues raised in this chapter.

What we have been able to show, albeit in a limited way, is that Gelfand et al.'s (1995) work in categorising GBV in terms of three overlapping but distinct parts (sexual coercion; unwanted sexual attention; degrading gendered harassment) can be found across both academic and professional services in our HE environment. The respondents' mention of this GBV being experienced in other institutions prior to working at Sunderland indicates a wider problem to be found at more than just one university. In many cities in the UK, universities are large employers and understanding and assessing the scale and severity of gender-based violence amongst staff is a crucial endeavour if these institutions are to contribute meaningfully to achieving the interlocking ambitions of both SDG16 and SDG8.

Acknowledgements The authors would like to thank Sarah Connelly, Lecturer in Criminology at the University of Sunderland, for her help with the analysis of the quantitative data used in this research.

References

Acker, J. (1992). Gendering Organizational Theory. *Classics of Organizational Theory, 6*, 450–459.

Anitha, S., & Lewis, R. (2018). *Gender Based Violence in University Communities: Policy, Prevention and Educational Initiatives.* Bristol University Press.

Attenborough, F. (2014). Rape Is Rape (Except When It's Not): The Media, Recontextualisation and Violence Against Women. *Journal of Language Aggression and Conflict, 2*(2), 183–203.

Banet-Weiser, S. (2018). *Empowered: Popular Feminism and Popular Misogyny.* Duke University Press.

Bull, A., & Page, T. (2021). Students' Accounts of Grooming and Boundary-Breaking Behaviours by Academic Staff in UK Higher Education. *Gender and Education, 33*(8), 1057–1072. https://doi.org/10.1080/09540253.2021.1884199

Dziech, B. W., & Hawkins, M. W. (2012). *Sexual Harassment and Higher Education: Reflections and New Perspectives.* Routledge.

Finniear, J., Morgan, N., Chambers, D., & Munar, A. M. (2020). Gender-Based Harassment in Tourism Academia: Organizational Collusion, Coercion and Compliance. In P. Vizcaino, H. Jeffrey, & C. Eger (Eds.), *Tourism and Gender-Based Violence: Challenging Inequalities* (pp. 30–45). CABI Publishing.

Flores, N. M. (2020). Harassment at conferences: will# MeToo momentum translate to real change? *Gender and Education, 32*(1), 137–144.

Forbes-Mewett, H., & McCulloch, J. (2016). International Students and Gender-Based Violence. *Violence Against Women, 22*(3), 344–365.

Gelfand, M., Fitzgerald, L., & Drasgow, F. (1995). The Structure of Sexual Harassment: A Confirmatory Analysis Across Cultures and Settings. *Journal of Vocational Behavior, 47*(2), 164–177. https://doi.org/10.1006/jvbe.1995.1033

Gill, R. (2016). Post-postfeminims? New Feminist Visibilities in Postfeminist Times. *Feminist Media Studies, 16*(4), 610–630. https://doi.org/10.1080/14680777.2016.1193293

Gov.uk. (2021, June 10). *Review of Sexual Abuse in Schools and Colleges.* Retrieved July 19, 2022, from https://www.gov.uk/government/publications/review-of-sexual-abuse-in-schools-and-colleges/review-of-sexual-abuse-in-schools-and-colleges

Humphreys, C., & Towl, G. (Eds.). (2023). *Stopping Gender-Based Violence in Higher Education: Policy, Practice, and Partnerships.* Routledge.

Kelly, L. (1987). The Continuum of Sexual Violence. In J. Hanmer, & M. Maynard, (Eds.), *Women, Violence and Social Control.* London: Palgrave.

Kirkner, A. C., Lorenz, K., & Mazar, L. (2022). Faculty and Staff Reporting & Disclosure of Sexual Harassment in Higher Education. *Gender and Education, 34*(2), 199–215.

Lewis, P. (2006). The Quest for Invisibility: Female Entrepreneurs and the Masculine Norm of Entrepreneurship. *Gender, Work and Organization, 13*(5), 453–469.

Lewis, P., & Simpson, R. (2017). Hakim Revisited: Preference, Choice and the Post-Feminist Gender Regime. *Gender, Work and Organization, 24*(2), 115–133.

Mahlori, X. F., Byrne, D. C., & Mabude, L. A. (2018). Perceptions of Gender-Based Violence Among University Staff: Interim Results. *SAGE Open, 8*(3), 2158244018800163.

Mair, J., & Frew, E. (2018). Academic Conferences: A Female Duo-Ethnography. *Current Issues in Tourism, 21*(18), 2152–2172.

Marine, S., & Lewis, R. (Eds.). (2020). *Collaborating for Change: Transforming Cultures to End Gender-Based Violence in Higher Education.* Oxford University Press.

McDermott, C. (2022). *Feel-bad Postfeminism: Impasse, Resilience and Female Subjectivity in Popular Culture.* Bloomsbury.

McRobbie, A. (2009). *The Aftermath of Feminism: Gender, Culture and Social Change.* Sage.

Nayak, M. S. D. P., & Narayan, K. A. (2019). Strengths and Weaknesses of Online Surveys. *Technology, 6*(7), 31–38.

NUS. (2010). Hidden Marks: A Study of Women Students' Experiences of Harassment, Stalking, Violence and Sexual Assault.

Off, G., Charron, N., & Alexander, A. (2022, August 15). Who Perceived Women's Rights as Threatening to Men and Boys? Explaining Modern Sexism Among Young Men in Europe. *Frontiers in Political Science.* https://doi.org/10.3389/fpos.2022.909811

Phipps, A. (2020). *Me Not You: The Trouble with Mainstream Feminism.* Manchester University Press.

Pilkington, E. (2011, May 6). SlutWalking Gets Rolling After Cop's Loose Talk About Provocative Clothing. *The Guardian*. Retrieved July 19, 2022, from https://www.theguardian.com/world/2011/may/06/slutwalking-policeman-talk-clothing

Smith, A. (2017). *Introduction. Re-Reading Spare Rib*. Palgrave Macmillan.

Smith, A. (2018). Gender in 'Crisis': Everyday Sexism and the Twittersphere. In M. Patrona (Ed.), *Crisis and the Media* (pp. 231–260). John Benjamins.

Topping, A. (2021, March 27). 'Moment of reckoning' for UK schools as 5,800 accounts of abuse published. *The Guardian*. Retrieved July 19, 2022, from https://www.theguardian.com/uk-news/2021/mar/27/moment-of-reckoning-for-uk-schools-as-5800-accounts-of-abuse-published

Vizard, S. (2013, December 13) The Marketing Year. Marketing Week. Retrieved July 19, 2022, from https://www.marketingweek.com/the-marketing-year/

Watts, C., & Zimmerman, C. (2002). Violence Against Women: Global Scope and Magnitude. *The Lancet, 359*(9313), 1232–1237.

Walter, N. (2010). *Living Dolls: The Return of Sexism*. Virago.

Whelehan, I. (2000). *Overloaded: Popular Culture and the Future of Feminism*. The Women's Press.

Williamson, J. (2003, May 31). Sexism with an Alibi. The Guardian. https://www.theguardian.com/media/2003/may/31/advertising.comment

CHAPTER 10

Relating the UN's Sustainable Development Goals to Trans and Marginalised Gender Identities: Are They Adequate?

Katie Ward

Introduction

In 2015 The United Nations (UN) released its sustainability agenda outlining 17 Sustainable Development Goals (SDGs) to help the betterment of society and the preservation of the planet. The focal point of the UN's goals is threefold; eradicating poverty, protecting the environment, and promoting social inclusion (United Nations, 2022a). With the onset of the Covid-19 pandemic and the negative impacts it has had, the UN has increased its efforts to ensure the goals are met by 2030.

Despite the UN scaling up its effort, this chapter will argue that some of the SDGs still are not adequate for some people of marginalised genders, particularly trans and non-binary people. To explore trans and marginalised gender identities in relation to the UN's sustainability goals, this chapter focusses on the three goals in particular: Goal 3, Good Health and

K. Ward (✉)
Newcastle-upon-Tyne, UK

D. Dalton, A. Smith (eds.), *Gender, Sexuality and the UN's SDGs*, Sustainable Development Goals Series,
https://doi.org/10.1007/978-3-031-31046-1_10

Wellbeing; Goal 5, Gender Equality; and Goal 10; Reduced Inequalities (United Nations, 2022b).

Gender equality is described by the UN (2022b, no pagination) as a 'fundamental human right'. However, the goal overlooks trans and non-binary genders, who are at increased risk for gender-based violence (Bachmann & Gooch, 2018; Gyamerah et al., 2021), with 2021 being cited at the most violent year on record for trans people (HRC Foundation, 2021). Additionally, higher rates of violence are an indicator for poorer quality of life, lower economic status and adverse health outcomes (Donovan & Hester, 2014; Gyamerah et al., 2021). Therefore, as trans people are at higher risk for gender-based violence, and the UN's SDG 5 does not include gender-diverse identities, it follows that Goals 3 and 10 cannot be met for trans and non-binary people.

This chapter will explore this by analysing the representation of trans and gender-variant people in British news media, both historical and contemporary. Using critical discourse analysis and narrative analysis, this chapter will argue that media narratives create a cultural fiction (Butler, 1990) about gender diversity and either legitimise hostility towards or create an idealised version of trans people.

Trans Identities and the UN Sustainable Development Goals

The aim of this chapter is to address and explore the gender gap which is prevalent amongst the UN's sustainable goals (2022a), particularly in relation to representation. In reviewing the goals, it is clear that they assume a gender binary and there are three goals which stand out as fundamentally lacking for trans and gender-variant people.

Goal 5, *Achieve Gender Equality*, works towards full gender equality and the empowerment of women and girls by looking at societal issues such as female genital mutilation, domestic and intimate partner violence, and unpaid domestic labour (this list is not exhaustive). It is imperative that these issues are addressed however, what is conspicuous in this goal is the lack of trans and gender-variant voices. For example, in their study, Peitzmeier et al. (2020) conclude that there are higher rates of intimate partner violence for trans people when compared to cis people. This is supported by other studies which puts trans people at increased risk of violence (Bachmann & Gooch, 2018; Gyamerah et al., 2021), yet it is striking that throughout the goal's aims, there are no indicators that trans and marginalised identities have been considered.

Closely linked to Goal 5 is Goal 3, *Ensure Healthy Lives and Promote Wellbeing*. As part of Goal 3 the UN is looking to level up access to affordable healthcare and social services, eradicate diseases and improve infant mortality rates. Additionally, the UN has stated the prevalence of depression and anxiety is rising (2022b) in part due to the Covid-19 pandemic. However, it can be argued that the erasure of trans and non-binary identities, both within the UN's SDGs and also within wider society, contributes to poor health and wellbeing for these communities. This is again supported by studies into trans wellbeing (Bachmann & Gooch, 2018; Gyamerah et al., 2021; Peitzmeier et al., 2020) which suggest levels of discrimination and lack of access to health and social services for trans people could contribute to the level of intimate partner violence within the community. Essentially, the negative consequences of Goal 5 (gender equality) contributes to adverse outcomes for health and wellbeing targets in Goal 3.

Finally, the erasure of trans and gender-diverse people from the goals discussed above, and the consequences from that have an impact on Goal 10, *Reduce Inequality*. Briefly, not aiming for equality for communities outside the gender binary leaves trans and gender-variant people vulnerable for further discrimination. It follows that discrimination leads to poorer social and health outcomes which contributes to overall inequality.

Fundamentally, groups of people vulnerable for discrimination due to their gender identity have been erased from the UN's wider agenda. It could be argued that this is purposeful as the language used in the SDGs is vague and left open to interpretation. For example, Target 10.2 looks to reduce inequalities 'irrespective of age, sex, disability, race, ethnicity, origin, religion or economic or *other status*' (United Nations, 2022c, emphasis added). Here, 'other status' can be assumed to relate to sexuality and gender identity, but is ambiguous enough not to dissuade countries in which gender identity and homosexuality are condemned, if not illegal: homosexuality is illegal in at least 72 countries, most of whom have signed to participate in the Sustainable Development Goals (Scolaro, 2020).

To explore this idea, I have used data which looks at the historical and contemporary representations of trans people in news media, as well as some lived experiences of trans people in North East England. Collected as part of a wider research project, the data includes trans and non-binary individuals' experiences living in North East England (Ward, 2020); in particular, representations of trans people compared to lived experiences. I will also be referring to five individuals who relayed their personal experiences to me; Donna, Terri, Rachel, Michael, and Sophie. This data has been included to support the analysis of news media and to enrich the data with lived experiences. These narratives were collected in 2015 via in-depth, semi-structured qualitative interviews in which they were asked to describe their experiences navigating their gender identity. Each participant related to their gender in different ways. Donna and Rachel described themselves as trans women, Terri as a girl, Michael as non-binary, and Sophie as female—each of these categories being self-defined.

What emerged were cultural fictions of trans people which were being perpetuated via the media and within these fictions we can see barriers to gender equality and wellbeing. Additionally, we can see how the erasure of gender-variant identities from the UN's agenda supports the otherising of trans people and how media discourses have, and still are, taken trans people out of their own stories.

Data and Analysis

This chapter draws upon topics discussed through a lens of critical discourse analysis (CDA) and narrative analysis, and the data to be analysed consists of media and personal stories. 'Media' is a broad term which encompasses a number of communication outlets however, in the context of this chapter, I will be using media to refer to UK printed newspapers and their online counterparts because, more often than not, cis people gain their knowledge and understanding of trans people from their consumption of media (McInroy & Craig, 2015).

Critical discourse analysis (CDA) provides the bases for analysis of the texts. Intertextuality is used particularly in CDA, as it enables a text to be studied within its wider context. Methods of analysing discourse outside of CDA analyse discourses and texts in isolation, without any reference to other texts and away from its historical context (Fairclough, 1989). However, it is argued that discourse is historical, produced with context, and cannot be understood without reference to that context (Fairclough & Wodak, 1997).

Since discourse, according to CDA, both reflects and produces society, then it is evident that texts are intrinsically linked and their meaning shaped by other texts. Additionally, the discourse historical approach (DHA) to discourse analysis attempts to assimilate all background information into the analysis (Fairclough & Wodak, 1997) in order to uncover prejudices. The background information the DHA alludes to not only includes public discourses and textual context but also a social-psychological dimension of the discourse producers and consumers, including culture, gender, class, personality, and so on (Titscher et al., 2000).

In narrative discourse, performance is important (Thornborrow & Coates, 2005) and particularly Goffman's (1959) and Butler's (1990) theories of performativity. In the production and repetition of stories we see the repeated stylised acts which Butler ascertains produces gender. This is also prevalent in media narratives, which go some way to solidify wider society's opinions of trans lives, whilst not necessarily representing real lived experiences. In addition, the stories we tell are a powerful form of cultural capital and help construct single and group identities, as well as life-histories (Thornborrow & Coates, 2005).

In newspaper media, trans people have habitually been used for sensationalist stories and as curiosities (Oram, 2007), often focusing on either deception or peculiarity. Stories of people like Lucy Meadows (Greenslade, 2013; Pike, 2012) and Kate Stone (BBC News, 2014) brought how the press reports about trans people into the spotlight. Both Lucy and Kate received severe press intrusion which highlighted the press's use of gender identity for reader titillation. Additionally, they were trans women who experienced public outing and, in Lucy's case, job loss and death by suicide. Just within these two stories, you can see the negative outcomes which relate to the UN Goals 3, 5, and 10. The rest of this chapter will highlight further instances of gender inequality and poor wellbeing, leading to wider inequality, ultimately illustrating why the sustainability goals are not suitable for trans and gender-variant people.

The Narratives of Trans Identities in News Media

Debating Identity

Stories of trans identities have historically perpetuated the news media been used for sensationalist stories and as curiosities (Oram, 2007). These stories discussed trans people as either deceptive or peculiar and focused on individual experiences. Often, trans people (whether willingly or not) gained a celebrity status because of their gender identity (ibid.) and people like Christine Jorgensen and April Ashley built on their celebrity status to advocate for trans rights (Feinberg, 2006). These narratives can still be seen in media outlets today, however, there has been an increased visibility of trans identities, which has formed an increased awareness of how transgender people are spoken about.

In more recent times, stories which focus on gender identity have shifted to talk about wider issues and rights of trans people as a homogenised group; often from the perspective of people who claim to be 'gender critical'. Gender critical viewpoints are not new and have inhabited some feminist, political, and academic discourses for some time (Phipps, 2020). However, over the last decade, these discourses have spilled into public narratives as social media platforms, such as Twitter, have enabled people to express their viewpoints to a wider audience. For example, author JK Rowling built a career as a highly successful writer of children's books, but in more recent times, has taken to social media to express her gender critical views. As a result, media outlets have picked up on her opinions and used them for stories which discuss trans identities, but are centred around a cis woman. This is damaging to trans and gender-variant people as Rowling's celebrity has enabled gender critical views to reach a wider audience. Additionally, Rowling's views are used by the media to legitimise the demonisation of trans people—trans women in particular. As Phipps suggests, this narrative, and centring of cis women, 'generates outrage through constructing trans women as dangerous in response to isolated incidents' (Phipps, 2020, p. 104).

To illustrate this point, we can look at the case of Maya Forstater. Forstater is a researcher and was working as a visiting fellow at the Centre for Global Development where her employment was terminated as a result of her social media output. In 2019, Forstater posted tweets expressing biological essentialist views and, as a result, her employment contract was not renewed. The story made headlines due to public support from JK Rowling, whose celebrity status and social media presence enabled her opinions to reach a wide audience. Rowling tweeted in direct support of Forstater, stating:

> Dress however you please. Call yourself whatever you like. Sleep with any consenting adult who'll have you. Live your best life in peace and security. But force women out of their jobs for stating that sex is real? (Rowling, quoted in Kindred, 2019, paras 10–11).

The tweet above caused a strong reaction from her followers and the media; on either side of the argument. In reading the tweet, it is clear Rowling anticipates by starting with what might be perceived to be 'liberal' views then reverts her narrative. Here Rowling is using a double voice in which she is anticipating backlash for her controversial opinion (Baxter, 2014). By starting with 'liberal views' Rowling is satiating critics, before presenting an opinion she is aware will receive criticism. It reads as Rowling allowing people to live how they want to, before criticising the consequences of anyone critical of this; the consequences in this case being a loss of employment.

Wider reporting on Forstater and Rowling is similar across various news outlets as it centres on both Forstater's situation and Rowling's outspoken support. The language and tone of the articles often downplay Forstater's and Rowling's opinions, and overstate the consequences for these. In an article on the *The Sun*'s website (Kindred, 2019) it is stated in the strap line that Forstater 'was sacked for sharing her views'; however, it is revealed further in the article that her contract was not renewed. Whilst these both amount to a loss of employment, using the word 'sacked' evokes stronger feelings—from both supporters and detractors—than not having a contract renewed; something which happens often for those on temporary contracts. Additionally, teaming 'sacked' with 'expressing her views' can be seen as antagonistic as it leads the reader to assume that this person was forcefully removed from employment for having an opinion, ultimately overstating the situation to provoke outrage. Further in the article, Forstater's views were referred to as a 'twitter spat', which again downplays the situation as 'spat' is often used to describe petty quarrels. In other articles on *The Daily Mirror*'s (Newman, 2019) and *The Guardian*'s (Noor, 2019) websites, Forstater's opinions were shared in more detail, one of which is that she would refuse to use the pronouns a gender-variant person would use to describe themselves, and use the ones she deemed appropriate.

Pronoun use for trans and non-binary people is imperative as it affirms their gender identity in a wider societal context, to not use them is not communicating in a respectful way. Additionally, it is increasingly becoming common practice for workplaces and institutions to have guidance on pronoun usage as they can be used to model trans allyship (Stonewall, 2022). To not use a person's pronouns, therefore, can be used to delegitimise a person's identity which amounts to more than a 'spat'.

More recently, Rowling and Forstater returned to the headlines as Forstater's loss at employment tribunal was overturned. This was described by Rowling as making life safer for women who 'express gender critical views' (Swerling, 2022), and the case as a whole was described as 'about protected beliefs, not trans rights' (Hinscliff, 2019). It can be argued that this case, and others like it, has set a precedent for people to be able to 'debate' the existence of another human being, and those gender critical views should be protected akin to religious views; Forstater herself has described the original tribunal loss as 'like forcing Jewish people to eat pork' (Kindred, 2019). These contemporary news articles of trans issues do not centre around trans people themselves and present identities as worthy of debate. However, a protester for trans rights, as quoted in a news article by Ferreira (2022, para 2), sums up the impact these articles have:

> Trans people cannot simply exist. We must justify our existence in the public arena – in a format that is inherently dehumanising because it assumes that a fundamental aspect of our personhood is up for discussion.

Overall, these articles take autonomy away from trans people for their own identities and invite criticism of trans lives under the guise of debate. Again, it erases trans and gender-variant people from their own stories and legitimises narratives which demonise them. This is reflective in the UN's sustainability goals in which trans rights are conspicuous by their absence. The goals discuss human rights in terms of gender, whilst erasing a whole community of people actually marginalised because of gender. However, these articles did not appear out of a vacuum, the news media has a history of presenting trans stories in this way.

Trans People as Drains on Resources

In contrast to the identity debate which is prevalent in news media now, only a decade ago there was an interesting subset of stories about trans people which are presented as hard news, yet the content can be categorised as soft news. This can be seen most blatantly in tabloid journalism, and often on the front page. Additionally, these stories often lead with 'being trans' to present trans people as either novelties or peculiarities, or as a vessel for outrage. For example, a *Daily Star* front-page headline about a trans woman begins:

> Sponger wants sex swap op reversed ... And YOU will end up footing bill again. (Robins, 2014, p. 1, emphasis in original)

The headline is sensationalist and provocative. It personally appeals to the reader by the use of the personal pronoun 'you', which is capitalised for maximum effect. In contrast, Chelsea, as the subject of the story, is depersonalised being referred to only as 'sponger', which is a highly provocative category. In the context of this article, 'sponger' carries with it certain implications of a person who takes advantage of the generosity of others, lives off the money of others and someone who may not be employed. These implications are common sense cultural understandings (Sacks, 1974), because they do not need to be explained and readers of this article will implicitly know what the newspaper is trying to suggest about Chelsea.

Also in the headline is the term *sex-swap*, a sensationalist way to refer to people who transition medically. The term is steeped in historical medical discourses originating from early gender studies (Benjamin, 1966; Cauldwell, 1949), which contributed to the medicalisation of gender identity; still a pervasive viewpoint. Terms like *sex-swap* and *sex-change* are reductive and medicalised, essentially reducing Chelsea's identity to her genitalia. Use of these terms erase Chelsea's overall experience and adds to the wider discourse of medicalised gender identity. *Sex-swap* also reduces the experience of transitioning to the gender binary. With it comes the insinuation that transitioning is a switch, which leaves out the nuance of transitioning and simplifies what may be a difficult and ongoing process. This is reinforced further in the story of Chelsea as the article describes a desire to 'swap back'; delegitimising transitioning, and implying that Chelsea is erratic in her decisions. Additionally, the use of 'swap' in this context can be argued to trivialise what is a lengthy and often emotional process.

The strapline of the article is steeped in bias and provocation, and presents a number of assumptions and stereotypes:

> Jobless transgender Matthew Attonley, who had a £10,000 sex change on the NHS, now wants another op to reverse it because being a girl is too 'exhausting'. (Robins, 2014, p. 1)

The first word used is 'jobless', a provocative opening which is used in conjunction with references to the NHS and taxpayers. Something which is already part of the public consciousness. Robins (2014) uses concern for the NHS to reposition the story for one of anger over public services rather than one of trans people as peculiarities. However, what Robins does is highlight the unequal access to public services that trans people often face. Additionally, there is an implicit assumption that it is okay for Chelsea to be trans, but not okay for her to use public-funded organisations in order to facilitate her transition; hence an assumption that gender dysphoria is a lifestyle choice. Like the articles discussed earlier in the chapter, this is also a form of double-voicing (Baxter, 2014) in which the author of the story expresses acceptance for trans people and trans lives, in order to appear accepting and sympathetic. In this instance, Robins does not attack Chelsea personally, and expresses acceptance of her gender identity, but the criticism of trans lives comes under the guide of concern for resources.

It is worth noting the ambiguity in the sentence as it is unclear in the strapline what the word class of transgender is. It could be read here as either an adjective or a noun in this context. Using transgender as a noun is problematic as it creates a discrete category of person outside of male and female, which suggests that gender-variant people are neither. This adds to the othering of Chelsea and, by association gender-variant people, as they have been put in a category of their own.

Finally, the strapline contains another layer of stereotyping against both women and unemployed people. The use of *exhausting* here, when used in conjunction with being jobless, suggests that Chelsea is 'lazy'; a prejudice which is pervasive in society for people without employment and reliant on state welfare (Russell, 2016). Additionally, the idea that it is exhausting 'being a girl'; (Robins, 2014, p. 1) both infantilises woman and perpetuates stereotypes of women as 'high maintenance'.

Overall, the article is written in a reductive way in which readers are manipulated into being angry with Chelsea for desiring NHS treatment. Chelsea's story also highlights specific narratives about trans lives which are often found in the media. It covers what might be called a 'regret narrative', and also the narrative of trans people as 'scroungers', 'spongers', or drains on the NHS. At no point during the article was Chelsea's mental health taken into consideration, or her potential struggle with gender dysphoria which is likely to cause distress (according to the Trans Mental Health Study 84% of respondents had considered suicide, McNeil et al., 2012). This highlights how Chelsea is othered and how her health and wellbeing is being used as a vessel for outrage. Additionally, parts of her identity, namely her gender and her socio-economic status, are being used to manipulate readers into propping up stereotypes. This is ultimately contravening the targets set by the UN to deliver their SDGs as Chelsea is not presented as equal or deserving of adequate healthcare.

Chelsea's story is well known and it was discussed by participants in semi-structured interviews which were used to gather qualitative data exploring the lived experiences of transgender people in North East England. One interview participant, Rachel, a self-defined trans woman, discusses the problematic reporting of the story and calls it 'sensationalist beyond belief'. She picks out specific tools used by newspaper authors when talking about trans people, such as the use of before and after photos, birth names and inconsistent pronoun use. In addition, there is an unnecessary emphasis on money and cost, which is all focused on the taxpayer. These, Rachel says, are tools used in a lot of articles, which often downplay the real experiences of the person in the article:

> [A]nd that article about Chelsea, I can't remember her surname, who wanted to revert I actually did a bit more reading because I remember this case from a little bit- from when it actually happened and I had something in my head and it's right, she was later interviewed again afterwards and she hasn't had surgery, she's had HRT, she actually hasn't had GRS [gender recognition surgery] so where they get all this like this person wants to have surgery to rebuild a penis, that was never- there's nothing to revert there. (Ward, 2018, p. 168)

Rachel here makes the salient point that the news article omitted facts regarding Chelsea in order to be provocative, something, she points out, that it used in many articles which feature trans and gender-variant people. To support this, Rachel uses the example of Billy-Joe Newington (Evans, 2014), a trans man, who was in the process of undergoing various surgeries and, having had a mastectomy, was embarking on bottom surgery. His story was reported in the *Daily Mail* (Evans, 2014) which reported on Newington's future having penis construction surgery, with the focus being the use of the tattooed skin on his forearm for the surgery. Throughout the article, 'NHS' is used three times, whilst 'taxpayer' is also used twice when describing the operations that Billy-Joe has undergone. When describing his upcoming surgeries, the author also highlights the exact cost of the operation. However, as Rachel highlights:

> [T]he trans guy that's going in for surgery and he's got a tattoo on his arm and it mentions that he's had top surgery which costs £6000, well they very much downplay the fact that they also found a tumorous lump that they removed so it's like well he would have needed that anyway. (Ward, 2018, p. 168)

Both these articles show how stories about trans lives often have underhanded motives. Both articles juxtapose one another in that the ideologies in Chelsea's story are more blatant. The article in *The Daily Star* was written with the intention to cause outrage; however, Billy-Joe's story was written in the style of a lifestyle/human interest piece containing references to the NHS and money in order to drum up outrage. The motives here are hidden within the outward presentation of a positive piece. However, there is an assumption that trans people consume resources from the NHS, and therefore the taxpayer, without contributing themselves. It is also implied that surgery for gender-variant people is cosmetic and therefore does not warrant NHS spending. This intent is recognised by the readers of the newspapers who will also be aware of other contextual knowledge like the paper's political affiliation and ideologies. As a result, these implications about gender-variant people become 'mutual knowledge' (Blum-Kulka, 1997, p. 39) between newspaper and media.

Rachel highlights perhaps the most important points about these articles; the fact that they either downplay, or completely ignore, any health aspects which may lead gender-variant people to opt for surgery yet focus on the supposed 'peculiarity' of both Chelsea's and Billy-Joe's lives. Both Chelsea's and Billy-Joe's mental health is omitted from the articles, and Billy-Joe's cancerous tumour are understated and overtaken by overt and implied displays of outrage on behalf of their readership. What these articles also demonstrate is how the media uses gender identity to further their political and social ideologies, often at the expense of the person featured. The UN's goal for wider health and wellbeing is being undermined by a large social institution such as the media with the implicit and explicit suggestions that trans people are 'draining' health resources and therefore not deserving. As a result, it could be argued that trans people are seen as unequal.

Trans People as Peculiarities and Novelties

In 2015 *The Sunday Mirror* ran the story of Roxy whose relationship with her young autistic son had improved since her transition. Again, the story was front-page news, however with a more understated headline: 'Daddy Became Mummy and Now I Love Her Even More' (Gilmour, 2015, p. 1). This edition of *The Daily Mirror* was published on the run-up to the 2015 UK general election; however, stories covering the election, the NHS, and other political matters did not appear until page 6 in the paper, with Roxy's story taking precedence. Roxy's transition story took the entire front page and was touted as an 'exclusive', which adds to the idea that Roxy is a novelty that needs to be read about. The story presents itself from the angle of Roxy's relationship with her son before her transition, and how her transition has seemed to improve that relationship. Throughout there is nothing negative said about gender variance and transitioning and on the surface this is a positive representation of trans lives. When analysing the language used and the angle of the story however, it becomes clear that even this positive story is problematic.

Roxy, according to the article, came out to her wife in 2013, two years prior to the publication of the story. However, throughout the article, Gilmour (2015) uses male pronouns and Roxy's birth name. In fact, male pronouns are used to describe Roxy for the first four paragraphs of the article, with female pronouns not being used in the lead of the story on the front page, and only introduced in paragraph 7 out of the 25-paragraph article. In addition, Roxy's birth name is used eight times by the author to refer to Roxy, this is without counting direct quotes from family members. The frequent use of male pronouns and Roxy's birth name delegitimises her identity as a woman. This, teamed with the 'before and after' pictures, reinforces the idea of Roxy as a novelty, something to be stared at. Another way of delegitimising Roxy's identity is consistently referencing masculinity throughout the article. Roxy is described as 'a former bodyguard' by the author, and there are direct quotations, including 'Bob was so masculine and afraid to show emotions' (Gilmour, 2015, p. 5). Being a bodyguard and being afraid to show emotions reflects what we might think of as traditional masculinity, this also adds to the 'novelty' value of Roxy's story. The reader is constantly reminded of Roxy's sex assigned at birth and, as a result, is subtly led to question her gender identity.

There is further delegitimisation of Roxy's gender identity in the way the article is written. Despite the story centring on Roxy's transition, she is not actually at the centre of her own story, rather her son is. The first direct quote in the article is from Roxy's son, William, who says 'I love mummy Roxy and never want Bob back. He was grumpy' (Gilmour, 2015, p. 1), and continues on describing how William has reacted to Roxy's transition. This is a common trope in reporting on stories about trans people, where cis gender people's thoughts and feelings are more often used to tell the trans person's story. It could be argued that presenting stories in this was enables them to be accessible to a largely cisgender audience and thus promotes trans issues. However, it also reflects a cisnormative society which prioritises cisgender people's thoughts, feelings and experiences and ultimately undermines trans people. By not being the subject of their own story, trans people and their experiences are further erased and delegitimised. This erasure of trans identities in mass media is indicative of the erasure of trans identities in further areas of society. At the beginning of this chapter, I discussed how Goal 5 does not reference gender variance in any target related to gender equality, and it is clear to see how trans people are widely erased when they are not presented as the subject of their own story—particularly when the community is vulnerable to discrimination because of their gender identity.

The Problematic Language of Gender-Variant Identities in the Media

Interview participant Sophie discusses how trans people are written about compared to their actual experiences and she makes some salient points. Firstly, with the overuse of birth names, Sophie states:

> I don't think we introduce ourselves as our former names and 'born a boy', it isn't a personality trait. (Ward, 2018, p. 175)

The overuse of these journalistic techniques, and the focus on medical and monetary aspects of gender identity, takes away the intersectional identity of the individual. Often trans people are represented in the media as just that, trans. This is supported by Michael, who says:

> [I]f your blueprint of what a trans person is comes from just your consumption of news media, then I think you would just end up with this view of who gets up, takes a bucket of hormone pills then goes out and tricks some-

> body to having sex with them, then gets beaten up on the way home, then loses their job, then goes to bed and then the next day just does the same thing with more tragic things put in. (Ward, 2018, p. 175)

Here Michael references further tropes that are found in media narratives; the medicalisation of trans people and trans people as deceivers. In her research, Oram (2007, 2016) highlights how gender variance was written about in the nineteenth and early twentieth centuries, where it was widely perceived that trans people were seen to be masquerading. At that point, the 'masquerade' itself was newsworthy, and the narrative of deceitful trans people emerged. However, trans identities in themselves no longer have tellability, and it is rare to find a story about a trans person without another story alongside; whether that be the improvement of a relationship with a child, or the 'concern' for taxpayers' money.

Having explored some of the more pervasive media narratives about trans people, it is important to look at how these are perpetuated. A lot of the news outlets I have referenced and read throughout this research have a set of common phrases and words used to describe gender-variant people. However, one word or phrase may not reflect the experiences of most trans people. One of the most pervasive words used is 'become' which is used to describe the transition process and is common in newspaper reporting. Roxy, Chelsea, and Lucy are all described by the authors as wanting to 'become' women. The verb 'to become', as defined by the Oxford Dictionaries (2017), is 'to begin to be', which suggests that a person's transition is the commencement of their gender identity.

However, it is argued that for most trans and gender-variant people, there is no 'becoming' involved, as one was always male, female, non-binary, or any other gender-variant identities. To suggest someone becomes male or female, erases the history of the individual, the potential distress and mental struggles the person may experience, and also how that person came to transition. It is, in itself, a binary concept in which the individual is, for example, a man, but then suddenly starts their life as a man; much like the eponymous hero of Woolf's (Woolf, 1928) *Orlando*, who starts their story as male and then wakes up one morning as female.

When the participants spoke about their gender identity throughout the interview, no one referred to themselves as becoming a man or woman. In fact, the participants spoke about having always known, in some capacity, that their gender identity did not align with their sex assigned at birth. Terri states, 'I've always been a girl in my mind' (Ward, 2018, p. 176), and when Donna was asked about whether she saw herself transitioning, she said, 'the way I see it, it's probably more a normalisation' (Ward, 2018, p. 176). These quotes are particularly interesting because, at the time of interview, Terri had no plans for hormonal and surgical intervention, and Donna was at the very beginning of her transition. Both these quotes from the participants suggest that they both do not consider themselves to have to become anything, as they are already their preferred gender identity.

Another phrase most often found, particularly in headline, is sex-swap or sex-change. *The Daily Star* article, written about previously uses, 'sex swap op' (Gilmour, 2015, p. 1) in its front-page headline. It is a tactic of tabloid papers to use alliteration and puns in their headlines; designed to be catchy and draw in readership. However, they are often reductive and, again, erase the diverse experiences of trans people whilst also medicalising them. For example, a headline from *The Mail Online* refers to the subject of the article as 'sex-change father' (Winter, 2014), again, reducing this person's experiences to surgery.

Donna describes the term sex-change as 'hideous' (Ward, 2018, p. 176); however, goes into no more detail. However, Michael explains that 'you cannot change your sex, most people don't know their sex, and what even is sex anyway as we're all made up of so many different things' (Ward, 2018, p. 176), which underpins why 'sex-change' or 'sex-swap' is problematic. These terms make assumptions about people and identities. Not only does it conflate sex and gender identity, but it assumes that we all know our chromosomal make-up and that there is a binary choice between male and female that every gender-variant person makes. As mentioned, discussing the term 'become' or 'sex-change/swap' also assumes that to be trans you must have surgery and also erases the experience of people who may not choose to have surgery.

The reductive nature of news media reflects an archaic attitude towards gender identity as a whole. Before Butler's (Butler, 1990) performativity theory, which proved to be a significant moment in gender theory, concepts of gender development were reduced to biology and sexual characteristics. However, whilst academic and theoretical discourses around gender may have moved away from essentialism, wider understanding of gender still places people into two categories. As Eckert and McConnell-Ginet (2013) outline, biological essentialism endures in society and can be seen permeating public spheres such as social media and newspaper comments spaces. Throughout the media there is a common discourse about gender-variant people which is reinforced by a constant representation of one experience of being trans.

Conclusion

What this chapter highlights is how British news media presents trans people in a particular manner which perpetuates a specific narrative about gender variance. If gender identity is a cultural fiction (Jagose, 1996) then news media as cultural outlets are creating a fictional trans person, especially when we consider that the majority of society's experiences with trans people come from media consumption (McInroy & Craig, 2015).

Trans people are not presented as being the centre of their own stories. In more recent times, trans and gender issues have been presented through those who 'disagree' with people affirming their gender identities. Trans issues, therefore, are being discussed and 'debated' in a forum in which they are not a part. This erasure is reflective of trans people's erasure in the UN's SDGs, in which women's and men's issues are discussed without including one of the most marginalised groups of people.

Additionally, the articles from the 2010s provided a contrast in story subjects, but still manages to delegitimise or erase trans identities. In these articles, gender-variant people are represented as a homogenised group who experience gender in the same way. Each trans person is expected to cross a binary line from either male to female, or male to female, and this is always done with hormone treatment and surgery. After speaking to the participants, it is clear how much news media erases experiences and lacks nuance when discussing trans stories; however, these narratives are so pervasive that not only do they inform wider society, but often gender-variant people feel they need to adhere to them to be considered 'legitimate'.

Additionally, there are often tropes which are discussed frequently, such as knowing you were trans since early childhood or having been born in the wrong body, or undergoing extensive and 'expensive' surgeries. It is clear that the participants do not adhere to these tropes. Terri, for example, self-identifies as a girl yet is undergoing no medical transition and also refuses hormone treatments. Also, Rachel, as we just discussed, did not fully understand her gender identity until she was in her twenties and never necessarily felt it in early childhood. Donna identified as a cross-dresser for the majority of her life, only transitioning in her forties. Already here we have diverse experiences of gender variance, each as legitimate as the rest; however, consuming media stories would lead an audience to believe there is only one way of being trans. Cis audiences in particular may get their knowledge and understanding of trans people from the media and when representations are limited to a very narrow lens of trans experiences and stories, this knowledge and understanding also limited. Media discourses on gender variance prop up certain tropes of trans identities and build a picture of what trans people should be. Consumed by cis audiences, these tropes become expectations and if not met, may lead to further discrimination.

It is clear, therefore, that the UN's sustainability goals lack adequate targets for a community which faces widespread discrimination because of gender. The sustainability goals, whilst important, do not do enough to acknowledge the specific issues and needs for gender-variant people. In living with a backdrop of discriminatory discourses, whether overt or covert, there is extra pressure for trans people to adhere to certain ideas of gender. Not adhering to these expectations creates a feeling of otherness and can lead to questioning the validity of one's identity. Media discourses on gender variance prop up certain tropes of trans identities and build a picture of what trans people should be. Consumed by cis audiences, these tropes become expectations and lead to further discrimination in laws, socio-economic status, health, and education outcomes.

Overall, the goals themselves cannot be attained if a person's identity is undermined and questioned repeatedly by a powerful institution such as the media, which perpetuates stereotypical narratives. What has been discussed demonstrates that the lived experiences of trans and gender-variant people are as intersectional as cis people but the reductive nature of trans stories leads to identity erasure. This is reflected in the sustainability goals which are fighting for gender equality but at the same time omitting a highly marginalised group. This erasure, therefore, props up discrimination rather than eradicates it, and does not help in the eradication of other societal inequalities or promote good health and wellbeing. Until the UN addresses this oversight, the SDGs cannot be fully met.

References

Bachmann, C. L., & Gooch, B. (2018). *LGBT in Britain: Trans Report*. Stonewall. Retrieved October 4, 2018, from https://www.stonewall.org.uk/sites/default/files/lgbt-in-britain-trans.pdf

Baxter, J. (2014). *Double-Voicing at Work: Power, Gender and Linguistic Expertise*. Palgrave Macmillan.

BBC News. (2014). *Stag Gore Victim Dr Kate Says Press 'Trampled on Private Life'*. Retrieved November 20, 2017, from http://www.bbc.co.uk/news/uk-england-27405267

Benjamin, H. (1966). *The Transsexual Phenomenon*. The Julian Press Inc.

Blum-Kulka, S. (1997). Discourse Pragmatics. In T. A. Van Dijk (Ed.), *Discourse as Social Interaction* (pp. 38–63). Sage.

Butler, J. (1990). *Gender Trouble: Feminism and the Subversion of Identity*. Routledge.

Cauldwell, D. O. (1949). Psychopathia Transexualis. *Sexology: Sex Science Magazine, 16*(5), 274–280.

Donovan, C., & Hester, M. (2014). *Domestic Violence and Sexuality: What's Love Got to Do With It?* Bristol University Press.

Eckert, P., & McConnell-Ginet, S. (2013). *Language and Gender* (2nd ed.). Cambridge University Press.

Evans, S. J. (2014, August 1). Sex-Swap DJ to Have New Genitalia Made out of Skin from His Tattooed Arm… Leaving Him with Tribal-Print Organ. *Daily Mail*. Retrieved August 12, 2014, from http://www.dailymail.co.uk/news/article-2712474/Transgender-Cardiff-man-new-genitalia-skin-tattooed-arm.html

Fairclough, N. (1989). *Language and Power*. Longman.

Fairclough, N., & Wodak, R. (1997). Critical Discourse Analysis. In T. A. Van Dijk (Ed.), *Discourse as Social Interaction* (pp. 258–284). Sage.

Feinberg, L. (2006). Transgender Liberation: A Movement Whose Time has Come. In S. Stryker & S. Whittle (Eds.), *The Transgender Studies Reader* (pp. 205–220). Routledge.

Ferreira, L. (2022, January 11). British Media, 'Your Bigotry is Killing Trans People'. *Open Democracy*. Retrieved October 1, 2022, from https://www.opendemocracy.net/en/5050/british-media-your-bigotry-is-killing-trans-people/

Gilmour, P. (2015, 17 April). Daddy Became Mummy and Now I Love Her Even More. *The Daily Mirror*.

Goffman, E. (1959). *The Performance of Self in Everyday Life*. Reprint, Penguin Books, 1990.

Greenslade, R. (2013, March 22). Daily Mail Urged to Fire Richard Littlejohn After Death of Lucy Meadows. *The Guardian*. Retrieved November 20, 2017, from https://www.theguardian.com/media/greenslade/2013/mar/22/richard-littlejohn-transgender

Gyamerah, A. O., Baguso, G., Santiago-Rodriguez, E., Sa'id, A., Arayasirikul, S., Lin, J. … Wesson, P. (2021). Experiences and Factors Associated with Transphobic Hate Crimes Among Transgender Women in the San Francisco Bay Area: Comparisons Across Race. *BMC Public Health*. [Online Publication 2 June]. https://doi.org/10.1186/s12889-021-11107-x

Hinscliff, G. (2019, December 22). *Maya Forstater's Case Was About Protected Beliefs, Not Trans Rights. The Guardian*. Retrieved October 1, 2022, from https://www.theguardian.com/commentisfree/2019/dec/22/maya-forstater-case-about-protected-beliefs-not-trans-rights

Jagose, A. R. (1996). *Queer Theory: An Introduction*. New York University Press.

Kindred, A. (2019, December 20). Who Is Maya Forstater and What Was JK Rowling's Tweet About? *The Sun*. Retrieved October 1, 2022, from https://www.thesun.co.uk/news/10592038/who-is-maya-forstater-and-what-was-jk-rowlings-tweet-about/

McInroy, L. B., & Craig, S. L. (2015). Transgender Representation in Offline and Online Media: LGBTQ Youth Perspectives. *Journal of Human Behaviour in the Social Environment, 25*(6), 606–617.

McNeil, J., Bailey, L., Ellis, S., Morton, J., & Regan, M. (2012). *Trans Mental Health Study 2012*. Scottish Transgender Alliance.

Newman, V. (2019, December 19). JK Rowling Under Fire as She Throws Support Behind Maya Forstater. *The Daily Mirror*. Retrieved October 1, 2022, from https://www.mirror.co.uk/3am/celebrity-news/jk-rowling-under-fire-throws-21129342

Noor, P. (2019, December 19). JK Rowling in Row Over Court Ruling on Transgender Issues. *The Guardian*. Retrieved October 1, 2022, from https://www.theguardian.com/books/2019/dec/19/jk-rowling-trans-row-court-ruling-twitter-maya-forstater

Oram, A. (2007). *Her Husband Was a Women! Women's Gender Crossing in Modern British Popular Culture*. Routledge.

Oram, A. (2016). Woman as Husband: Gender, Sexuality and Humour in the News of the World 1910–1950s. In L. Brake, C. Kaul, & M. W. Turner (Eds.), *The News of the World and the British Press 1843–2011*. Palgrave Macmillan.

Oxford Living Dictionaries. (2017). *Become*. Retrieved November 26, 2017, from https://en.oxforddictionaries.com/definition/become

Peitzmeier, S. M., Malik, M., Kattari, S., Marrow, E., Stephenson, R., Agenor, M., & Reisner, S. L. (2020). Intimate Partner Violence in Transgender Populations: Systematic Review and Meta-analysis of Prevalence and Correlates. *American Journal of Public Health* [Online Publication 12 August]. https://doi.org/10.2105/AJPH.2020.305774

Phipps, A. (2020). *Me, Not You: The Trouble with Mainstream Feminism*. Manchester University Press.

Pike, S. (2012, December 19). School's Letter to Parents Tell them Male Teacher Will Return to Class as a Woman After Christmas. *Accrington Observer* (Accrington edn). Retrieved November 20, 2017, from http://www.accringtonobserver.co.uk/news/local-news/accrington-schools-letter-parents-tells-1273948

Robins, P. (2014, October 1). Sponger Wants Sex Swap Op Reverse ...and YOU Will End Up Footing the Bill Again. *Daily Star*, pp. 1, 7.

Russell, L. (2016). The Realities of Being Young, Unemployed and Poor in Post-Industrial Britain. *Power and Education, 8*(2), 160–175.

Sacks, H. (1974). On the Analysability of Stories by Children. In R. Turner (Ed.), *Ethnomethodology* (pp. 216–232). Penguin.

Scolaro, B. (2020). LGBTI and the Sustainable Development Goals: Fostering Economic Well-Being. *LGBTQ Policy Journal.* [Online Publication 24 June]. https://lgbtq.hkspublications.org/2020/06/24/lgbti-and-the-sustainable-development-goals-fostering-economic-well-being/#_edn3

Stonewall. (2022). *A Beginner's Guide to Pronouns and Using Pronouns in the Workplace.* Retrieved October 2, 2022, from https://www.stonewall.org.uk/workplace-trans-inclusion-hub/beginner%E2%80%99s-guide-pronouns-and-using-pronouns-workplace

Swerling, G. (2022, July 6). JK Rowling Says Women Making Gender-Critical Claims Safer After 'Free Speech' Tribunal. *The Telegraph.* Retrieved October 1, 2022, from https://www.telegraph.co.uk/news/2022/07/06/maya-forstater-wins-two-claims-fresh-employment-tribunal-following/

The Human Rights Campaign Foundation. (2021). *Fatal Violence Against the Transgender and Gender Non-Conforming Community in 2021.* Retrieved July 27, 2022, from https://www.hrc.org/resources/fatal-violence-against-the-transgender-and-gender-non-conforming-community-in-2021

Thornborrow, J., & Coates, J. (2005). *The Sociolinguistics of Narrative.* John Benjamins.

Titscher, S., Meyer, M., Wodak, R., & Vetter, E. (2000). *Methods of Text and Discourse Analysis.* Sage.

United Nations. (2022a). *The Sustainable Development Agenda.* Retrieved July 10, 2022, from https://www.un.org/sustainabledevelopment/development-agenda/

United Nations. (2022b). Take Action for the Sustainable Development Goals. *Sustainable Development Goals.* Retrieved July 10, 2022, from https://www.un.org/sustainabledevelopment/sustainable-development-goals/

United Nations. (2022c). *10 Reduce Inequality Within and Among Countries.* Retrieved October 10, 2022, from https://sdgs.un.org/goals/goal10

Ward, K. (2018). *Building an Identity Despite Discrimination: A Linguistic Analysis of the Lived Experiences of Gender Variant People in North East England.* Unpublished PhD Thesis, University of Sunderland, Sunderland.

Ward, K. (2020). Understanding Gender Categorisation in a Binary Society. In A. Smith (Ed.), *Gender Equality in Changing Times.* Palgrave Macmillan.

Winter, K. (2014, June 26). He Ain't Heavy... She's My Mother: 28st 7lb Sex Change Father-Of-Three Loses TEN Stone. *Mail Online.* Retrieved August 12, 2014, from http://www.dailymail.co.uk/femail/article-2670509/He-aint-heavy-shes-mother-28st-7lb-sex-change-father-three-loses-TEN-stone.html

Woolfe, V. (1928). *Orlando: A Biography.* Reprint, Hertfordshire: Wordsworth Classics, 1995.

CHAPTER 11

Hate, Disgust, and Restrictive Eating: Abusive Comments on Body-Inclusive Posts on Instagram

Tina Kristensen

Introduction

In line with the overarching theme of the book this chapter will be aligned with the United Nations' 17 goals for sustainable development. Specifically, this chapter will align with two goals—Goal 5, which aims to 'achieve gender equality and empower all women', and Goal 3 which will 'ensure healthy lives and promoting well-being for all at all ages' (United Nations, 2015).

This chapter aims to show the juxtaposition of these two goals and the reality for women on Instagram. Women are scrutinized and harassed for existing in bodies, which are larger than the perceived social ideal, to the point where starvation is encouraged to decrease the size of one's body.

T. Kristensen (✉)
University of Sunderland, Sunderland, UK
e-mail: tina.kristensen@research.sunderland.ac.uk

D. Dalton, A. Smith (eds.), *Gender, Sexuality and the UN's SDGs*, Sustainable Development Goals Series,
https://doi.org/10.1007/978-3-031-31046-1_11

Throughout this chapter the word 'fat' will be used, rather than obese or overweight. Overweight implies that there is an ideal weight and obese has negative medical connotations, so in line with existing research 'fat' will be used (Lupton, 2012).

What Is Instagram?

Recently, a large amount of research has been done on the social media app Instagram (Are, 2020; Cohen et al., 2019; Kim, 2020; Tiggemann et al., 2020). Instagram originally started as a social media app where people would post pictures of their everyday life and follow their friends and family. However, as social media became an increasingly bigger part of everyday life Instagram grew and its purpose changed. An estimate from Business of Apps (2022) suggests that Instagram currently (2022) has about 1.45 billion users worldwide, which is up from one billion in 2018, and 70% of its users are under 35 years of age. Furthermore, Business of Apps (2022) states that Instagram's annual revenue in 2020 was $24 billion. Compared to traditional media social media is interesting because social media is interactive in its nature and the creation of context is happening in a much more participatory manner than what is the case for traditional media. This means that the people who consume the content are not just consumers in the traditional sense (KhosraviNik & Unger, 2016; Kim, 2020), but rather 'prosumers' who 'are not only viewers of creative content and advertisements, but also the co-creators and co-distributors of the very content themselves' (KhosraviNik & Unger, 2016, p. 207).

As Instagram grew it became a marketing tool where popular public users, named influencers, can promote products in return for payment (Business of Apps, 2022). Brown (2022, p. xx) defines an influencer as someone who has cultivated a large number of online followers, who in some cases pay to get 'a peep show' into their life. Additionally, Leaver et al. (2020) explain that influencers are characterized by a high follower to following ratio and that they can reach a 'microcelebrity' status, where they engage in self-branding and can turn their high visibility and engagement from followers into a fulltime career. As such Instagram has changed from a networked intimacy to a 'networked public' (Leaver et al., 2020). Brown (2022, p. ix) states that the current number of people who make a living of their social media presence has reached millions. Instagram has indeed become a business for many, and influencers treat it as such as they curate their Instagram feed by staging photos and often portraying an idealized version of their lives, giving followers the impression that they are 'living their best life' (Leaver et al., 2020).

Body Positivity, Body Love, and Body Neutrality

There are, however, groups of influencers on Instagram who devote the majority of their social media presence to destroy prevalent beauty standards. One of the first mainstream media campaigns to discuss and challenge the beauty standards for women was Dove's 'Real Beauty' campaign (Unilever, 2017). They started their campaign in 2004 and stated that the campaign was to feature and celebrate real women. Today they have made a pledge to never use models in their advertisement and to help girls build confidence (Unilever, 2017). Gill and Orgad (2015) explain that Dove's 'real beauty' campaign gave rise to what they call 'body love' discourse (Gill & Orgad, 2015, p. 329). Both the Dove campaign and the 'body love' discourse were made possible because of the fat rights movement in the 1970s, which, along with the internet, was the catapult for the body positivity movement (BBC Bitesize, n.d.). The body positive movement was created by fat people of colour, in order to create visibility for fat minority bodies, who had previously been excluded from the fat rights movement (BBC Bitesize, n.d.; Robyn, 2021). The body positivity movement sits within post-feminism, which argues that women's problems can be solved with an increase in self-confidence. Generally, post-feminism does not focus on structural or institutional issues, but rather it argues that women should turn the gaze inwards and focus on changing themselves as the culture around them will not change, thereby overlooking the scrutiny that society puts on women's bodies (Gill & Orgad, 2015).

When collecting Instagram photos and comments to use in this chapter, it was found that they did not fully align with the body positive movement. The majority of the women, whose posts were collected, did not live in fat minority bodies but were much more aligned with the midsize movement. Midsize is representing people who fall between petite and plus size (Robyn, 2021). Many of the influencers whose posts were collected have explicitly stated that they are aware that they do not belong in the body positive movement and acknowledge the privileges which come with a midsize body. One thing that the women in the midsize movement seem to have in common is that they lean more towards body neutrality with the primary philosophy that you don't always have to love how your body looks but you do need to respect it and love the functions it performs (Fuller, 2022; Weingus, 2018). Unlike the body positive movement, which is rooted in post-feminism, the midsize movement is more aligned with fourth wave feminism. When discussing fourth wave feminism Banet-Weiser (2018, p. 1) defines what she calls popular feminism by three points. Firstly, it exists in online spaces, such as social media and secondly, the 'popular' in the term popular feminism refers to 'the condition of being liked or admired by like-minded people'. Lastly, she explains that popular feminism is also built on an understanding of Stuart Hall's (1998) theory of 'a terrain of struggle, a space where competing demands for power battle it out' (Banet-Weiser, 2018, p. 1). While the two movements do share a similar discourse the midsize movement exists heavily on social media, which is a key element of fourth wave feminism (Prendergast & Quinn, 2020). Furthermore, the influencers in this study are certainly 'liked or admired' as their combined following, at the time of writing, is 891,000 people. Lastly, the 'terrain of struggle' will be seen throughout the chapter. As Banet-Weiser (2018, p. 1) explains popular feminism and what she calls popular misogyny battle it out for visibility in online spaces. Which means that the midsize movement is in constant battle with the misogyny of dominant culture, which takes the form of hate comments. It is this clash between two ideologies which becomes clear in this chapter.

The midsize movement is challenging the status quo and does not accept that society will not change. Instead, it uses social media to call out and challenge the normalization of scrutiny of women's bodies. It tells women that they can learn to accept their bodies and want society to change at the same time.

The two movements are closely related and without the body positive movement the midsize movement would most likely never have come to be. For the purpose of this chapter definitions and boundaries between the two movements have been drawn, but it is important to note that these lines are fluid, and the movements overlap. The main aim of this chapter is not to decide the scope and limitations of the two movements but to show the abuse and hate women receive online for existing in their own bodies.

As such this chapter will focus on the work that influencers are doing to challenge dominate ideologies around the thin ideal and the hate and abuse this is generating. The chapter will, amongst others, draw on Tiggemann et al. (2020) who explained that on Instagram the work to dismantle the thin ideal includes women showing perceived flaws such as cellulite and stomach rolls and is to be understood as any message, visual or written, that challenges dominant ways of viewing the physical body in accordance with beauty ideals and encourages the reclaiming of embodiment and control over one's self-image. Body positivity encompasses any individual or movement actions which aim to denounce the societal influences and construction of body norms, and instead promotes self-love and acceptance of bodies of any shape, size, or appearance: including rolls, dimples, cellulite, acne, hairy bodies, bleeding bodies, fat bodies, thin bodies and (dis) abled bodies. (Cwynar-Horta, 2016, p. 38)

Online Abuse and Hate

Chakraborti et al. (2014) define hate crime as 'acts of violence, hostility and intimidation directed towards people because of their identity or perceived "difference"'. The influencers in this research were targeted with hate because of their gender and because they are challenging the societal expectations of what a woman's body should look like. KhosraviNik and Esposito (2018) explain that gender-based abuse helps maintain equality imbalances both online and offline. A report by Center for Countering Digital Hate (2022) found that Instagram has failed to act on 90% of reports of abusive DMs (direct message) towards women and that Instagram failed to act on nine out of ten reports of violent DMs. The report also made it clear that Meta, the company which owns Instagram, has previously failed to act on a letter from the Women's Disinformation Defence Project.

The Center for Countering Digital Hate report found that many female influencers alter their content or refrain from posting due to fear of abuse. This echoes Megarry (2017) who stated that both political feminist activists and general users of social media had doubts about posting opinions online. Are (2020, p. 741) explains that 'the same platforms that were going to give them [women] voice are also giving users new opportunities to harass, insult and silence them'. Are (2020, p. 741) adds that 'offline vulnerabilities have followed women online'. One reason why online hate is so prevalent is the anonymity which is possible online (KhosraviNik & Esposito, 2018) and the fact that women in online spaces are more easily accessible to men (Megarry, 2017). Additionally, this also means that men have more access to online feminist activism, and they can therefore more easily influence and disrupt this work (Megarry, 2017).

As evidenced in the above hate against women who challenge main ideology in online spaces is an issue. It is clear from the report from the

Center for Countering Digital Hate that Meta so far has failed to protect its female influencers and as such continues to leave them vulnerable to harassment.

Method and Methodology

Who can see a photo posted to Instagram depends on the settings of the user, either private, meaning only preapproved followers can view shared photos, or public which means that everyone can see the photo. All accounts used in this analysis were public and usually had between a couple of hundred to thousands of comments on their photos. Some of the comments which were collected are from the influencers' DM, which is private, but was shared by the influencers on their story. As such it was not always clear what photo the comment was a reaction to, this is the case for Photo 11.2. The influencers whose photos and comments will be used in this chapter all speak out about various feminist issues they meet both offline and online. Photos from several influencers were collected but ultimately only photos from two influencers were used in this chapter. Both influencers are white. One influencer can be defined as fat whereas the other exists in a straight midsized body, which means they live in a body which comfortably fits into clothing from high street clothing brands (Waheed, 2022).

Despite the limitations in terms of racial diversity this research stands to show the abuse women receive online, but it recognizes that other forms of hate and discrimination may have been present had data from racial minorities been included. Ultimately, the goal is to draw parallels between the UN's goals of gender equality and well-being and the fact that women are abused for existing in their bodies. The aim of this chapter is not to suggest that these goals are not worthwhile, but rather to juxtaposition them against the realities women face online.

This research will be using Cwynar-Horta's (2016) definition of body positive activism where all actions to challenge the idealized body and move to normalize perceived flaws, such as stomach rolls, stretchmarks, and cellulite count as body positive actions. As this research is more interested in the comments than the influencers themselves a minimum number of followers was not a selection requirement, as has been the case with other studies (Cohen et al., 2019; Cwynar-Horta, 2016). However, like Cwynar-Horta (2016) it was required that the influencer had posted at least one photo in the last two weeks to ensure the content for analysis was recent. All data was collected in summer 2020.

Following Cwynar-Horta's (2016) lead photos were selected based on one or more of the following criteria

- Photos that challenge norms around body shape and size
- Photos where advocates share experiences with eating disorders

When a photo fulfilled one or both of the above criteria, the comments were manually scanned for negative comments and sub-comments. An unexpected challenge arose when it became clear that some influencers delete the negative comments on their photos or make comments invisible to other users, so only the influencer would be able to see it. To counter this, screenshots were taken of the post and comments, but some comments may no longer exist on the actual photo. When selecting comments and sub-comments this research again followed Cwynar-Horta's (2016) lead and chose to not have any pre-set criteria and categories. Instead, selection was guided by familiarity with the topic of online abuse. The reason for this was to collect a variety of comments, including some, which may not at first seem overtly abusive.

In the end seven photos were collected, all with at least one negative comment and subsequently three photos were chosen for analysis with a combined total of 16 comments. All photos and comments have been numbered for ease. Two photos came from a fat influencer and one photo from a midsized influencer. Following collection, the comments were categorized, and the categories are as follows:

- Food restriction
- Dignity and disrespect
- Disgust
- Weight bias

The methodology which will be used in this chapter is Social Media Critical Discourse Studies (henceforth SM-CDS), which is a relatively newer area of Critical Discourse Studies (CDS). CDS is 'not interested in investigating a linguistic unit per se but in analysing, understanding, and explaining social phenomena that are necessarily complex and thus require a multidisciplinary and multi-methodical approach' (Wodak & Meyer,

2016, p. 2). Therefore, discourse cannot be seen in isolation, and one must always keep in mind the social environment in which it exists. 'Such analysis aims to be clear in the way that it provides "evidence" from texts to reveal discourses—and therefore the ideas, values, and priorities—that define our societies' (Bouvier & Machin, 2018, p. 178). Bouvier (2020) explains that in society there will always be one ideology which is the dominate one, and which has previously been the main focus of CDS, but with the emergence of social media it provides the opportunity to look at how other ideologies compete and challenge the dominate one, and how these ideologies are supported and challenged.

KhosraviNik and Esposito (2018) explain that when conducting SM-CDS analysis it is important to consider the platform itself and how it enables people to communicate. Instagram allows for a sizeable amount of text to accompany the photo, which offers influencers the opportunity to provide in-depth thoughts and arguments about various topics and in return people can comment and sub-comment. This creates the possibility for several different conversations to take place under one post. Two of the main arguments that KhosraviNik and Unger (2016, p. 231) and KhosraviNik and Esposito (2018, p. 61) put forward are that SM-CDS still needs to focus on the same central questions as CDS and that SM-CDS should never see social media as an isolated environment but rather as a symptom of what is happening in offline society. Which is why KhosraviNik and Unger (2016, p. 212) argue that social movements need to be viewed as such even if they take place primarily online. The social media platform is only a resource used to further the movement. Social media in itself is not the movement. 'It is still the society, its discursive structures, cultural contexts, genealogies of knowledges, discourses-in-place and issues around discrimination and inequalities to represent the core object of study. Accounting for communicative structures and norms of new media technologies should not result in reducing the notion of society into a cybernetic space' (KhosraviNik & Esposito, 2018).

One method which will be used to analyse the comments is semantic fields. Gao & Xu (2013, p. 2031) explain that semantic fields are 'the relationship between genus and species of lexical study' and 'since the vocabulary of a language is semantically related, we are not supposed to study the semantic change of individual words in isolation, but to study vocabular as an integrated system'. This method fits well with the overarching methodology of SM-CDS as both argue that language must be understood in relation to its wider settings as opposed to an isolated unit. With this methodology and method as the lead this chapter will continuously draw parallels between the abusive comments and the two UN goals.

Data Analysis

Food Restriction

The first photo to be analysed is Photo 11.1, which is of the fat influencer, Kenzie Brenna, photographed from a low angle with the words 'eating food is complicated' written across the photo.

The text that accompanied the photo talks about difficulties with eating the amount of food that your body needs and experiences of both under-eating and overeating. Kenzie further philosophizes if the perfect balance will ever be reached. Comment 1 says:

> I don't think eating food is that complicated for you unless you're taking a deit [diet] or trying to avoid certain foods, which you clearly don't do enough. (Comment 1)

It is interesting to note that Kenzie is addressed directly in comment 1 by the sentence 'which you clearly don't do enough'. Kenzie is being blamed for not being thin and not restricting her food in order to become thin.

Photo 11.2 is of the midsized influencer, Alex Light, standing in her underwear and around her she has included hateful and shaming comments she has received.

In the text Alex asks how comments like these are okay and what motivates people to leave these kinds of comments. The comments on the image say:

> Perhaps you should lay off the calories for a while? (Comment 2)

> Beauty why just don't stop eat junk food? Find an activity You love (CrossFit, gym, yoga) ♥♥ (Comment 3)

As with comment 1, these two comments are advocating restrictive eating, by suggesting to 'lay off the calories' and 'stop eat junk food'. The idea of food restriction as a 'common sense' way of losing fat is widespread, which Wright et al. (2006) showed as they found that the female participants in

Photo 11.1 Kenzie Breena's post

their study 'equated "being healthy" with a slim body shape' and that they choose to focus on controlling food intake in order to obtain and maintain a thin body. Some women have internalized the pressure to reach the thin ideal (Wright et al., 2006). To avoid getting fat one must ensure to only eat the 'right' things (Plotz, 2020). This is what is seen in comment 3. Because Alex is not meeting the thin ideal it is automatically assumed that she is only eating the 'wrong' things, such as fast food. Alex has previously disclosed having had an eating disorder and in the text accompanying the photo, she talks about how these comments trigger her eating disorder. She says 'and that ED [eating disorder] voice that is normally so small and so quiet tends to rear its ugly head when I read things like this. Because despite all the work I've done, I'm still a human being with the ability to

Photo 11.2 Alex Light's post

feel hurt'. Despite having recovered from her eating disorder Alex is struggling not to internalize the thin ideal in these situations. The fact that a thin body is preferred over being physically and mentally healthy is worrying, especially when it is known that out of all mental disorders eating disorders have the highest mortality rating (The Checkup by Single Care, 2022). It seems dominant discourse would rather see women ill, unhealthy, and starving than for them to deviate outside of the perceived ideal body and as such it is unsurprising that it is estimated that 1.2 million people in the UK have an eating disorder (Beat Eating Disorders, n.d.). One of the main issues is that thin is generally seen as 'healthy' no matter the circumstances, and the two main strategies to becoming thin are 'taking more exercise and reducing food consumption' (Lupton, 2012, p. 15). Even the

Department of Health England (2011, p. 3) has declared a war on food when they state that 'overweight and obesity are a direct consequence of eating and drinking more calories and using up too few'. It is therefore unsurprising that the general attitude is to restrict eating in order to lose fat. However, Lupton (2012, p. 20) shows that yoyo dieting and poor eating habits can have a negative effect on a person's health and states that there is no data to prove 'that significant weight loss improves fat people's health status'.

When explaining society's obsession to keep women thin Wolf (1991, p. 187) states that

> a culture fixated on female thinness is not an obsession about female beauty, but an obsession about female obedience. Dieting is the most potent political sedative in women's history; a quietly mad population is a tractable one.

Wolf's explanation of thinness is in line with Bordo (1993, cited in Plotz, 2020, p. 92), who states that

> such restrictions on appetite, moreover, are not about food intake. Rather, the social control of female hunger operates as a practical "discipline" (to use Foucault's term) trains female bodies in the knowledge of the limits and possibilities. Denying oneself food becomes the central micro-practice in the education of feminine self-restraint and containment of impulse.

It can be suggested that all of the comments above have less to do with how the influencers look and more to do with the fact that they are straying outside of the social norm and challenging the dominate ideology. The analysis shows that gender equality and women's right to well-being, UN's Goals 5 and 3 respectively, are not achieved for Kenzie and Alex. They are being targeted for being women who dare to not obey the norms of the thin ideal and challenge the main ideology by doing so. Additionally, while the idea of restricting food to become thin is presented by dominant discourse as a 'common sense' way to achieve a healthy body, it is clear that Kenzie and Alex's actual health statuses are being ignored and their health is judged only on their appearance.

Dignity and Disrespect

Photo 11.1 will be looked at again. Comment 4 says:

> it is against the human dignity to say it's ok to be that fat! It's fking unhealthy and you should definitely NOT tell people that they are beautiful and it's "normal" to be like this. It's a fking illness and it was her own choice! As long she doesn't have a hormone disorder! DON'T tell people it's ok to be fat! It ISN'T! It's even deadlier than smoking a pack of cigarettes a day! Open your eyes! (Comment 4)

The comment implies that fat people have no dignity and deserve no respect. This implicature stems from the use of taboo language, which Culpepper (2019, p. 29) defines as 'negative attitudes towards its use in specific contexts, and those attitudes are underpinned by societal thinking', which ultimately 'has negative emotional consequences for at least one participant' (Culpepper, 2019, p. 29). In comment 4 the taboo word is 'fat' as it is used to shame Kenzie. The word fat is in and of itself not taboo but as Culpepper (2019) explains it is context dependent. For example, throughout this chapter fat has been used many times, however it is used as a neutral descriptor, whereas in comment 4 it is used negatively by saying Kenzie is ugly and ill because she is fat. In comment 4 fat is meant to cause emotional harm to Kenzie. It is also worth noting the use of 'normal' in this comment. This implies that being bigger than the ideal is not normal, when the reality is that in 2013 45% of UK women were a size 16 and the ideal UK dress size was a size 12 (Dahlgreen, 2013; Etherington, 2017). Therefore, the 'norm' may be to be bigger than the ideal.

Comment 5 left on Photo 11.3, among other things, says:

> when u work for a good body u have earned the right to have ppl respect ur body. If you sit around eating pancakes all day like Kenzie then im sorry but ur not gonna get the same respect. U have to earn it. (Comment 5)

It is clear from the comments that some do not believe that fat people deserve the same respect as thin people. Comment 5 talks about earning the right to have people respect your body, so by this logic everyone is entitled to be disrespectful towards fat people, because they haven't 'earned' the right to respect. By drawing on the previous section 'work for a good body' could likely mean to restrict eating in order to become thin, so again we see how food restriction is a 'common sense' way of losing weight. Only through starvation can someone claim to 'work for a good body' and thereby get respected.

Photo 11.3 Kenzie's bikini post

In light of this it can be argued that fat and midsize people may have their human rights violated, particularly their right to dignity, as they are frequently 'subjected to discrimination and ill treatment based on their appearance, attacks on their privacy and reputation and coercion in the interests of losing weight' (Lupton, 2012, p. 23). 'According to Foucault, in the disciplinary society individuals are ranked within a hierarchical order/system, dependent on how close their bodies or behaviour are to what is postulated as norm and thereby as ideal, which is how they are disciplined to conform to this postulate' (Plotz, 2020, p. 13). Additionally, 'Female fatness carries connotations of being in opposition to hegemonic gender roles' and they can therefore be 'demonized or ridiculed' (Plotz, 2020, p. 68). Fat and midsize people are discriminated against because their body size places them outside of the perceived norm and this in turn means that they are placed lower on the societal hierarchy and therefore people feel entitled to be disrespectful towards them. This discrimination clearly hinders not only health and well-being, UN's Goal 3, but also general equality, not just between gender but between fat people of all genders and the dominant ideology. With mainstream ideology seeing fat as a reason to place people lower in the social hierarchy no one who is larger than the thin ideal will be able to reach true equality and well-being as they will always be disrespected and discriminated against.

Disgust

Comment 6 on Photo 11.1 says:

> Also I don't think any camera angle would flatter you (Comment 6)

This comment implies that Kenzie is ugly because she is so fat that it is impossible to find a flattering angle. This is building on the societal notion that only thinness is attractive, and no one could or should be attracted to fat people. Prohaska and Gailey (2009) studied 'hogging', which is when a man picks up with a fat woman, a 'hog', and then jokes to his friends about it afterwards. They found that men who were attracted to fat women would disguise it as 'hogging'. This idea that women who do not have the ideal thin body are unattractive is clearly seen in the comments below. All of these comments are from Photo 11.2.

> You = (Sick emoji, puking emoji) (Comment 7)
> Horrible (Comment 8)
> This is absolutely disgusting stio [stop] posting up rotten stuff like this (Comment 9)
> This is gross (Puking emoji) (Comment 10)
> Ew I did not ned to see this (Comment 11)

From these comments a semantic field, with 'fat' as the genus, can be created, with the following species (Table 11.1):

This shows a mentality that fat is disgusting and unattractive. This is in line with both Prohaska and Gailey (2009) and Vartanian (2010) who found that disgust was an important reason for negative attitudes towards fat people. Women's bodies, and particularly fat women's bodies, are at

Table 11.1 Semantic field: Fat 1

Fat						
Nauseous	Throwing up	Horrible	Gross	Disgusting	Ew	Rotten

risk of 'invoking disgust' as 'the leakiness and permeability of the female embodiment' 'challenge the dominant western ideals of containment and control of the body/self' (Lupton, 2012, p. 28). 'Due to the conflation of eating and consumption, thinness is viewed as the embodiment of responsibly consumption' (Plotz, 2020, p. 17). Fatness falls outside of what is socially acceptable and everything which falls outside of the norm is often met with disgust (Plotz, 2020). As such fatness becomes a moral issue as it shows how fat people are unable to show the proper restraint and control, and they are therefore seen as disgusting and lazy. This stands in contrast to the UN's Goal 5, which aims for gender equality and to empower women. Kenzie and Alex are not being empowered, but rather seen as disgusting, unattractive, and lazy. No data on fat male influencers was collected so it is not possible to compare if harassment is happening more to female influencers than male influencers. However, it can be suggested that this is happening primarily because the influencers are female and while online harassment 'can happen to anyone' it seems to be greatly targeted towards women (Chemaly, 2014).

Weight Bias

Photo 11.3 is a side by side set up of Kenzie and a model both in bikinis.

Kenzie wrote that the size of a person's body doesn't matter, and people should wear a bikini if they want to. Several people believed that the model and Kenzie were the same person at different stages of her life.

Comment 12 says:

> You looked way better before, being healthy is not a choice, it is very important (Comment 12)

The below comments are all from Photo 11.2:

> This isn't normal. Stop promoting obesity. It is unhealthy and there's nothing good about it. Going to the gym and eating healthy and getting rid of this fat is a better option. Why not promote that? (Comment 13)

> This isn't normal (sick emoji) (throwing up emoji) (Comment 14)

> If that's normal I don't like normal (sick emoji) I like the model bodies not this mess (Comment 15)

> Please look up for the disease #lipedema ❤ (Comment 16)

It is clear from these comments that two semantical fields can be created. In the first semantic field 'fat' would be the genus and the species would be as follows (Table 11.2):

Whereas the semantic field of thinness has the following species (Table 11.3):

The two fields almost stand as antonymous—where fat is unhealthy thinness is healthy, thinness is attractive while fat is not, thinness is important while fat needs to be gotten rid of. It is clear from the 'fat' semantic field that fatness is generally seen as something dangerous which needs to be eliminated.

Goal 3 of the UN is focusing on well-being for all and particularly female well-being. The comments above are disguised as health concern, but they are judging the person's health only on their lack of thinness. The comments show a tendency for weight bias in society, as they believe the person must be unhealthy due to their size. Puhl, Luedicke, and Grilo (Puhl et al., 2013) found that weight biases are frequent in healthcare and up to 65% of the healthcare students in their study had observed colleagues and teachers making jokes or derogatory comments about fat patients. Based on this study fat or midsized people who seek healthcare

Table 11.2 Semantic field: Fat 2

Fat							
Obesity	Unhealthy	Getting rid of this fat	Not good	Not attractive	Not normal	Mess	Disease

Table 11.3 Semantic field: Thinness

Thinness					
Gym	Eating healthy	Looking good	Healthy	Important	Model

are likely to be met with bias and prejudice due to their size and their health issues might often be put down to their perceived excess of fat. In fact, The World Health Organization has classified obesity as a chronic disease, so despite their actual well-being a fat person will always be classified as ill (Lupton, 2012). Unfortunately, fatness is not only perceived to be a danger to personal health, but also public life. A 2011 report from the Department of Health England stated that 'most people in England today are overweight or obese. Excess weight is a leading cause of type 2 diabetes, heart disease and cancer, adding costs to the NHS—money that could be spent on other priorities' (Department of Health, 2011, p. 3). 'At a time when our country needs to rebuild our economy, overweight and obesity impair the productivity of individuals and increase absenteeism' (Department of Health, 2011, p. 3).

It is clear from the above that weight biases in society and within the healthcare profession are likely to hinder well-being and adequate healthcare for midsized and fat people. This is not only in relation to physical health but consider what comments like the above have done to the mental well-being of the influencers. It seems unlikely that hateful and harassing comments will disappear as long as the main ideology dictates that fat is a detriment to both personal health and societal economic wealth.

Conclusion

In conclusion, this chapter has looked at hateful comments made on Instagram posts which work to challenge the dominate ideal of the thin body. The chapter has explained that these Instagram posts exist within the body positive and midsize movements which belong to post-feminism and fourth wave feminism, respectively. Furthermore, it was shown that online platforms such as Instagram have consistently failed to protect and support their female influencers from online abuse. This chapter analysed three different photos and 16 comments and divided these into four categories. Throughout the analysis it was shown that existing in bodies which do not meet the thin ideal evokes feelings of disgust and lack of respect. Additionally, it was shown that society would rather see a woman restrict her eating to achieve the thin ideal than to stray away from this but be mentally and physically healthy. Throughout the chapter the findings were aligned with existing research, and with Goals 3 and 5 of the United Nations Sustainable Development. It has been made clear that the hateful comments made on the Instagram posts are clear examples of the wider society's views on the female body and how the need to control the female physic speaks to a greater tendency of control and oppression towards women.

References

Are, C. (2020). How Instagram's Algorithm Is Censoring Women and Vulnerable Users But Helping Online Abusers. *Feminist Media Studies, 20*(5), 741–744.

Banet-Weiser, S. (2018). *Empowered: Popular Feminism and Popular Misogyny.* Duke University Press.

BBC Bitesize. (n.d.). *From New York to Instagram: The History of the Body Positivity Movement.* The history of the body positivity movement – BBC Bitesize, Retrieved July 17, 2021.

Beat Eating Disorders. (n.d.). *How Many People Have an Eating Disorder in the UK?* Retrieved July 16, 2022, from https://www.beateatingdisorders.org.uk/get-information-and-support/about-eating-disorders/how-many-people-eating-disorder-uk/

Bouvier, G. (2020). From 'Echo Chambers' to 'Chaos Chambers': Discursive Coherence and Contradiction in the #MeToo Twitter Feed. *Critical Discourse Studies.* https://doi.org/10.1080/17405904.2020.1822898

Bouvier, G., & Machin, D. (2018). Critical Discourse Analysis and the Challenges and Opportunities of Social Media. *Review of Communication, 18*(3), 178–192. https://doi.org/10.1080/15358593.2018.1479881

Brown, S. (2022). *Get Rich or Lie Trying.* Atlantic Books.

Business of Apps. (2022). *Instagram Revenue and Usage Statistics.* Instagram Revenue and Usage Statistics (2022) - Business of Apps. Retrieved July 17, 2022.

Center for Countering Digital Hate. (2022). *Hidden Hate.* Hidden Hate | CCDH (counterhate.com). Retrieved July 17, 2022.

Chakraborti, N., Garland, J., & Hardy, S. (2014). The Leicester Hate Crime Project. Findings and Conclusions. University of Leicester. Retrieved July 17, 2022, from https://le.ac.uk/hate-studies/research/the-leicester-hate-crime-project/our-reports

Chemaly, S. (2014). *There's No Comparing Male and Female Harassment Online.* There's No Comparing Male and Female Harassment Online | Time. Retrieved August 28, 2022.

Cohen, R., Irwin, L., Newton-John, T., & Slater, A. (2019). #bodypositivity: A Content Analysis of Body Positive Accounts on Instagram. *Body Image, 29*, 47–57.

Culpepper, J. (2019). Taboo Language and Impoliteness. In K. Allan (Ed.), *Oxford Handbook of Taboo Words and Language* (pp. 28–40). Oxford University Press.

Cwynar-Horta, J. (2016). The Commodification of the Body Positive Movement on Instagram. *Stream: Culture/Politics/Technology, 8*(2), 36–56.

Dahlgreen, W. (2013). *Size 12 is Britain's 'Ideal' Dress Size, Size 12 is Britain's 'Ideal' Dress Size*. YouGov. Retrieved August 29, 2022.

Department of Health. (2011). *Healthy Lives, Healthy People: A Call to Action on Obesity in England*. Department of Health.

Etherington, J. (2017). One Size Fits All? These Women are Different Heights and Shapes But Are Considered to Be UK's 'Mrs Average'... Because They're Size 16. *The Sun*. Retrieved August 29, 2022.

Fuller, K. (2022). *Body Positivity vs. Body Neutrality* (verywellmind.com). Retrieved July 17, 2022.

Gao, C., & Xu, B. (2013). The Application of Semantic Field Theory to English Vocabulary Learning. *Theory and Practice in Language Studies, 3*(11), 2030–2035.

Gill, R., & Orgad, S. (2015). The Confidence Cult(ure). *Australian Feminist Studies, 30*(86), 324–344. https://doi.org/10.1080/08164649.2016.1148001

Hall, S. (1998). Notes on Deconstructing 'the Popular'. In J. Storey (Ed.), *Cultural Theory and Popular Culture: A Reader* (p. 442). London: Routledge.

KhosraviNik, M., & Esposito, E. (2018). Online Hate, Digital Discourse and Critique: Exploring Digitally-Mediated Discursive Practices of Gender-Based Hostility. *Lodz Papers in Pragmatics, 14*(1), 45–68.

KhosraviNik, M., & Unger, J. W. (2016). Critical Discourse Studies and Social Media: Power, Resistance and Critique in Changing Media Ecologies. In R. Wodak & M. Meyer (Eds.), *Methods of Critical Discourse Studies* (pp. 205–233). Sage.

Kim, H. M. (2020). What do Other's Reaction to Body Posting on Instagram Tell Us? The Effects of Social Media Comments on Viewers' Body Image Perception. *New Media and Society, 23*(12), 3448–3465.

Leaver, T., Highfield, T., & Abidin, C. (2020). *Instagram: Visual Social Media Cultures*. Polity Press.

Lupton, D. (2012). *Fat*. Taylor and Francis.

Megarry, J. (2017). Under the Watchful Eyes of Men: Theorising the Implications of Male Surveillance Tactics for Feminist Activism on Social Media. *Feminist Media Studies*, 1–16. https://doi.org/10.1080/14680777.2017.1387584

Plotz, B. (2020). *Fat on Film*. Bloomsbury.

Prendergast, M., & Quinn, F. (2020). Justice Reframed? A Comparative Critical Discourse Analysis of Twitter Campaigns and Pint Media Discourse on Two High-Profile Sexual Assault Verdicts in Ireland and Spain, *Journalism Practice*. https://doi.org/10.1080/17512786.2020.1786436

Prohaska, A., & Gailey, J. (2009). Fat Women as "Easy Targets" Achieving Masculinity Through Hogging. In E. Rothblum & S. Soloway (Eds.), *The Fat Studies Reader* (pp. 158–166). New York University Press.

Puhl, R. M., Luedicke, J., & Grilo, C. M. (2013). Obesity Bias in Training: Attitudes, Beliefs and Observations among Advanced Trainees in Professional Health Disciplines. *Obesity: A Research Journal, 22*(4), 1008–1015.

Robyn. (2021, January 8). *What Is Mid Size Fashion and How It Can Change Your Life, Midsize Millennial* (midsizemillennial.co.uk). Retrieved July 17, 2022.

The Checkup by Single Care. (2022). Eating Disorder Statistics 2022. Retrieved July 16, 2022, from https://www.singlecare.com/blog/news/eating-disorder-statistics/#eating-disorder-prevalence

Tiggemann, M., Anderberg, I., & Brown, Z. (2020). #Loveyourbody: The Effect of Body Positive Instagram Captions on Women's Body Image. *Body Image, 33*, 129–136.

Unilever. (2017). *Announcing the Dove Real Beauty Pledge, Announcing the Dove Real Beauty Pledge*. News | Unilever global company website. Retrieved July 17, 2022.

United Nations. (2015). *Do You Know All 17 SDGs?* Retrieved January 7, 2021, from https://sdgs.un.org/goals#goals

Vartanian, L. R. (2010). Disgust and Perceived Control in Attitudes Toward Obese People. *International Journal of Obesity, 34*, 1302–1307.

Waheed, J. (2022). *The Midsize Movement Is Taking Over Fashion TikTok*. Glamour. Retrieved July 17, 2022.

Weingus, L. (2018). Body Neutrality Is A Body Image Movement That Doesn't Focus On Your Appearance. *HuffPost Life*. Retrieved July 17, 2022.

Wodak, R., & Meyer, M. (2016). Critical Discourse Studies: History, Agenda, Theory and Methodology. In R. Wodak & M. Meyer (Eds.), *Methods of Critical Discourse Studies* (pp. 1–22). Sage.

Wolf, N. (1991). *The Beauty Myth*. Vintage.

Wright, J., O'Flynn, G., & Macdonald, D. (2006). Being Fit and Looking Healthy: Young Women's and Men's Constructions of Health and Fitness. *Sex Roles, 54*, 707–716.

CHAPTER 12

'T'Ain't Right, T'Ain't Fair, T'Ain't Proper': Examining the Representations of Women in *Poldark*

Barbara Sadler

The United Nations General Assembly set out the 17 Sustainable Development Goals in September 2015 as part of the UN-GA Resolution 2030 Agenda. Notwithstanding the contradictory nature of some of the goals, and the connection between the United Nations and the controversial World Economic Forum via Memorandum of Understanding, the issues relating to Sustainable Development Goal 5, gender equality, are of genuine concern for a large proportion of the global population. Gender is one of the most hotly debated categories in contemporary Western culture. For evidence of this look no further than the UK press where there is debate and (heated) discussion about gender almost every day. From the inequality in medicine related to women's health, 'Why wasn't it mandatory for doctors to be taught about women's issues before now?' (Thorp, 2022), the issues related to transgender sport, 'Here's how trans people

B. Sadler (✉)
University of Sunderland, Sunderland, UK
e-mail: barbara.sadler-1@sunderland.ac.uk

D. Dalton, A. Smith (eds.), *Gender, Sexuality and the UN's SDGs*, Sustainable Development Goals Series,
https://doi.org/10.1007/978-3-031-31046-1_12

feel about YouGov's survey on trans rights' (Stone, 2022) to men experiencing 'social body pressures' and 'feeling under threat from rising equality' in 'Oh boy! The scourge of topless men in London parks' (Muston, 2022). The issues and debates around gender spill into social media too—on Twitter in particular—where the name of J K Rowling is currently tantamount to an explosive device. The concerns in most of the stories relate to gender inequality and issue of what gender means and its relationship to human bodies and how they are categorised. The exclamation of this chapter title is often uttered by Jud, Prudie or Demelza, in the *Poldark* stories and it may prove a fitting description of the discourses and discussions of gender within popular culture where the battle over gender is currently raging. Popular culture as an item of study is very useful for it acts as a barometer of contemporary concerns because it is an 'arena of struggle' (Storey, 2003, p. 51) where competing ideas aim for supremacy: essentially popular culture is an ideological battleground. I have selected the case study of *Poldark* because it offers a unique opportunity to review gender and related inequalities over several different time periods. The 12 Winston Graham *Poldark* novels were written over a period spanning seven decades from 1945 to 2002 with stories within the novels set within the period 1783–1820. The stories are well-loved, with Leggot and Taddeo (2015, p. xxvii) mentioning the notion of a 'Cult of Poldark'. This popularity has led to three television adaptations: in 1975–1977 for BBC, in 1996 by HTV/ITV, and 2015–2019 for BBC and Mammoth Screen. The latest of the adaptations has already received some academic scrutiny related to the depiction of masculinity (Goodman & Moseley, 2018; Taddeo, 2015; Sadler, 2022; Wheatley, 2016). And yet, the *Poldark* stories include some complex and well-loved female characters who have not had the same critical attention. This only serves to highlight the existing gender inequality. This chapter will aim to redress that deficit and focus upon the representation of the female characters and femininity and make links to the concerns of gender theory and feminist politics. As problematic as the notions of 'waves' may be in feminist politics, the historicising aspects of the 'waves' offer an opportunity to map some theoretical ideas to the time frames of the story and its various versions with the social world at the time of production. The awkward concept of postfeminism spans some of the 'waves' but it is useful as a concept for our purpose of analysing female representation over time. To paraphrase Gill on postfeminism she suggests (2007, p. 161) the media now seems to be the place where feminist debate takes place. In this case each of the versions of the story will be reviewed to check how they respond to aspects of feminist politics. Consequently, the story of Demelza and the themes relating to the status (legal and social) and role (function) of women will be a central concern. There are at least five time periods to consider, although the main focus will be the first four novels and corresponding adaptations. Throughout the analysis of female characters and female concerns there will be connections made to gender theory which will enable assumptions and issues about gender to be foregrounded and a measure taken of any changes over the decades—perhaps a consideration of how far we have to travel to achieve gender equality.

Representation, Gender and Adaptation

The focus of how women are portrayed on screen has been a concern of Rosen's (1973) *Popcorn Venus: Women, Movies and the American Dream* which explored women's roles and characterisation in films from 1900s to 1970s. This book was a significant part of the coming to consciousness in the second wave of feminism and following on from it the examination of representation became an important aspect of scholarly work. Nevertheless, depictions on screen are not 'real life' so why should anyone be bothered by representation of characters? Why is representation so important? According to Storey, 'modes of representation seek to construct us as particular subjectivities' (2003, pp. 80–81). It is the identity positions which representations offer and encourage audiences to occupy and the repetition of types of representation which make representation of gender such a key cultural battleground in the drive for gender equality. Essentially, media culture articulates the concerns, identities and debates circulating in a given culture in a given time. The *Poldark* story offers an opportunity to discuss gender representation in relation to the time frame of the setting, source text and era of production to highlight any similarities or changes in how gender is portrayed. As the waves of feminism progressed scholars began to question more about women's position of inequality; was the issue a lack of legal rights (Liberal Feminism), a lack of access to property (Marxist Feminism), or cultural systems (Radical Feminism) or psychology (Psychoanalytical Feminism). The work of Judith Butler (*Gender Trouble* 1990) created a fundamental shift in asking serious questions about what gender means and where in fact it originates. Butler argued that gender is socially constructed and performative and that it is reinforced through repetition and can change depending upon contexts.

'There is no gender identity behind the expressions of gender…identity is performatively constituted by the very "expressions" that are said to be its results' (1980, p. 25). The struggle about this still rages. This may be compounded by a lack of accuracy about the terms 'sex' and 'gender' within Western culture more generally, where the two words are used interchangeably when in fact they refer to quite different referents. For the purposes of this chapter 'sex' will refer to a sex act or biological sexed body, and 'gender' will refer to how a body is enacted or performed. Whether or not the binary terms masculine or feminine are sufficient descriptors are further ongoing debates. Clearly none of the discourses about gender are straightforward. For some there is a deep-rooted belief that gender is biological and from the body and yet for others there is evidence that gender is socially determined, the results of social and cultural influences. Even if there is a tiny proportion of cultural impact upon gender, then gender representation really does matter. Constant repetition of specific attributes makes those attributes seem natural and normal and have the effect of regulating human behaviours. This is especially true when media stories illustrate the consequences of any 'transgressive' behaviour. In film analysis the transgressive woman is punished through death, illness, or isolation (Doane, 1987) and this trope is mirrored in the *Poldark* stories with Keren Daniels' death after her affair with Dwight Enys and Aunt Agatha's death after maliciously planting seeds of doubt in George's mind about Valentine's paternity. In both cases the characters have transgressed boundaries of so-called ideal feminine behaviour. Historian Yuval Noah Harari (CBS News, 2021) has warned about the danger of humans being 'hacked' by algorithms on social media, but all media—including period drama television—has this potential to have impact on attitudes and beliefs which in turn influence behaviour and lead to real world impact. It is crucial to pay attention to what exactly is being represented and how, and consider the consequences.

In this chapter that means looking closely at the depiction of gender within the *Poldark* stories and also taking account of the genre. There is a multitude of research about genres being aligned with gender (Ang, 1985; Geraghty, 2000; Hobson, 1980; Morley, 1986) and that period drama is particularly associated with a female audience. All genres are cultural constructs and the generic boundaries are policed variously by critics, audiences and academics. The extent to which a genre is thought to be aligned with the masculine (news, documentary) or the feminine (soap operas, period dramas) is also culturally decided and this aspect has much to demonstrate about how a culture values certain characteristics over others and perpetuates the lack of visibility of females in public roles. As Tong describes this is the focus of liberal feminism which argues that 'female subordination is rooted in a set of customary and legal constraints that blocks women's entrance and /or success in the so-called public world' (1992, p. 2). For example, soap opera is aligned with femininity and feminine concerns, and it is no accident that soap operas are denigrated. Very often soap operas deal with the concerns of working-class women in the private realm of the home rather than public worlds and roles, so the lack of value attached to the genre is doubly meaningful. The intersections of class and gender also work in the examples of genres which are highly valued, such as news genres or documentaries which are historically the television programme choice of middle-class males and are focused on the concerns of public life. As a period drama, *Poldark* is aligned with middle-class, middle-aged women. This intersection of age, class and gender is important to consider because culturally this group is usually consigned to invisibility. A postfeminist viewpoint here might suggest that it is the women's buying and viewing power which makes them valuable (Keller & Ryan, 2018).

The middle-aged female fans achieve a level of recognition as an audience, though existing fans are more likely to tune in and a new adaptation will open the stories to new audiences. Naturally, a whole series of well-loved novels, such as *Poldark*, is the 'Holy Grail' for producers because of the opportunity for returning seasons. Saunders, writing about adaptations, explains:

> Adaptation is frequently involved in offering commentary on a source text. This is achieved most often by offering a revised point of view from the 'original', adding hypothetical motivation, or voicing the silenced and marginalised. Yet adaptation can also constitute a simpler attempt to make texts 'relevant' or easily comprehensible to new audiences and readerships via processes of proximation and updating. (2006, p. 19)

In adapting the *Poldark* novels for television the producers enter a dialogue with the source novels and its themes and characters. The 'proximations and updating' that Saunders discusses are specifically relevant to the time when the adaptation is produced and articulates concerns within the culture at the time of production. The representation of Demelza is a useful example to illustrate how this works.

Winston Graham introduces Demelza in the first novel *Ross Poldark* (1945). She is described as thin and looking like 11 or 12 years old when she and Ross meet at the fair and he rescues her from a beating by some village boys who are using her beloved dog in an animal fight. Ross offers Demelza a position as a kitchen maid at his house, Nampara, and this rescues her from her home life of acting as surrogate mother to her six brothers, and housekeeper, cleaner and cook for her father, who would regularly beat her when he was drunk. At this point Demelza is represented as an abused teenager. The exact age of Demelza is somewhat unclear, she tells Poldark she is 14, but this is later disputed by her father (1945, p. 133). It is explained that in law a girl of 14 can decide where she lives, so this may be an attempt by Tom Carne to ensure Demelza is returned home to her household duties. Later when she has been at Nampara a short while it is confirmed, 'the child was like a young animal which had spent fourteen years in blinkers' (Graham, 1945, p. 192), immediately the legal and social position of females is apparent. Demelza is a chattel, used by her father as unpaid help and subject to abuse and beatings. Even as Ross Poldark offers her an escape route the legal position of female children is clear: 'There is a law to these things. I must hire you from your father' (1945, p. 113). Demelza will not receive any money for her work but will obtain food, lodging and better clothing. At the time the novel was written (1945) feminism was not established, yet Graham wrote a female character who actively resisted her life of poverty and abuse—Demelza had already attempted to run away from home at age 12—and continues to seek improvements to her circumstances once she is at Nampara. Indeed, the way Demelza strives for her opportunities against a system which only offers disadvantages highlights the injustice of her gendered situation. Tong states these are foremost concerns of liberal feminism: 'gender justice…requires us, first, to make the rules of the game fair' (1992, p. 20). Taddeo goes so far as to suggest that Graham himself has a feminist perspective (2015, p. x) which is commendable considering he wrote the novel prior to feminism emerging.

Whatever Graham's motivation for Demelza, it is certain that he did not appreciate the first four episodes of the 1975–1977 BBC adaptation of *Poldark*. Writing his memoirs, Graham exclaimed, 'What stuck in my crop beyond all swallowing were the ridiculous liberties taken with the characters and with the stories' (2003, p. 203). Graham had sold the rights to *Poldark* to London Films/BBC and as he laments, he had 'no more than parental control over how she developed'. The main issue being that in this iteration of Demelza she is depicted as a promiscuous thief. Demelza (played by actor Angharad Rees) first appears in Episode 2 where she steals bread and cash and offers to remove her knickers for a shilling. All representations are in dialogue with the anxieties of the time of production and in this case a dialogue with source text too. At the time of production second wave of feminism was in full bloom. Humm points out that in the 1970s 'Critics focused on sexist vocabulary and gender stereotypes in the work of male authors and highlighted the ways in which these writers commonly ascribe particular features, such as "hysteria" and "passivity" only to women' (1998, p. 196). This must have been awkward for the *Poldark* producers and show script writers. What transpires is evidence of the struggles playing out in the 'life world' via the inherent complications of 'proximations and updating'. In the 1975–1977 version, Demelza moves from an abused girl to a work-shy, thieving, promiscuous teen until she is 'saved' by the hero Ross Poldark (played by actor Robin Ellis). In several aspects, Demelza's story only serves to bolster the position of Ross as a hero. He rescues her from the village boys, feeds her and overlooks her thieving and laughs when she explains the promiscuous aspects of her life (1975, S1, E2).

Ross: Why don't you grow your hair?
Demelza: It is growing – a man cut it off – he said I stole his watch.
Ross: Did you?
Demelza: It fell out of his pocket when he was dressing.

Demelza transgresses expected gender behaviour in her battle to eat and remain safe. However, it is her place within the law which puts her in such a bind as she protests later in the same episode when her father is given the wages she worked for: 'A woman's got no rights, no nothing. Men, you're all the same when it comes to it, you stick together' (1975, S1, E3). Throughout the 1970s series, Demelza is represented as a mix of traditional femininity and fiery independence. During her first years at Nampara she develops a close friendship with Ross and they chat together frequently. On the day of Jim's trial, Ross returns home drunk. Demelza provides his supper and more rum. She is already in love with him and tries hard to speak properly to please him and ask about the trial proceedings that day. She then makes an effort to seduce him by asking if she is pretty and showing him her stockings. She jokes she'd remove them for a shilling echoing their very first meeting. Ross realises what is occurring and tells her to go to bed. She then confides her love for him and asks him to take her to bed. At this point Ross is seated upright in his chair and Demelza is on her knees on the floor begging and grasping his leg. He stoops down and kisses her. The scene is set up to foreground the inequality in the relationship through the physical size and relative position of the two characters. Demelza is diminutive and emotional—literally begging on the floor; Ross is tall, even whilst seated, and composed, even whilst drunk. What is expressed here is Demelza taking control and following what Tong describes as the feminist position of 'following the lead of her own desires', (1992, p. 5) but being simultaneously subject to stereotyped framing devices within the scene as it was shot.

On the morning Ross explains to Demelza that he will find her a suitable position in another household and that she must leave for he will use her. Demelza believes she is being punished and says she 'should have been like Margaret and asked for money this morning, but I did it for nothing and said I loved you'. Demelza's desire here is outside of marriage and as Doane discusses related to woman's film of the 1940s, such excessive female sexuality poses a threat and must be eliminated or punished (1987, p. 99). This is a very clear expression of the difficulties feminism posed as it disrupts cultural systems of hierarchy, family and domination/subordination. How the issues are handled within the story suggests the ways media culture expresses arguments that are ongoing within a culture in a given moment. After some discussion Demelza gets angry and takes control: 'You don't owe me anything, you needn't worry on that score. I haven't lost anything being here. I have done my work and given nothing short, so we're equal and that's fair' (1975, S1, E3). She walks out and returns to her father who has now remarried and lives a life of sobriety. In the 1970's adaptation Demelza becomes pregnant to Ross from their night together. This is a significant plot divergence from the novel and places Demelza in a difficult situation. Her father insists they go to Ross for financial support for 'there's no marriage there, he's gentry'. In this aspect the intersection of gender and class has a double impact upon Demelza's options. She refuses and leaves to live with Ginny. In another plot divergence, Elizabeth Poldark (played by Jill Townsend) is set to leave Francis Poldark (played by Clive Francis) and be with Ross. They even speak of her divorce from Francis. However, everything changes when Ross realises Demelza is pregnant with his child and she is on her way to Truro to meet a woman who will perform an abortion. Prudie explains: 'I've heard of her, doesn't stay around to see what happens. Takes her money and lets it in the lap of the Almighty. Like as not, there'll be two dead afore morning' (1975, S1, E3). Demelza has limited choices. No one expects Ross to marry her because of their differing social status, and her pride will not allow for Ross to support her without marriage. If she remains unmarried her reputation is ruined and if she has the abortion she will likely die along with the child. It is almost as though Demelza is at war with herself torn between being independent and being feminine. What is articulated are the extra behavioural sanctions which exist for women but not for men and this has long been an area of concern for feminists. Various branches of feminism seek to challenge essentialist ideas on sexuality (Jackson, 1998, p. 139) and question the 'natural order' (Tong, 1992, p. 3) which ultimately 'controlled women's sexuality for male pleasure' (Tong, 1992, p. 5). In the story Ross catches up with Demelza and tells her she won't be alone and that they will be married. Taddeo points out that this scene is deliberately constructed to demonstrate Ross' chivalry: 'Viewers cheered (and still cheer) this seemingly romantic gesture and recall with pleasure those beautiful scenes of Ross carrying her (Demelza) to his horse' (2015, p. 210). In the process, she points out, Demelza herself is reduced as Ross is elevated. When Ross tells Elizabeth that he cannot now marry her, Elizabeth responds with anger, calling Demelza a trollop and encouraging Ross to give Demelza up. Such plot changes only serve the purpose of emphasising Ross' benevolence and simultaneously emphasising both women as unscrupulous and transgressive. In doing so it re-establishes the dominant system of females only being valuable whilst chaste and restores male supremacy. Figuratively gender equality is dismissed.

The scripts for the first four episodes of the 1975–1977 series were written and edited by Jack Pullman and Simon Masters. Winston Graham was provided advance copies of the first scripts during the early part of the production. He was so displeased with the changes that he tried to have the whole series cancelled, but the BBC and producers London Film Productions refused as so many scenes were already filmed. In his autobiography Graham provides anecdotes and detail about the fury he felt. Throughout his memoir he comes across as a gentle and intelligent man, but his reaction to the plot changes moved him to thoughts of violence: 'If anyone had offered me a helicopter and a bomb, I should have leapt at the chance and should have known just where to drop it' (2003, p. 203). The liberties taken with the characters and storyline were doubly problematic where Elizabeth was to seek a divorce from Francis, because as

Graham pointed out divorce was only achieved through an act of parliament which took years to secure and would cost over £10,000. The absurdity of Elizabeth being able to afford this when she has no income of her own made the adaptation of that part of the story unrealistic. Similarly, the use of modern phrasing and language evident from the first episode when someone exclaims that 'they must be joking!'. This serves to highlight the care and attention to historical accuracy that Graham lavished on his novels and also that all adaptations are in a dialogue—not only with the source material, but with the social and economic context of the time of production. Viewed in context, the 1975 script articulates the issues of the era; the 'problem' of unmarried mothers, the changes the Feminist Movement had brought, the increased numbers of divorces, the contradictions of traditional femininity, and the role of women as married, domesticated chattels of their husbands. The male script writers seem to struggle to represent the female experience and instead elect to strengthen the role of the male hero.

Domesticity, Laws and Sexual Violence

Narratives in popular culture help to construct and re-enforce specific meanings, and social roles through repeated representations. In the time frame setting of *Poldark*, 1783–1820, there were very limited options for women, but crucially it is during this period that Wollstonecrafts' *Vindication of the Rights of Women* was first published in 1792. Despite Graham's feminist perspective he still focused on representing the conditions of the period with precision. Demelza's situation as a housekeeper to her father and then to Ross—both before and after marriage—is normalised. Indeed, the domestic labour of women is taken for granted and not questioned. What is interesting in the 2015 adaptation is that the scriptwriter Debbie Horsfield admits to finding any possible ways to provide Demelza with additional storylines.

> It is true to say that she [Demelza] recedes a little in books 3 and 4 in terms of feistiness [...] and she becomes more of a housewife [...] and we did feel that was a bit of a shame. (BFI, 2016)

This seems to position the newer iteration *of Poldark* as having a post-feminist sensibility. Horsfield develops plot deviations to give Demelza the role she deserves: she interferes in politics, fundraises, and manages the mine and farm while Ross is away. All the while Demelza still manages her usual household duties and a side line as a midwife to some of the local women. This foregrounds the subtle ways that much of women's work goes unseen and is only valued when work is in the public sphere. Demelza (played by Eleanor Tomlinson) typically steps up to manage the Poldark business, and discusses this fact with Prudie her housekeeper when Ross does not return from France with the others but sends his hat and apologies (2017, S3, E3). The scene is constructed with the two women side by side kneading bread dough and throwing the dough down on the table with such force to make a loud thud. What seems to occur here is that 'feminist notions are systematically reworked to accommodate mainstream ideas' (Keller & Ryan, 2018, p. 4). Their anger is evident, but so is their shared experience and friendship. Essentially, it has the appearance of feminism but without the activism.

Demelza:	'Young Captain Ross do most sincerely regret' [mimicking Tholly's voice]...Oh he'll regret ever sending home his hat for it won't fit his head when I've done with him.
Prudie:	T'ain't right.
Demelza:	T'ain't fit.
Prudie:	T'ain't fair.
Demelza:	T'ain't proper.
Prudie:	And a child to raise and another on the way.
Demelza:	With a farm to run and a mine beside. What a cheek the menfolk expect us to do their bidding. [Throws bread dough on the table with a thud.]
Prudie:	Lucky we never do. [Smirking].

In the novels, the servant role is taken by Prudie and later Jane Gimlett. Horsfield is compelled to conflate several characters from the novels into one for the sake of brevity and ease of understanding for a television audience. She does so with Dr Dwight Enys and Prudie, and in each case produces more meaningful characters as a result. The female friendship between Prudie and Demelza is a further plot change, but one that reflects female experience and the importance of female friendships which is not developed in the novels and initial 1970s adaptation. The impact of Horsfield as a writer is evident here making a difference to the authenticity of the female characters and their associated plotlines. Demelza's character as written by Horsfield disrupts male dominance several times. When Ross returns from his night with Elizabeth Demelza responds by slapping his face so hard he falls over (2016, S2, E8); she questions why she should love, honour and obey Ross when he is reckless and absent (2017, S3, E3), and by continuing as a midwife to local women, Demelza disrupts the male medical practice of attending and controlling childbirth (2017, S3, E4). Her refusal of male medical help at the birth of Clowance demonstrates her defiance of the social class convention of paying for medical care to demonstrate higher social status. She dismisses this idea because it puts her body into the hands of Dr Choake who she does not trust. In this way she privileges the support of Prudie and her own knowledge of childbirth. What this suggests is that postfeminism is a media phenomenon (Keller & Ryan, 2018, p. 4) where feminist politics are expressed, and some aspects accepted and some rejected.

Not all of the female characters are as independent as Demelza. Very few of the *Poldark* women have means to take care of themselves with two notable exceptions; Caroline Penvenen is an heiress so does not need a husband—indeed she has several suitors who seek her fortune for themselves. Caroline is strong-willed and Upper Class and decides to marry Dr Enys who is of lower rank. Her independent wealth enables more options, and she marries for love. Margaret Vosper is a marginal character who makes a living as a prostitute and is frequented by Francis, George and Ross. She is interesting in that she seems to overcome the notion that 'prostitution is irrecuperable' (Doane, 1987, p. 119) because she marries a lord. Such transgression usually leads to illness, death, madness or isolation, but Margaret prevails.

The more usual representations are evident in characters such as Verity Poldark. She remains unmarried at 23 and it is presumed she will be a spinster forever and augment the household staff making preserves, sewing and mending and looking after the family. When Verity elopes to marry Captain Blamey, her family think of her as selfish for leaving them although the grounds for this belief relate to her value in the domestic sphere. She is a valuable free extra help. However, marriage is seen as a solution for many female characters, even if it most benefits the male characters. This is due to the Common Law of Coverture where a women's rights are subsumed to her husband on marriage. This legal situation makes marriage a double bind for women such as Morwenna Chynoweth. In the life world this is the justification for many of the concerns of first wave of feminism. Morwenna is Elizabeth's cousin and the Chynoweths have several daughters and little money. George encourages Elizabeth to hire Morwenna as a governess for her son, Geoffrey Charles. George is motivated to divert Elizabeth's attention away from Geoffrey Charles in order that she can focus upon the baby she is expecting. Subsequently, George uses Morwenna again by arranging a marriage between her and Osbourne Whitworth. He achieves the marriage by coercion. Morwenna agrees to marry Whitworth to save Demelza's brother, Drake Carne from hanging for stealing the Bible. This charge was engineered by George to ensure the marriage occurred—the purpose of which was to secure a useful connection for George's parliamentary ambitions. The matter highlights that women had little power and were regularly used by men for their own purposes. Morwenna's marriage to Osbourne is disastrous for her and leads to two years of marital rape. Projansky (2001) discusses the history of rape and points out that it is significant that in 1382 legislation in England gave fathers and husbands legal rights to bring a charge of rape to protect women of their family but that far from being protective of the woman who had suffered this was an issue relating to property ownership. This reduced women to chattels. In George's manipulation of Morwenna (forcing marriage to Osbourne, defeating Drake) he treats her as his property. Under such law, marital rape by Osbourne was 'theoretically impossible, since she "belonged" to him' (2001, p. 4). Byrne and Taddeo comment that in the story George and Elizabeth and even Dr Enys bear some responsibility for Osbourne being able to continue to rape Morwenna and they suggest that 'society as a whole is complicit in rape' (2022, p. 152). These storylines were written by Winston Graham in the 1970s when rape and sexual violence against women was a key focus of feminist activism. Notably Graham's writing is careful to illustrate the psychological and physical damage that marital rape has upon Morwenna. However, Projansky points out that such narratives promote 'psychological interiorisation' which despite Graham's feminist perspective, function to provoke fear. Unsurprisingly, Osbourne Whitworth tries to justify his actions through law and religion to have Morwenna acquiesce to his sexual demands. When she repeatedly refuses, he aims to have Morwenna committed to an asylum for failure to perform her wifely 'duties'. It is shocking to consider that such beliefs prevailed for so long and that marital rape was not considered a crime in the United Kingdom until Criminal Justice and Public Order Act 1994. There is no ambiguity in the rape of Morwenna and the fact that Osbourne is a thoroughly bad man, but it is notable that there is another significant rapist in the story.

In the earlier *Poldark* novel *Warleggan* (1953) a rape is perpetrated by the hero Ross Poldark. This rape has a different tone and there is great debate in the *Poldark* fandom about whether it is or is not a rape. It is worth considering the representation in detail in the novel and 2016 television adaptation. The novel written in 1953 was produced before the second wave of feminism. The relevant episode (2016, S2, E8) was first screened in the United Kingdom on 23 October 2016—one year prior to #MeToo and #TimesUp and produced in the era of later postfeminism. The story concerns Elizabeth, Ross and George. When Francis dies he leaves Elizabeth Poldark without money. She seeks support from Ross about financial matters and running her estate as it is assumed that she cannot run the estate alone. George Warleggan, Ross' sworn enemy, proposes marriage to Elizabeth. George offers stability and wealth and the security of marriage. Elizabeth sends a letter to Ross to advise him of the intended marriage. Ross rushes to Trenwith House and breaks in through a window. He enters Elizabeth's bedroom and confronts her aiming to prevent the marriage. In the book Ross is aroused when Elizabeth becomes angry 'her eyes were lit with anger. He's never seen her like it before, and he found pleasure in it' (1953, p. 313). Ross kisses her, she slaps his face, and tells him to stop but he picks her up and carries her to the bed. At this point it does not state he raped her; it's implied. Winston Graham's observations were accurate and the point that rape is often motivated by anger and power is supported by research (Anderson & Swainson, 2001). Ross is furious that Elizabeth would even consider marrying his enemy George and when she shows anger it serves to provoke further. The lack of detail in the novel leaves a little ambiguity which fans on social media debate regularly and passionately. Projansky takes a firm line with such implicit or offscreen actions particularly where the sexual violence is obscured but it motivates the narrative progression. She states, 'If rape is everywhere in film and yet often offscreen, alluded to, or not acknowledged as "really" rape', she insists 'on identifying all these types of representations and naming them as forms of rape within the narrative' (Projansky, 2001, p. 29). Such a political act may be a move forward towards equality.

Media representations such as Ross' rape of Elizabeth contribute to layers of misunderstanding about sexual violence. Additionally, pervasive rape myths which circulate in culture and complications about types of femininity that are valued make rape representations appear more ambiguous when they are not. One of the issues relates to the representations of the past and the sanctions facing female characters who transgress the ideals of femininity. In feminist terms this serves to deny a woman her own desires and make her chaste for male pleasure. Doane (1987) pinpoints the likely outcome to be punishment in the narrative. Over time such repeated patterns become internalised and seem natural. This in turn has subtle degrees of impact on the shared beliefs of readers and viewers that transgression of feminine ideals—sexual or otherwise- leads to negative outcomes. Belief systems form attitudes which ultimately regulate behaviour and re-enforce the ideal in the 'life world'. It is against this background that the defence of rape can be better understood. Byrne and Taddeo (2022) suggest period dramas often depict rape as 'eroticised ravishment' (2022, p. 8). The ravishment scenario is problematic because the woman does not transgress the feminine ideal and initiate or encourage sex whilst *secretly*, she desires it or enjoys it. Such a plotline perpetuates the rape myth that 'she said no but meant yes'. This is observable in the 2016 iteration of the rape scene. Ross is angry about Elizabeth's intention to marry George. He enters the house by kicking the door open, shouting for Elizabeth as he goes through the house. In her bedroom the two quarrel. As he moves towards her with his anger blazing across his face, he is also backing her towards the bed. He says, 'I oppose this marriage Elizabeth and I'd be glad of your assurance that you won't go through with it' (S2, E8). The threat of sexual violence here is evident. He is threatening her with rape unless she agrees to refuse George. Elizabeth responds saying he's hateful and she detests him to which he responds, 'No you don't, and you never will'. She looks at the bed realising what is about to happen and exclaims 'You'd not dare, you'd not dare' and he replies, 'Oh I would Elizabeth, I would...and so would you'. He throws her onto the bed. However, she appears to yield to his kissing and caressing and begins to kiss him back. There is no ambiguity that he was using the threat of sex as a weapon to prevent her marrying his enemy. As Byrne states such scenes are 'violence served up as entertainment but also that it is ultimately more about masculinity, and male identity, than it is about the victim' (2015, p. 185). The motivation for the visit was the feud between Ross and George—it is about Ross claiming rights over what he feels is Poldark property (Elizabeth is Francis Poldark's widow). In depicting Elizabeth as capitulating it strengthens the 'she meant yes' myth. The fact that she was threatened and coerced is obscured.

Whilst such gendered representations endure there can be no gender equality. The system is weighted in favour of masculinity at the expense of femininity. This privileging of masculinity is evident when examining the BBC and Mammoth Screen trying to manage the media promotion of season two of *Poldark* in 2016 to prevent a media backlash about Ross raping Elizabeth. In a BBC Breakfast interview between Aidan Turner, who plays Ross, and the host, Louise Minchin, both go to lengths to avoid using the term 'rape' when describing the scene they know will cause controversy (Aidan Turner BBC Breakfast, 2016). At the premier screening of *Poldark* season two at BFI 22 August 2016 writer Debbie Horsfield also tries to avoid using the 'rape' word, but ultimately must use the dreaded term as she reads a statement from Andrew Graham (Winston's son) who was an advisor to the production. Graham's statement said that there was:

> the potential for rape but what then happens is not described but is left entirely up to one's imagination. The only way to judge what my father intended is to read the novels as a whole. Doing so it becomes clear that from earlier scenes and Elizabeth's immediate reactions and later mixed emotions that what finally happened was consensual sex born of long-term love and longing. (BFI, 2016)

The attempted management of the controversy only serves to highlight the gender inequality in the story and in the life world. Where was actor Heida Reid in these discussions about what happened to her character, Elizabeth? If Graham's guidance to look to the novels is followed, answers become evident. In *The Four Swans* written in 1976 and set two years after the rape incident, Ross and Elizabeth meet and speak directly to each other for the first time since that fateful night in May 1803. Graham describes Ross' internal thoughts; 'He was only too aware of the indefensibility of his actions then…He knew it was something for which Elizabeth would never be willing to forgive him' (1976, p. 199). I argue that this is not the ruminations about a consensual sex act. The scene continues with Ross and Elizabeth discussing Valentine's paternity and George's suspicions. Ross provides Elizabeth with a plan to allay George's concerns, but this plan ultimately leads to Elizabeth's death. Even the fact that a plan is required brings into sharp relief the centrality and privileging of male identity and male concerns to the detriment of female identity and female concerns. If more evidence of rape is required there is a notable scene in season three (2017, S3, E9) where Elizabeth confirms to George by swearing on the Bible that she has only ever given herself to two men. The sentence she omits is that she did not give herself to Ross. It is clear that Ross did rape Elizabeth, but the fact that BBC/Mammoth resorts to a statement from the novelist's son does indicate the level of discomfort about the scene. There are efforts to protect the series, the story, the actor, and characters, and by extension their profits, by finding ways to excuse or defend the actions of the hero. A direct consequence of this reputation management is the response of some fans on Facebook fan pages taking the same line of argument and refusing to acknowledge Ross' crime. Instead of rape they call the incident VBT or the Very Bad Thing. This proves the importance of gender representations and as Storey avers texts and practices are 'reflections and expressions of power relations' which conceal the reality of domination and subordination (2021, p. 3). Only by close analysis of the details can the issues be foregrounded, and opportunities taken to redress the balance. Byrne and Taddeo are clear on the issue 'that rape should be an issue for society and state' (2022, p. 16). I am arguing that the case is the same for gender equality—there is a collective responsibility to be aware of the inequalities which exist and take collective steps to create balance.

Conclusion

If gender equality is to be achieved and it is everyone's responsibility then it is worth considering who are the women of *Poldark*, for it is not just the characters on screen; it is the writers, producers, actors, fans and audiences all expressing and adding to the textual environment. The analysis in this chapter of specific themes related to female experience and the representation of women indicates that many issues still exist and even while there are assertions of gender equality, particularly with Demelza, there are also simultaneously depictions of oppression, omission and exploitation. The complications brought about with the intersection of social class and age often make the gender inequality more keenly felt and this is evident when considering the economic position of characters—poverty limits the options of women in the story and in the life world. Demelza succeeds because she is rescued by Ross, but she also makes sure to educate herself at every opportunity. Winston Graham may indeed have some feminist credentials as Taddeo suggests (2015). He is ahead of his time in representing certain of the concerns about female experience such as the storylines for Morwenna and Verity. His attention to historical detail is laudable. This makes his fury at the changes in the 1970s adaptation more understandable. Pullman and Masters do capture the mood of the times in the 1970s and there is no doubt that having 15 million viewers is evidence of a successful show. The representation of women does not progress as might be expected. With the exception of the handling of the Elizabeth rape storyline, having a female writer, Debbie Horsfield, and female executive producer, Karen Thrussell, may have been beneficial in the 2015–2019 adaptation. There are some small but significant steps to provide Demelza with the storyline she deserves and develop the female friendship between Prudie and Demelza, but ultimately, it may be more of the same, where female friendship is foregrounded as a token at the expense of feminist activism. Keeler and Ryan suggest this is a trope of postfeminism which functions as 'a set of neoliberal cultural ideas that privilege the individual, apolitical empowerment of girls and women, who are hailed as productive feminized workers, citizens, and mothers' (2018, p. 4).

Despite the initial aim to redress the deficit of scrutiny on female representations there is a large section of this chapter concerned with men and masculinity. This echoes the structural inequalities and the myths which continue to uphold them. For even while the legal position has altered over time, such as the Equal Pay Act of 1970, the situation has not improved for everyone. Indeed, the persistent gender pay gap exists because of prevailing beliefs about femininity and masculinity and whilst representations of oppressed and exploited women continue to circulate real change will be hard to encourage. For representations influence thought and thought effects attitudes which impact behaviour. This is very clearly the case with sexual violence. Perhaps #MeToo will make a difference, but sexual violence is a daily concern for many women and that has not changed even over the long periods considered here. Byrne and Taddeo's position on rape that it is an issue for all society (2022) is instructive. For the same is true for gender equality. Everyone has their role to play to bring gender equality into being and a good starting point is to recognise how inequality is perpetuated through texts and practices of culture.

References

Aidan Turner BBC Breakfast. (2016). Full Interview, *online video*, https://www.vimeo.com/181021219

Anderson, I., & , Swainson, V. (2001). Perceived Motivations for Rape: Gender Differences in Beliefs About Female and Male Rape. Current Research in Social Psychology University of Iowa, 6, 8.

Ang, I. (1985). *Watching Dallas: Soap Opera and the Melodramatic Imagination.* London: Methuen.

BFI. (2016). *Poldark Season 2 Q& A with Aidan Turner, Debbie Horsfield, Damien Timmer*. Retrieved October 26, 2022, from https://youtu.be/OWRqkyLotcE

Butler, J. (1980). *Gender Trouble: Feminism and the Subversion of Identity*. Routledge.

Byrne, K. (2015). New Developments in Heritage: The Recent Dark Side of Downton 'Downer' Abbey. In J. Leggot & J. A. Taddeo (Eds.), *Upstairs and Downstairs: British Costume Drama Television from the Forsyte Saga to Downton Abbey*. Rowman & Littlefield.

Byrne, K. & Taddeo, J. A. (2022). *Rape in Period Drama Television: Consent, Myth and Fantasy*. Retrieved August 4, 2022, from Amazon Kindle.

CBS News. (2021, October 29). *Yuval Harari Warns Humans Will Be 'Hacked' If Artificial Intelligence Is Not Globally Regulated*. Retrieved July 29, 2022, from https://www.cbsnews.com/news/yuval-harari-sapiens-60-minutes-2021-10-29/

Doane, M. A. (1987). *The Desire to Desire: The Women's Film of the 1940's*. Macmillan.

Geraghty, C. (2000). *British Cinema in the Fifties: Gender, Genre, and the 'New Look'*. London: Routledge.

Gill, R. (2007). Postfeminist media culture: Elements of a sensibility. *European Journal of Cultural Studies, 10*(2), 147–166.

Goodman, G., & Moseley, R. (2018). Television Costume Drama and the Eroticised, Regionalised Body: Poldark and Outlander. In K. Byrne, J. Leggott, & J. A. Taddeo (Eds.), *Conflicting Masculinities: Men in Television Period Drama*. London: I B Tauris.

Graham, W. (1945). *Ross Poldark*. London, Pan 2008.

Graham, W. (1953). *Warleggan*. Pan 2008.

Graham, W. (1976). *The Four Swans*. Pan 2008.

Graham, W. (2003). *Memoirs of a Private Man*. Pan.

Hobson, D. (1980). Housewives and the Mass Media. In S. Hall, D. Hobson, A. Lowe, & P. Willis (Eds.), *Culture, Media, Language: Working Papers in Cultural Studies 1972–79* . London: Hutchinson.

Humm, M. (1998). Feminist Literary Theory. In S. Jackson & J. Jones (Eds.), *Contemporary Feminist Theories*. Edinburgh University Press.

Jackson, S. (1998). Theorising Gender and Sexuality. In S. Jackson & J. Jones (Eds.), *Contemporary Feminist Theories*. Edinburgh University Press.

Keller, J., & Ryan, M. E. (Eds.). (2018). *Emergent Feminisms: Complicating a Postfeminist Media Culture*. Routledge.

Leggot, J., & Taddeo, J. A. (2015). *Upstairs and Downstairs: British Costume Drama Television from the Forsyte Saga to Downton Abbey*. Rowman & Littlefield.

Morley, D. (1986). *Family Television: Cultural Power and Domestic Leisure*. London: Comedia.

Muston, S. (2022, July 21). Oh boy! The Scourge of Topless Men in London Parks. *Evening Standard*. Retrieved July 22, 2022, from https://www.standard.co.uk/insider/topless-men-summer-london-parks-put-it-away-b1013900.html

Poldark. (1975–1977). *The Complete Collection [DVD]*. BBC Worldwide.

Poldark. (2015–2019). 5 Seasons. Retrieved October 31, 2022, from Netflix.

Projansky, S. (2001). *Watching Rape: Film and Television in Postfeminist Culture*. New York University Press.

Rosen, M. (1973). *Popcorn Venus: Women, Movies and the American Dream*. New York: Coward, McCann and Geoghegan.

Sadler, B. (2022). Avoiding 'the faddlings of Dr Choake': the professionalisation of medicine in *Poldark*. In K. Byrne, J. A. Taddeo, & J. Leggott (Eds.), *Diagnosing History: Medicine in Television Period Drama*. Manchester: Manchester University Press.

Saunders, J. (2006). *Adaptation and Appropriation*. Routledge.

Stone, G. (2022, July 26). Here's How Trans People Fell About YouGov's Survey on Trans Rights. *HuffPost*. https://www.huffingtonpost.co.uk/entry/yougov-polled-the-public-about-trans-rights-heres-how-trans-people-feel-about-it_uk_62daa0c7e4b000da23ff4545

Storey, J. (2003). *Inventing Popular Culture*. Blackwell.

Storey, J. (2021). *Cultural Theory and Popular Culture*. Routledge.

Taddeo, J. A. (2015). Why Don't You Take Her?': Rape in the Poldark Narrative. In J. Leggot & J. A. Taddeo (Eds.), *Upstairs and Downstairs: British Costume Drama Television from the Forsyte Saga to Downton Abbey*. Rowman & Littlefield.

Thorp, N. (2022, July 22). Why Was It Not Mandatory for Doctors to Be Taught About Women's Issues Before Now? *Metro*. Retrieved July 22, 2022, from, https://metro.co.uk/2022/07/22/why-wasnt-it-mandatory-for-doctors-to-be-taught-about-womens-issues-before-now-17052718/

Tong, R. (1992). *Feminist Thought*. Routledge.

Wheatley, H. (2016). *Spectacular Television: Exploring Televisual Pleasure*. London: I B Tauris.

CHAPTER 13

Are Stay-at-Home Dads Real Men? The Potential of Critical Media Literacy to Enhance Teacher Training

Kim Gilligan

Introduction

Sustainability as a set of issues has become, a contemporary global trend with the sustainability agenda currently influencing many aspects of societies. Sustainability is underpinned by the requirements of the Sustainable Development Goals' 2030 agenda. The concept of sustainability is defined and interpreted in a number of ways but is often linked to meeting the needs of the present as well as consideration of the future (WCED, 1987). The sustainability agenda more generally, concerns itself with a number of themes including environmental health etc., but this chapter will only predominantly consider the goal related to gender (SDG5) but in addition will draw on the sustainability goal related to education (SDG4) to look at

K. Gilligan (✉)
University of Sunderland, Sunderland, UK
e-mail: kim.gilligan@sunderland.ac.uk

D. Dalton, A. Smith (eds.), *Gender, Sexuality and the UN's SDGs*, Sustainable Development Goals Series,
https://doi.org/10.1007/978-3-031-31046-1_13

how these two goals when examined together may contribute to economic welfare and social justice around gendered expectations.

The chapter will use the SDG5 focused on gender and SDG4 in equality of education as a vehicle to evaluate the potential of popular culture for teaching critical visual or critical media literacies (Janks, 2010). It will illustrate links between critical thinking, habits of reflexivity and the exploration of lived experiences to look at how we can influence university students' attitudes towards the sustainability goal of gender equality. Within the initial stages of the chapter is a discussion of some of the current debates relating to gender. This draws on the work of Adkins and Skeggs (2004) and McNay (1999) who question ideas of agency, in terms of the gender roles as they are experienced in everyday contexts adopted in the contemporary world. The chapter will then go on to consider the place of education in supporting a more nuanced understanding of the sustainability goal related to gender. The Universal Design for Learning approach (Cast, 2011) will be used to show how teaching approaches can be utilized to ensure that through a range of resources being drawn upon we can encourage critical thinking. The discussion will explore the potential of creative, but critical teaching approaches to engage students returning to study in HE with the concept of gender equality. It will illustrate how using academic papers charting the real lived experiences of stay-at-home fathers, coupled with the analysis of fictional depictions of mothers and fathers in popular culture can be used to challenge thinking around gender.

The fictional depictions are drawn from popular two series. One is *Motherland* a British series shown on the BBC between 2016 and 2021 written by Sharon Horgan, Graham Linehan and Holly Walsh. The other series *Working Moms* is a Canadian series originally shown on CBC from 2017 and then on Netflix from 2019. The series was written and produced by Catherine Reitman. Both the TV series are part of a growing trend for often comedic fictional focus on the lives of working women and their related partners and children. The series were chosen because they both contain stereotypical elements relating to gender and gender roles and lend themselves to careful analysis.

The context for the chapter comes from work with students using critical pedagogies in a module within an MA in Education. The sustainability goals of gender equality and education are part of a wider exploration of social justice in the module facilitated through critical thinking activities. The aims of the module are related to engaging students in ways that may transform their thinking around areas related to gender and social justice

(Mezirow, 1997). The module is aimed at teachers as it is very important that teachers particularly are encouraged to engage with the sustainability goals because of their role in the socialization process. The students studying on the module are qualified teachers pursuing continuing professional development. The chapter suggests ways in which as part of an MA course graduate teachers can explore the nature of complex issues like gender and reflexivity in order to understand the capacity for education to challenge gender inequalities and influence social justice in the wider world (Morales-Doyle, 2015). The module includes the use of multiple forms of representation in line with Universal Design for Learning and multiple forms of expression. Popular culture is extensively drawn upon in the module, as well as photography and other visual media as vehicles to question representations and reframe them during dialogic teaching sequences.

Sustainability Goals

The sustainability development goals are a set of goals or targets aimed at ending poverty by 2030. Gender equality is number five of the sustainability goals (SDG5) which were conceived in 2015 though the sustainability agenda emerged earlier probably in the 1970s (Ariffin & Ng, 2020). The sustainability goal related to gender is underpinned by concerns about inequality but for the purpose of this piece two key areas are the focus; occupational segregation and wage inequality which according to Elam and Terjesen in 2010 indicate wider issues related to areas like the division of labour, unequal distribution of awards and how different genders have different exchange value in specific contexts. Most discussions on the importance of the gender sustainability goal will illustrate examples of inequalities in the workplace for example studies by Stamarski and Son Hing (2015) and Heilman and Okimoto (2007) illustrate unfair practices related to Human Resources including different reactions to roles at work, and how mothers are perceived in the workplace. Both of these themes appear in the two series identified above, particularly during the work focused interactions of some of the main characters. The workplace is a key setting for the working moms in both series but features to foreground lack of 'fit' in the workplaces of the stay-at home fathers.

It is clear then within the rationale for the sustainability goal relating to gender, that gender inequalities are still deep-rooted in every society and may well 'stagnate social progress' (Freund & Hernandez-Maskivker, 2021) but to a different extent depending on geographical context. It is possible to find many examples illustrating how women and girls still suffer from a lack of access to decent work, and often face occupational segregation and continue to experience gender wage gaps (Haasler, 2014; Triventi, 2013). In addition to this, women are also underrepresented at decision-making levels, in senior roles and leadership positions (Thornton & Bagust, 2007). Though there is no denying that women and girls suffer from inequality in relation to their gender in many contexts, there is a case to suggest that work, and parenting patterns are changing, and it may be that in the contemporary world we need to consider the impact on both genders from more recent expectations related to heteronormativity and ideas related to patriarchy. Butler (2002) in her work on gender suggests that both men and women in society are subject to exclusionary gender norms which are to the detriment of all gendered subjects. In her work she calls for an end to the damaging effects of gender binaries on individuals who contradict them.

Changing Patterns in Gendered Expectations

Formerly scholarship in gender and gender related areas asserted that women in the main spent longer on unpaid domestic chores than men. More recent data from the US (Bianchi et al., 2012) suggests that women are now spending less time on household tasks and increasing amounts of time in paid employment. Conversely men are spending more time on household tasks and increasingly time is spent by men caring for their children. Despite these changes however there is evidence to suggest that although sex discrimination in the workplace has been illegal since the 1960s men and women still often remain in segregated occupations (Oswald, 2008). It is still also the case that women are the exception in careers like engineering and computer science (in 2021 in the US only 15.9% of engineers in the US were women and 19% of computer tech staff). Conversely men are underrepresented in the care professions including teaching and nursing. In 2021 in the US only 14.1% of primary teachers were men and only 10.4% of nurses were male.

Significant structural barriers exist supporting inequality between the sexes. The lack of gender equality in management positions indicated above is likely to be linked to family commitments. In 2016 for example according to the International Leadership Organisation (ILO) a considerable number of women lost to senior positions were as a result of leaving work to have children. Another aspect of inequality noted by women highlights stereotypes and the preconceptions of their skills and capabilities as a significant barrier to success as well as a segregating organizational culture (Johns, 2013). A significant barrier in the neoliberal context also identified is a lack of personal investment in production capacity which is effectively not engaging in education, training and additional experiences in order to progress.

The concepts of the glass ceiling, diamond ceiling, the cement ceiling and the sticky floor are worthy of discussion here in order to gain a deeper understanding of why gender inequality continues to exist. These represent invisible barriers that occur preventing career progression. The cement ceiling and the sticky floor are particularly prevalent to this piece as they represent a lack of agency in terms of particular subjectivities. The cement ceiling refers to the prejudices held by an individual (De Silva & Thulemark, 2022) about their capacity for progression and a lack of relatable role models being available to them. Women may witness higher levels of pressure on senior female colleagues in terms of having to prove themselves and decide not to step into such an arena. The sticky floor (Kee, 2006) on the other hand is an interesting one referring to the responsibilities allocated to women in the private sphere, for example the foundation parent or the main carer for others. These responsibilities hinder women in ways that make progression in the workplace harder.

From the above discussion it is clear that stereotypes related to capacities and skills can reinforce inequalities for women, and impact on men. It may be as authors suggest (Evans & Diekman, 2009) that gender stereotypes are a major contributory factor in why both men and women envisage themselves in specific kinds of careers. Stereotypes, in this case those related to gender, are both persistent and pervasive and may form without consciousness. Stereotypes are considered to be structured groups of beliefs, and dispositions thought desirable in a specific gender (Navarro Astor et al., 2017) and can be built on with exposure, leading to their further reproduction. It may also be the case however that forms of self-stereotyping occur. When individuals choose occupations or roles that relate strongly to how they see themselves in terms of their gender they may place themselves in roles that are expected of that particular gender.

A commonly accepted form of stereotyping relates to notions of women juggling work demands and home under the assumption that they take care of people and help them whereas men take control and focus on tasks commonly in the workplace (Hoyt & Murphy, 2016). Despite this there are an increasing number of men becoming stay-at-home fathers. Lamb

(2004) suggested that fatherhood should be understood as socially constructed and related to the period in which it is being carried out. In 2018, 144,000 male parents were stay-at-home fathers in Australia. In the US in 2016 there were approximately two million stay-at-home fathers. Despite their growing numbers stay-at-home fathers are still fairly under researched, but are in their choices challenging traditional norms of masculinity and caregiving. Kramer and Kramer (2016) suggested that the choice for fathers to stay at home and mothers to work was being made by both spouses and represents a shift in gendered behaviour patterns over time, despite claims that economic drivers that may be causing changes in work patterns between the genders stay-at-home fathers are likely to face stigma and stereotyping. Rudman and Glick (2001) comment that despite more positive labels, fathers staying at home with their children still face social backlash and isolation because they are considered Vanguards, those who adopt atypical positions (Rochlen et al., 2010). One area where we can witness the discursive constructions of contemporary fatherhood is in the media with Stevens (2015) suggesting it has a considerable influence on how we see gendered subjectivities. An important aspect of the role of the media is revealing which subject positions are admired and which ones are vilified (Sunderland, 2000). In the case of fatherhood many writers still report on the continuing discourses that suggest that 'real men' are providers and that men who take care of their children such as stay-at-home fathers may be seen as emasculated or feminized (Brandth & Kvande, 2009). On the other hand emerging in the literature is a growing emerging theme around the involved father with Marks and Palkovitz (2004) and Rehel (2014) remarking on fathers no longer fitting the stereotype of breadwinner or disciplinarian.

Different Ways of Understanding Gender/Agency

The changes in patterns of behaviour around work and parenting are debated by a number of authors (Doucet & Merla, 2007; Gregory & Milner, 2011) and the issues are part of wider debates about the impact of structure and agency. Lois McNay in *Feminism after Bourdieu* (Adkins & Skeggs, 2004) usefully suggests that a way forward in understanding contemporary gender issues is achieved through an understanding of the lived experiences of gender. In her discussion she utilizes a range of authors (Bourdieu, 2000; Butler, 2011; Fraser, 2000) to look at how the divisions between cultural and material analysis can be overcome through looking at the lived experiences of gendered subjects. She considers agency to be a mediating concept that can show how lived experiences can be impacted on ultimately affecting levels of agency. She argues that the structural forces at play in decision making for women and men can only be revealed by understanding their lived experiences. McNay utilizes the work of Young (1997) and Scott (1992) to show how by having a deeper understanding of how discourses position subjects we can also understand how experiences are produced. In the final part of the chapter McNay returns to Bourdieu and his approach utilizing the phenomenology of social spaces to show how experiences are lived out in different spatial contexts and suggests that social spaces are also symbolic spaces.

In addition to the work of Adkins and Skeggs in the same text *Feminism after Bourdieu* (2004) looks at how gender may be lived out at a pre-reflexive level and therefore is part of an embodied experience that may be less amenable to change. She suggests that men and women may then retain entrenched investments in conventional expectations of gendered behaviours, for example men as bread winners and women in roles that demand emotional responsibility. Despite claims above both Adkins and Skeggs (2004) assert that in order to fully understand notions of agency we need to understand the lived experiences of both genders. One way of understanding the experiences of gender is through critical engagement with representations in popular culture. This enables the questioning of the images we are presented with through critical approaches and deconstruction. Popular culture is often imbued with stereotypes and even 'dangerous stereotyping' unlike advertising which is under legislation (ASA, 2019). In order to prevent the influence of dangerous stereotyping, popular culture is not bound by the same laws and therefore stereotypes are a common feature of many TV depictions (Roth-Cohen et al., 2022).

Understanding Sustainability in Higher Education

In contemporary Higher Education contexts the theme of sustainability is widespread with many universities embedding sustainability goals in their overall frameworks and strategies. Some researchers including Shiel et al. (2020) suggest that educational organizations such as universities are in a unique position to utilize the sustainability goals as part of the teaching and learning process with the aim of preparing students to find solutions to complex issues and to take an active part in society more widely.

Goal 5 (SDG5), related to gender equality, makes specific reference to the empowerment of girls and women but is it not the case that gender inequality is also felt by boys and men depending on the context, for example, in the case of non-hegemonic males encountering discrimination in educational spaces such as schools (Gilligan, 2020) or in the case with the work of Pritchard et al. (2002) gendered spaces in urban landscapes? Sustainability Goal 4 (SDG4) champions the need for inclusive and equitable access to education for all, including provision for lifelong learning. It is clear then, that there is an interrelationship between education and its capacity to influence the realization of other sustainable goals including that of gender (Heleta & Bagus, 2021; Leal Filho et al., 2017).

The crucial role of education in supporting the implementation of the sustainability goals is often attributed to the Sustainability Development Solutions Network (SDSN, 2020). Here quality education is said to lead to improved development outcomes for individuals, communities and countries. This takes the form of better access to gainful employment, better nutrition and health, the reduction of gender disparities, greater resilience in disasters, more engaged citizens and so on. In 2012 Corcoran noted the commitment of a range of international bodies related to Higher Education to come together to utilize the goals within a broad range of curriculum areas but was ultimately disappointed in the number of universities not taking seriously the opportunity to embed this area into their curriculum. It is the case that universities have a part to play in ensuring that sustainability is understood and one such way is through engaging in the process of curriculum design where a critical understanding of the goals can be embedded influencing the teaching process. Universal Design for Learning (UDL) is a way of ensuring engagement with social justice through widening the opportunities offered to students.

The Contribution of Universal Design for Learning and Multiple Forms of Representation

A common approach to teaching and learning design within Higher Education is an approach centred around providing access and engagement to the widest possible range of students. Along with the impact of Access and Participation Plans, now a requirement of the Office for Students, and the more widespread use of technologies to support learning in Higher Education, it is possible to see how a range of interrelated agendas can be met. These current agendas may well have a related impact on students' investment in the sustainability goals and the potential for their contribution to work place environments later, when they leave university and take up roles in the workplace.

UDL approaches are inclusive and have regard for needs of diverse learners in Higher Education and take steps, including providing guidance in terms of key areas to be included when working with students. The core principles of UDL including the use of multimedia to teach a range of subjects, combined with critical thinking approaches, can be powerful tools in transforming ideas and beliefs. Critical thinking in itself has according to Barnett (1997) become a defining concept and is according to Chanock (2000) integral to academic practice across a range of disciplines. In relation to this piece, it is important to note that without critical thinking in universities there are implications when students go on to make meaning in the workforce. A lack of critical thinking ability for example may inhibit their confidence to influence gendered behaviours witnessed in organizations. This may then lead to a non-reflexive understanding of what is taking place in terms of constructions of gendered subjectivities. We know for example that leaders in organizations can have a significant influence in how gender is played out (Humbert et al., 2019; Kelan & Wratil, 2018) and so it seems reasonable to suggest that the teaching of critical thinking to graduates would be desirable in terms of equipping them for gender aware leadership later in their career trajectories.

Facione's (2011) model of critical thinking offers an approach that can be applied in a number of ways. His model includes six core critical thinking skills and of particular importance within the six are interpretation and inference. Both can be used in conjunction with interrogating media texts to reveal the gendered constructions present within them. In addition to the development of specific skills Facione suggests particular dispositions can then be developed; these include being inquisitive and being able to analyse and reason well. Both skills can be utilized to deconstruct gender stereotypes.

Graduate Skills

In addition to the above requirements of universities a common aim is to enable graduate skills through additions to students' main courses or embedding particular kinds of activities into modules. This is with a view to ensuring employability at the end of their term of study and perhaps more importantly to foster a propensity for ongoing critical thinking in order to encourage lifelong learning. Engaging in critical thinking at this stage of their careers will encourage the belief that they can go on to influence future working environments. Kopnina (2017) in her study in the Netherlands laments the fact that more could be done in universities to ensure that all students educated in university develop the ability to understand the complexities of societies and insights using critical thinking and argumentation. The involvement of individuals in issues related to sustainability and inequalities is important as their viewpoints will combine and contribute to a global collective. Reza (2016) commented on the vital contribution that universities can play in promoting all aspects of sustainable development and how discussion and a critical approach can support ongoing changes in attitudes to things like stereotypes. The ways that researchers view how students' commitment to understanding sustainability can be ensured varies immensely, but often includes pedagogical approaches that combine critical thinking, a range of ways of accessing information and a suitable environment for the challenging discussions that may ensue.

One way of working with the sustainability goals is through critical literacies and as a body of approaches they may then fall into more nuanced approaches related to specific disciplines. Scientific literacy (OECD, 2009) for example may include the consideration of psychology and how we can come to critically understand the complexity of the relationship between individual decision-making and the enabling of challenges to gender inequality in society. This approach highlights gendered differences in how people engage with the goals themselves and whether they would take opportunities to galvanize ideas and knowledge into everyday actions. One of the tenets of this approach is the belief that through interdisciplinary approaches that deal with sustainability it is possible to initiate challenges to gender constructions and other areas of inequality (Probst et al., 2019). The hope is that this may instill the propensity for thinking about gender then lead to individual action. Later when students view gender inequality being played out in organizational settings like workplace they may then act.

Another approach used within universities is the use of critical media literacy. Popular media can according to Kelly and Currie (2021) operate as a site of education providing a source for the construction of identities. It is, they suggest, an arena where ideas can circulate and social injustices can be challenged. Media educationalists including critical feminists, for example Iyer and Luke (2011), call for action beyond contending stereotypes, asking for close attention to how stereotypes are sustained over time and how work like that of Gee (2011) can be used through analytical approaches to challenge power. The practice of critical media literacy focusing on power and how notions of power are embedded within media representations is an effective approach. Exponents of critical media literacy including Alvermann and Hagood (2000) suggest by using specific techniques to look differently at media, resistance to stereotypes can be achieved. This kind of approach often addresses issues of prejudice within media representations in areas like gender, as an effort to challenge thinking around constructions of selfhood. Tosi for example (2011) is one author who suggests that the media often reflects particular ideas and values related to society more generally. He suggests that what is needed in university settings for example is for facilitators to provide appropriate interventions with a view to challenging perhaps long-held assumptions and beliefs which are outmoded or worthy of challenge. In addition to the work above, Spanierman et al. (2008) would suggest that the understanding of inequality may differ between individuals but they can all be enabled to take part in activities that raise their awareness.

Intersectionality (Crenshaw, 1991) is a consideration in this area, highlighting the constant changes that take place in terms of gender constructions and how they operate. Gill's work in 2009 is an example of an approach where we are made aware that the gender does not operate independently but is often within a nexus with other power dynamics like class and ethnicity, which when applied alongside gender impact on how subjects are represented. Intersectionality is a threshold concept (Meyer & Land, 2005) in the MA module and is explored in a range of other related activities across the Masters provision. The next section of the chapter will exemplify how the gendered archetypes and stereotypes are depicted in the two series and how the students are enabled in addition to explore the findings of the academic research. The exploration of the two different representations of gendered subjectivities, the real and the fictional together capture the lived experiences of gender. The students then work with a critical awareness of the media representations in order to counteract the influence that these may have in settings that they work within. In the next part of the chapter the discussion will centre around the fictional depictions of the stay-at-home fathers in the two series mentioned above.

Analysis of Stay-at-Home Fathers in *Motherland* and *Working Moms* with Students

It is common in the module to select visual media to illustrate social justice issues. The UDL principles of multiple forms of representation ensure that staff engage students in a range of mediums that depict lived experiences of gender including academic papers and in relation to this discussion visual media.

Motherland and *Working Moms* both focus on a range of gendered relationships and include working and non-working parents. The characters in the series are analysed with the students thematically. This is in order to look at both the male and female characters with a view to understanding how they are constructed and perhaps for what purpose. In the module we also explore relevant academic papers that deal with related topics. Littler (2020) for example is one academic who combines analysis of popular culture and implications for the perception of gender and gender positions in real-world settings. She has published a range of research on motherhood and archetypes associated with contemporary females for example the 'ladette' and the 'Yummy Mummy'. In a 2019 piece on *Mothers Behaving Badly*, Littler included *Motherland* in an extensive analysis of what she describes as 'chaotic hedonism' looking at motherhood in the light of neoliberal social reproduction and the relationship of contemporary motherhood to overworking and the precariousness of employment. In this piece she divides the constructions of mothers into two broad categories: those in the midst of chaotic spaces largely devoid of domesticity; and hedonistic mothers behaving perhaps in ways stereotypically associated with young childless males. She links the imagery in the series with a period of neoliberal crisis where inequality and overwork are at the heart of the depictions captured in popular culture. The students on the MA are used to critically explore the impact of neoliberalism on a range of areas including both gender and education. In an earlier piece of research Littler (2013) explored the phenomenon of the 'Yummy Mummy' and this contemporary type of motherhood is particularly useful when exploring the female characters in *Motherland* and *Working Moms* in terms of comparison. The stay-at-home fathers in particular can be explored in relation to them both in terms of what the research across the world says about changing typologies of masculinity and femininity in real and fictional contexts. The Yummy Mummy for example is characterised by her ability, because of her middle-class position, to ensure she is always well groomed and sexually attractive. This model of femininity can then be analysed in terms of how the masculine models including the stay-at-home and working fathers relate to her. Amanda in *Motherland* and particularly Kate and Jenny in *Working Moms* would fit this Yummy Mummy stereotype and act as yardsticks for other characters including the male ones. Littler (2020) provides a valuable insight into contemporary maternal figures which are usefully categorized, but in my discussion with students the different models of motherhood are explored only in order to utilize them to look at the male figures in relation to them.

The use of the critical literacy approaches outlined earlier enables a focus on the fathers partnered in various ways with the contemporary mothers in the two series. The module focuses on how fathers, specifically the stay-at-home ones, are considered in terms of how other characters react to them. The work of Tyler (2008) is useful here as she noted that particular gendered models can be repeated and may then solidify into stock social types or what may be described as 'difficult stereotypes'. These difficult stereotypes are drawn upon in the visual media and aspects of them are overemphasized. During the critical analysis phase of the teaching activities on the module some of the depictions of masculinity relating to fatherhood act as difficult stereotypes. These are then deconstructed by the group and reframing can occur as well as the development of reflexive awareness as to the implications of the depictions. Activities include exploration of how the stay-at-home father is constructed and the penalties they face for stepping outside of gendered expectations. The revealing of the 'invisible' is achieved here in the ways suggested by Adkins and Skeggs (2004) earlier. Part of the discussion in the session is what impact this may have on viewers who may then choose to reject the newer gendered positions due to perceived penalties (Rudman et al., 2012). Because the students are teachers there is often a discussion of the implications of the visual representations for pupils in schools. Here there is an opportunity to embed a discussion of the sustainability Goals 4 and 5.

In *Motherland* and *Working Moms* there are a number of male characters but unlike the women they are not depicted as frequently or in the same carnivalesque way that women are. When they are shown it is largely to highlight particular traits and the often act either as a contrast to the female characters around them to draw attention to the expectations of the different genders. There are significant differences in how Ian and Kevin the two stay-at-home fathers are constructed with one inviting ridicule and derision (Kevin played by British actor Paul Ready) for example shown as being overly 'needy' and sexually inept. As Littler (2020, 16) noted in her brief mention of the notion of the stay-at-home dad in *Motherland* 'there is no progressive mode of fatherhood to be found in this programme'. In contrast Ian in *Working Moms* (played by Canadian actor Dennis Andres) is shown sympathetically and is contrasted positively. His credibility as a father develops as the series goes on but this is unfortunately achieved to the detriment of his wife who is shown as failing to bond with her child and this reinforces Ian's position as hero and rescuer. In one scene in particular he is called by the police as Jenny, his estranged wife, has left their little girl in the car whilst going shopping. His arrival and his exchanges with the police for example, showing photographs of his child and him at breakfast construct him as responsible and his wife is 'shamed' for her inability to perform acceptable forms of motherhood. The encounter is captured in a public space mirroring the findings of Massey (2013) and Mattila (2020) in terms of the importance of the spatial elements discussed in more detail below. Although in *Working Moms* there are many significant males depicted alongside Ian and the female characters there is very little comparison to Ian and when there is he is depicted as being attractive to women because of his apparent sensitivity and physical strength. He is accepted into the group of all-female parents at the daycare centre but remains a hegemonic male character.

In *Motherland* we are presented with a range of male characters combining the intersections (Crenshaw, 1991) of class, ethnicity and masculinity. Kevin the stay-at-home father is the most conspicuous male and also the most problematic from a stereotypical point of view. He exemplifies the repercussions related to the backlash that can ensue when men particularly step outside of the gendered expectations of them (Phelan et al., 2008). He is feminized in all episodes of the series, and in common with the real dads analysed by Mattila (2020) is depicted in a wide range of contested spaces. Ian, the stay-at-home dad in *Working Moms*, is constructed very differently in terms of masculinity. He is seen in different spatial locations and these are always significant when looked at in terms of gender and the use of space. Massey's work from (Massey, 2013) on spaces and the gendered use of them is usefully drawn on by Mattila (2020) in her study of home-based fathers. She explores the everyday encounters of real stay-at-home fathers like Kevin in *Motherland* and the spaces they inhabit in their everyday lives. The real fathers are analysed to reveal the part played by space and place in the constructions of their gender in line with the suggestions made by Adkins and Skeggs (2004) mentioned earlier in the chapter. Mattila's empirical study of stay-at-home fathers involved the experiences of nine white middle-class married fathers living with their spouses. They were recruited from a specific geographical area on the East Coast of America. The men were recruited through their membership of local associations for stay-at-home fathers. Mattila's analysis reveals their constructions and how they occur by classifying distinct social spaces for example public spaces like parks, grocery stores and cafes. Mattila then analysed their experiences in a number of distinct social spaces and looked at how the fathers are seen to operate within them. She utilized data from the lived experiences of stay-at-home fathers in a total of five social spaces and explored the incidences of different 'types'. The five types she identified are:

- the nurturing father identified in the grocery store,
- the pervert in the playground,
- the unwelcome intruder in an early years setting,
- the man among men in a men and children's group,
- and the community man (within a more generalized schooling space).

All five are stereotypes and the data from the analysis revealed specific reactions by others depending on the setting and looked at the fathers felt sense of acceptance or rejection depending on the spatial context. The lived experiences of the fathers in the empirical study were mixed, but on the whole very positive compared to the tv versions.

It is important to note within the tv series there are significant differences to the empirical work that has been done in academic papers. The depictions in the tv series generally draw much more on stereotypes and the form of masculinity depicted particularly in motherland is demonized much more than in the real-life examples. It may be of course that the very positive experience of the men interviewed in America was as a result of the protection afforded by a middle-class milieu and the picture may have been very different had the study collected data from non-white or working-class males.

The spatial aspects featured in *Motherland* and *Working Moms* are remarkably similar to Matilla's empirical study with the school or nursery setting a key space where specific forms of masculinity are displayed and the 'fit' of the masculine model ascertained. Goodsell (2005) suggested that the nature of a spaces can have a significant impact on the performance of masculinity and fatherhood. In Mattila's research, the men when in cafes and shops reported feeling positive about the experiences and the author notes not a single father reported a negative experience. They felt in fact that they were seen as heroic in their nurturing father role. The men in the study felt that the validation they received reflected the changing nature of fatherhood in contemporary America. The positivity felt by the fathers reinforced the importance of their role in the eyes of others about looking after their children. In the fictional series Ian is seen as a very positive figure and receives support and admiration for his role as father.

In contrast to the positive experiences of the fathers in the study and the depiction of Ian, Kevin the stay-at-home father in *Motherland* is very rarely seen in a positive light. His presence in the café where the other parents (mothers) gather is highly problematic as he is seen as feminized and is often made to look ridiculous. His construction is as an 'unwanted intruder' but more as a problematic form of female rather than a threat as a man. This is as a result of his depiction as emasculated, emphasized by his clumsy efforts to fit in through engaging in activities that would be considered stereotypical of women, such as gossiping and being overly anxious about his impact on others. His attempts at breaking into the female group are discouraged and his suggestions ignored or criticized. Matthew Jenkins, a freelance journalist reviewing Kevin's role in *Motherland,* describes him as 'deeply unfunny' and an unwelcome step back in time. In his article he constructs him as emasculated, effeminate, needy and neurotic, adjectives often levelled at women rather than men. Jenkins (2021) further suggests that Kevin is a dangerous cliché, a man '*robbed of his manhood*'. Kevin's interactions in the café are highly problematic in terms of sterotypes with one of the most significant scenes showing Kevin attempting to 'compete' with a new male in the group. This other father is a working father and appears as a hegemonic version of masculinity with a successful job. He is presented as an old flame of Amanda's (the Yummy Mummy) and in contrast to Kevin is depicted as being entirely comfortable in the presence of all the women. He is welcomed into the women's group, placed at the head of the table and is very clearly depicted as a sexually attractive male. He perhaps represents 'new man' and a form of contemporary fatherhood (Pleck, 2004) that successfully combines sensitive but strong male. This man and the masculine version presented in *Working Moms* are nearer a 'sensitive new age man' than the Kevin figure. They are depicted as men who can outdo other men but in ways that foreground care and reflexive approaches to their masculinity.

Conclusions

Ian and Kevin represent two ends of polarized depiction of the manhood/fatherhood dyad. One is successful, dominant in the 'right' ways and powerful, what Kimmel and Aronson (2004) describes as a 'winner'. Kevin on the other hand is feminized and depicted as a 'loser' (Bosson et al., 2006) and suffers all of the penalties of stepping out of heteronormative expectations. The two father figures are important sources of critical evaluation and are used in the module to explore the nature of contemporary gender models and their impact on viewers including young people susceptible to the messages contained in visual media.

SDG 5 sadly only relates to equality for women and girls and this belies the complexity of contemporary debates around gender and gender equality. The use of visual media is a powerful source of material to illustrate the complex nature of gender and gender equality. The MA module enables the critical evaluation of the backlash effects that men and boys face when in specific kinds of contexts performing masculinity that does not 'fit' the gendered expectations of them. The teachers taking the module deal with young people of both genders daily and are required as part of the teaching standards to have a deeper understanding of areas involving equality. The Universal Design for Learning as an approach enables the bringing together of critical thinking with different forms of representation with the aim of building understanding and ensuring that Higher Education does fulfil its potential as a space for the exploration of sustainability.

References

Adkins, L., & Skeggs, B. (Eds.). (2004). *Feminism After Bourdieu* (pp. 191–210). Blackwell.

Alvermann, D. E., & Hagood, M. C. (2000). Critical Media Literacy: Research, Theory, and Practice in "New Times". *The Journal of Educational Research, 93*(3), 193–205.

Ariffin, F. N., & Ng, T. F. (2020). Understanding and Opinion on Sustainable Development Among Youths in Higher Educational Institutions in Penang, Malaysia. *Social Indicators Research, 147*(2), 421–437.

Barnett, R. (1997). *Higher Education: A Critical Business.* Open University Press.

Beck, U., Giddens, A., & Lash, S. (1994). *Reflexive Modernization: Politics, Tradition and Aesthetics in the Modern Social Order.* Stanford University Press.

Bianchi, S. M., Sayer, L. C., Milkie, M. A., & Robinson, J. P. (2012). Housework: Who Did, Does or Will Do It, and How Much Does It Matter? *Social Forces, 91*(1), 55–63.

Bosson, J. K., Taylor, J. N., & Prewitt-Freilino, J. L. (2006). Gender Role Violations and Identity Misclassification: The Roles of Audience and Actor Variables. *Sex Roles, 55*(1), 13–24.

Bourdieu, P. (2000). *Pascalian Meditations.* Stanford University Press.

Brandth, B., & Kvande, E. (2009). Gendered or Gender-Neutral Care Politics for Fathers? *The Annals of the American Academy of Political and Social Science, 624*, 177–189.

Butler, J. (2002). *Gender Trouble.* Routledge.

Butler, J. (2011). *Bodies That Matter: On the Discursive Limits of Sex.* Routledge.

CAST. (2011). *Universal Design for Learning Guidelines Version 2.0.*

Chanock, K. (2000). Comments on Essays: Do Students Understand What Tutors Write? *Teaching in Higher Education, 5*(1), 95.

Crenshaw, K. W. (1991). Mapping the Margins: Intersectionality, Identity Politics, and Violence Against Women of Color. *Stanford Law Review, 43*(6), 1241–1299.

De Silva, J., & Thulemark, M. (2022). Can You Break Through a Cement Ceiling? – Female Chefs' Possibilities for a Career in the Sri Lankan Culinary Industry. *Anatolia, 33*(3), 507–510.

Doucet, A., & Merla, L. (2007). Stay-at-Home Fathering: A Strategy for Balancing Work and Home in Canadian and Belgian Families. *Community, Work and Family, 10*(4), 455–473.

Elam, A., & Terjesen, S. (2010). Gendered Institutions and Cross-National Patterns of Business Creation for Men and Women. *The European Journal of Development Research, 22*(3), 331–348.

Evans, C. D., & Diekman, A. B. (2009). On Motivated Role Selection: Gender Beliefs, Distant Goals, and Career Interest. *Psychology of Women Quarterly, 33*(2), 235–249.

Facione, P. A. (2011). Critical Thinking: What It Is and Why It Counts. *Insight Assessment, 2007*(1), 1–23.

Fraser, N. (2000). Rethinking Recognition. *New Left Review, 3*, 107.

Freund, D., & Hernandez-Maskivker, G. (2021). Women Managers in Tourism: Associations for Building a Sustainable World. *Tourism Management Perspectives, 38*, 100820.

Gee, J. P. (2011). *How to Do Discourse Analysis.* Taylor and Francis.

Gill, R. (2009). Beyond the 'Sexualization of Culture' Thesis: An Intersectional Analysis of 'Sixpacks', 'Midriffs' and 'Hot Lesbians' in Advertising. *Sexualities, 12*(2), 137–160.

Gilligan, K. (2020). A Critical Analysis of Masculinity During Mentoring in Contemporary Schools. In *Gender Equality in Changing Times* (pp. 83–106). Palgrave Macmillan.

Goodsell, T. L. (2005). Fatherhood and the Social Organization of Space: An Essay in Subjective Geography. *Situated Fathering. A Focus on Physical and Social Spaces*, pp. 27–47.

Gregory, A., & Milner, S. (2011). What Is "New" About Fatherhood? The Social Construction of Fatherhood in France and the UK. *Men and Masculinities, 14*(5), 588–606.

Haasler, S. R. (2014). The Impact of Learning on Women's Labour Market Transitions. *Research in Comparative and International Education, 9*(3), 354–369.

Heilman, M. E., & Okimoto, T. G. (2007). Why Are Women Penalized for Success at Male Tasks?: The Implied Communality Deficit. *Journal of Applied Psychology, 92*(1), 81.

Heleta, S., & Bagus, T. (2021). Sustainable Development Goals and Higher Education: Leaving Many Behind. *Higher Education, 81*, 163–177.

Hoyt, C. L., & Murphy, S. E. (2016). Managing to Clear the Air: Stereotype Threat, Women, and Leadership. *The Leadership Quarterly, 27*(3), 387–399.

Humbert, A. L., Kelan, E., & Van den Brink, M. (2019). The Perils of Gender Beliefs for Men Leaders as Change Agents for Gender Equality. *European Management Review, 16*(4), 1143–1157.

International Labour Office. (2016). *Women at Work: Trends 2016.* ILO.

Iyer, R., & Luke, C. (2011). Gender Representations in the Media and the Importance of Critical Media Literacy. In S. Tozer, A. M. Henry, P. G. Price, M. B. Geiner, & B. P. Gallegos (Eds.), *Handbook of Research in the Social Foundations of Education* (pp. 434–449). Taylor & Francis.

Janks, H. (2010). *Doing Critical Literacy: Texts and Activities for Teachers and Students.* Routledge.

Jenkins, M. (2021). https://inews.co.uk/opinion/motherland-bbc-stay-at-home-dad-kevin-damaging-cliche-1024843

Johns, M. L. (2013). Breaking the Glass Ceiling: Structural, Cultural, and Organizational Barriers Preventing Women from Achieving Senior and Executive Positions. *Perspectives in Health Information Management*, (Winter).

Kee, H. J. (2006). Glass Ceiling Or Sticky Floor? Exploring the Australian Gender Pay Gap. *Economic Record, 82*(259), 408–427.

Kelan, E. K., & Wratil, P. (2018). Post-heroic Leadership, Tempered Radicalism and Senior Leaders as Change Agents for Gender Equality. *European Management Review, 15*(1), 5–18.

Kelly, D. M., & Currie, D. H. (2021). Beyond Stereotype Analysis in Critical Media Literacy: Case Study of Reading and Writing Gender in Pop Music Videos. *Gender and Education, 33*(6), 676–691.

Kimmel, M. S., & Aronson, A. (Eds.). (2004). *Men and Masculinities: AJ* (Vol. 1). Abc-Clio.

Kopnina, H. (2017). Future Scenarios for Sustainability Education. In P. B. Corcoran, A. Wals, & J. Weakland (Eds.), *Envisioning Futures for Environmental and Sustainability Education.* Wageningen Academic Publishers.

Kramer, K. Z., & Kramer, A. (2016). At-Home Father Families in the United States: Gender Ideology, Human Capital, and Unemployment. *Journal of Marriage and the Family, 78*, 1315–1331.

Lamb, M. (Ed.). (2004). *The Role of the Father in Child Development*. Wiley.

Leal Filho, W., Jin Wu, Y., Brandli, L. L., Avila, L. V., Azeiteiro, U. M., Caeiro, S., & Madruga, L. R. R. G. (2017). Identifying and Overcoming Obstacles to the Implementation of Sustainable Development at Universities. *Journal of Integrative Environmental Sciences, 14*(1), 93–108.

Littler, J. (2013). The Rise of the "Yummy Mummy": Popular Conservatism and the Neoliberal Maternal in Contemporary British Culture. *Communication, Culture & Critique, 6*(2), 227–243.

Littler, J. (2020). Mothers Behaving Badly: Chaotic Hedonism and the Crisis of Neoliberal Social Reproduction. *Cultural Studies, 34*(4), 499–520.

Marks, L., & Palkovitz, R. (2004). American Fatherhood Types: The Good, the Bad, and the Uninterested. *Fathering, 2*(2), 113.

Massey, D. (2013). *Space, Place and Gender*. John Wiley & Sons.

Mattila, H. (2020). The Social Construction of Stay-at-Home Fathering Across Everyday Spaces. *Qualitative Psychology, 7*(2), 185.

McNay, L. (1999). Gender, Habitus and the Field: Pierre Bourdieu and the Limits of Reflexivity. Theory, *Culture & Society, 16*(1), 95–117.

Meyer, J. H., & Land, R. (2005). Threshold Concepts and Troublesome Knowledge (2): Epistemological Considerations and a Conceptual Framework for Teaching and Learning. *Higher Education, 49*(3), 373–388.

Mezirow, J. (1997). Transformative Learning; Theory to Practice. *New Directions for Adult and Continuing Education, 74*, 5–12.

Morales-Doyle, D. (2015). *Science Education as a Catalyst for Social Change? Justice-Centered Pedagogy in Secondary Chemistry*. Unpublished Doctoral Dissertation, University of Illinois Chicago.

Navarro Astor, E., Román-Onsalo, M., & Infante-Perea, M. (2017). Women's Career Development in the Construction Industry Across 15 Years: Main Barriers. *Journal of Engineering Design and Technology, 15*(2), 199–221.

Organisation for Economic Cooperation and Development. PISA. (2009). Assessment Framework: Key Competencies in Reading, Mathematics and Science*;* OECD Publishing, 2010.

Oswald, D. L. (2008). Gender Stereotypes and Women's Reports of Liking and Ability in Traditionally Masculine and Feminine Occupations. *Psychology of Women Quarterly, 32*(2), 196–203.

Phelan, J. E., Moss-Racusin, C. A., & Rudman, L. A. (2008). Competent Yet Out in the Cold: Shifting Criteria for Hiring Reflect Backlash Toward Agentic Women. *Psychology of Women Quarterly, 32*(4), 406–413.

Pleck, E. H. (2004). Two Dimensions of Fatherhood: A History of the Good Dad-Bad Dad Complex.

Pritchard, A., Morgan, N., & Sedgley, D. (2002). In search of Lesbian Space? The Experience of Manchester's Gay Village. *Leisure Studies, 21*(2), 105–123.

Probst, L., Bardach, L., Kamusingize, D., Templer, N., Ogwali, H., Owamani, A., Mulumba, L., Onwonga, R., & Adugna, B. T. (2019). A Transformative University Learning Experience Contributes to Sustainability Attitudes, Skills and Agency. *Journal of Cleaner Production, 232*, 648–656.

Rehel, E. M. (2014). When Dad Stays Home Too: Paternity Leave, Gender, and Parenting. *Gender and Society, 28*(1), 110–132.

Reza, M. I. H. (2016). Sustainability in Higher Education: Perspectives of Malaysian Higher Education System. *SAGE Open, 6*(3).

Rochlen, A. B., McKelley, R. A., & Whittaker, T. A. (2010). Stay-At-Home Fathers' Reasons for Entering the Role and Stigma Experiences: A Preliminary Report. *Psychology of Men & Masculinity, 11*, 279–285.

Roth-Cohen, O., Kanevska, H. S., & Eisend, M. (2022). Gender Roles in Online Advertising. *Journal of Gender Studies*, 1–15.

Rudman, L. A., & Glick, P. (2001). Prescriptive Gender Stereotypes and Backlash Toward Agentic Women. *Journal of Social Issues, 57*(4), 743–762.

Rudman, L. A., Moss-Racusin, C. A., Glick, P., & Phelan, J. E. (2012). Reactions to Vanguards: Advances in Backlash Theory. In *Advances in Experimental Social Psychology* (Vol. 45, pp. 167–227).

Scott, J. (1992). Experience. In J. Butler & J. W. Scott (Eds.), *Feminists Theorize the Political*. Routledge.

Shiel, C., Smith, N., & Cantarello, E. (2020). Aligning Campus Strategy with the SDGs: An Institutional Case Study. In *Universities as Living Labs for Sustainable Development* (pp. 11–27). Springer.

Spanierman, L. B., Oh, E., Poteat, V. P., Hund, A. R., McClair, V. L., Beer, A. M., & Clarke, A. M. (2008). White University Students' Responses to Societal Racism: A Qualitative Investigation. *The Counseling Psychologist, 36*, 839–870.

Stamarski, C. S., & Son Hing, L. S. (2015). Gender Inequalities in the Workplace: The Effects of Organizational Structures, Processes, Practices, and Decision Makers' Sexism. *Frontiers in Psychology, 6*, 1400.

Stevens, E. (2015). Understanding Discursive Barriers to Involved Fatherhood: The Case of Australian Stay-at-Home Fathers. *Journal of Family Studies, 21*(1), 22–37.

Sunderland, J. (2000). Baby Entertainer, Bumbling Assistant and Line Manager: Discourses of Fatherhood in Parentcraft Texts. *Discourse & Society, 11*(2), 249–274.

Sustainable Development Solutions Network (SDSN). (2020). Accelerating Education for the SDGs in Universities: A Guide for Universities, Colleges, and Tertiary and Higher Education Institutions. *Report, Sustainable Development Solutions Network*, New York.

Thornton, M., & Bagust, J. (2007). *The Gender Trap: Flexible Work in Corporate Legal Practice* (Vol. 45, p. 773). Osgoode Hall Law Journal.
Tosi, P. (2011). Thinking About What We See: Using Media Literacy to Examine Images of African Americans on Television. *Black History Bulletin, 74*, 13–20.
Triventi, M. (2013). The Gender Wage Gap and Its Institutional Context: A Comparative Analysis of European Graduates. *Work, Employment and Society, 27*(4), 563–580.
Tyler, I. (2008). "Chav mum chav scum" Class Disgust in Contemporary Britain. *Feminist Media Studies, 8*(1), 17–34.
WCED, S. W. S. (1987). World Commission on Environment and Development. *Our Common Future, 17*(1), 1–91.
Young, I. M. (1997). *Intersecting Voices: Dilemmas of Gender, Political Philosophy, and Policy*. Princeton University Press.

Index[1]

[1] Note: Page numbers followed by 'n' refer to notes.

D. Dalton, A. Smith (eds.), *Gender, Sexuality and the UN's SDGs*, Sustainable Development Goals Series,
https://doi.org/10.1007/978-3-031-31046-1

FSC
www.fsc.org
MIX
Papier | Fördert gute Waldnutzung
FSC® C083411

Kolibri 360 GmbH
Ferdinand-Jühlke-Straße 7
99095 Erfurt, Deutschland
produktsicherheit@kolibri360.de